Here is a new and even more extraordinary collection of witty, amusing and memorable letters to *The Times*. From the irresistibly funny to the bitingly sarcastic, *The Times* letters have always displayed the very best in succinct prose from the pens of the famous and the infamous. This collection, expertly chosen for wit and style by Kenneth Gregory, offers the reader a fascinating range of hitherto unearthed gems dating from 1900 to the present.

The correspondence column of *The Times* is famous for its power. This is where records are 'put straight', where bombshells are dropped, where outrage is vented and iniquities laid bare—above all, it is where humour is most flamboyantly exhibited. You will therefore not be surprised to find in this volume: Queen Victoria delivering her 'blockbuster', Mussolini answering an awkward allegation, Bernard Shaw upholding 'sexual suggestiveness', Edith Sitwell blasting Dr Goebbels, Robert Graves on the art of generalship, Laurence Olivier on Shakespeare and A. P. Herbert on Civil Servant's English. No subject is beyond enquiry and comment: George III's bathing machine, the US President's jokes, suits for King Zog of Albania, uses for rat skins, behaviour in the Commons, footing the wedding bill . . . not to mention more classic sequences of letters.

Flitting from the sublime to the ridiculous, *The Third Cuckoo* alights on the most unexpected subjects and testifies, once again, to the genius of *Times* letter writers. Your bibliographic aviary will not be complete without it.

# THE THIRD CUCKOO

*More classic letters to*
**THE TIMES**
1900–1985

Chosen and introduced
by
KENNETH GREGORY

London
**UNWIN PAPERBACKS**
Boston          Sydney

First published by Allen & Unwin 1985
First published by Unwin Paperbacks 1986

**UNWIN ® PAPERBACKS**
**40 Museum Street, London WC1A 1LU, UK**

Unwin Paperbacks
Park Lane, Hemel Hempstead, Herts HP2 4TE, UK

Allen & Unwin Australia Pty Ltd.,
8 Napier Street, North Sydney, NSW 2060, Australia

Unwin Paperbacks with the Port Nicholson Press
60 Cambridge Terrace, Wellington, New Zealand

**British Library Cataloguing in Publication Data**

The Third cuckoo : more classic letters to
The Times, 1900–1985.
1. English letters
I. Gregory, Kenneth   II. The Times
826'.912'08     PR1347
ISBN 0–04–808061–6

Printed in Great Britain
by Cox and Wyman Ltd, Reading

# CONTENTS

# ACKNOWLEDGEMENTS

The editor and publishers wish to thank all those who have so readily given permission for inclusion of the letters which appear in this volume. The many writers, literary agents and executors to whom thanks are owed are too numerous to be named individually here but their friendly help and many interesting comments and postscripts have been invaluable.

Every effort has been made to trace the writers of the letters or their heirs and executors. Inevitably, we have not always met with success in tracking down the writers of letters in some cases published as many as eighty years ago. To those whom it has proved impossible to trace we would offer our sincerest apologies and express the earnest hope that they will find pleasure in the reproduction of their letters in these pages.

Kenneth Gregory would also personally like to thank all those who have helped him in his researches, especially the Air Historical Branch of the Ministry of Defence, and the staff of the Bath Public Reference Library.

# INTRODUCTION

*by Kenneth Gregory*

There are two sorts of letters, that written by A to be read by B, and A's more considered thoughts which he feels will benefit not only B but humanity. This second letter is undertaken with care: A takes a sheet of paper, writes 'To the Editor of *The Times*', and follows with 'Sir' and a comma. If the writer is Edith Sitwell, Bernard Shaw or Benito Mussolini, the odds are the letter will be published. But what of *the* letter, that which caused the editor to pluck at his beard and mutter 'I dare not print it', and – seconds later – 'I dare not NOT print it'? The editor, John Thadeus Delane, compromised: he did not print the letter, he merely included its contents in the pages of *The Times*.

Queen Victoria's letter to *The Times* had, and has, a curious history. Lytton Strachey's biography quoted three sentences, Elizabeth Longford's seven words; *The History of The Times* mentions primly that 'the text is printed in Cook's *Delane*, pp. 150–151'. The letter was the outcome of a leading article published on April 1, 1864:

> 'Her Majesty's loyal subjects will be very pleased to hear that their Sovereign is about to break her protracted seclusion.'

This seclusion had, of course, lasted since the death of the Prince Consort in December 1861. Rashly, *The Times* decided to flush Her Majesty out of Windsor Castle.

When Queen Elizabeth II visited New Printing House Square on February 28, 1985, and left carrying a copy of the next day's edition, it was stated that Queen Victoria, 'it is said, would not even allow the thing *The Times* in the house'. On the contrary, Queen Victoria was a most assiduous reader of *The Times*. Whether she propped it up against the morning marmalade pot and read snippets aloud is debatable; she was naturally keen to preserve her children's innocence. But read *The Times* – or have it read to her – on the day of publication she most certainly did.

1

## *Queen Victoria to Earl Granville*

Buckingham Palace, *13th June 1859*

The Queen is much shocked to find her whole conversation with Lord Granville yesterday and the day before detailed in this morning's leading article of *The Times*. What passes between her and a Minister in her own room in confidential intercourse ought to be sacred.

Lord Granville felt deeply this Royal reproof; he did not deny the accuracy of *The Times* account, though suggested its manner was 'vulgar and inflated'. A little more than two years later Her Majesty was urging the Prime Minister Lord Palmerston to use what influence he had to stop Delane from abusing everything Prussian. Delane fired off a witty squib:

My dear lord, – I shall be very glad to give the Prussians a respite from that most cruel of all inflictions – good advice. Indeed, I would not have intruded anything so unwelcome during the splendid solemnities of the Coronation had not the King uttered those surprising anachronisms upon Divine Right . . .

Palmerston interpreted the above to the Queen: '*The Times*, in order to maintain its circulation, criticises freely everybody and everything'.

Queen Victoria doubtless noted *The Times* leader of April 1, 1864: 'Her Majesty's loyal subjects will be very pleased to hear that their Sovereign is about to break her protracted seclusion.' She did not forget her dear Albert's words that 'soon there will not be room enough in the same country for the Monarchy and *The Times*.' Walking and driving in the grounds of Windsor Castle with Princess Louise, the Queen brooded. She brooded that evening when dining at Cliveden. The next day *The Times* turned its attention to the Schleswig-Holstein war, and published two letters – one on Greek and Latin Composition, the other on Pauper Idiots. The Queen walked and drove in the grounds of Windsor Castle.

On Monday, April 4, *The Times* considered the civil war in America; both sides, it seemed, were likely to be bankrupted. This reaction was less controversial than had been the paper's response a few months earlier to some remarks made by President Lincoln: 'Four score and seven years ago our fathers brought forth on this continent a new nation, conceived in liberty, and dedicated to the proposition that all men are created

2

equal.' *The Times* concluded: 'Anything more dull and commonplace it wouldn't be easy to reproduce.'

On Monday, April 4, 1864, Queen Victoria reached for her pen.

To the Editor of *The Times*.

Sir,
    An erroneous idea seems generally to prevail . . .

General Grey, Her Majesty's private secretary, was by now either booted and spurred, watching his carriage being made ready, or seeing if he had sufficient small change to purchase a railway ticket from Windsor to Paddington, via Slough. Queen Victoria finished her letter and handed it to General Grey.

'Grey took it straight from Windsor to Delane,' wrote Lord Clarendon to his wife on April 7, so suggesting that HM's private secretary used a carriage, for by chance he met Lord Granville on the way.

'Good afternoon, Grey.'

'Good afternoon, Puss.'

'And what are you doing in town?'

'I am bearing a letter from Her Majesty.'

'Good God!'

'To the Editor of *The Times*.'

'You mean she has written a . . . But my dear fellow, she can't! You must consult some of Her ministers before Her Majesty commits herself.'

General Grey regarded Lord Granville, then said to his coachman: 'Printing House Square.'

John Thadeus Delane read Queen Victoria's letter. In her own hand. Better sit on it for a day thought Delane. On Tuesday, April 5, Delane stood up and called in his letters editor who, we may suspect, was himself. Was *The Times* mail bag full of interesting letters? The best of the lot would appear to be one on Sugar Duties – unsigned. It contained more meat, so to say, than Intercessory Prayer, though this was signed. Delane weighed the two: unsigned Sugar, or Prayer signed by 'Indignant'. A third letter, University Mission to Central Africa, was added as a vague link.

'An erroneous idea seems generally to prevail . . .'

A letter in *The Times*, or any other newspaper, must be given a heading. 'Sugar Duties' constitutes such a heading, so does 'Intercessory Prayer'; 'Erroneous Idea' does not. Had Queen Victoria and Delane been living today, then perhaps 'The Queen denies re-entry' would suffice; in the event of Delane returning the letter to sender, with the usual regrets, and its being tried on

3

a less august journal, then 'VICKY SLAMS TIMES!' But Queen Victoria and Delane were in 1864 when a certain decency prevailed. It prevailed, above all, in the Court Circular whose prose – then as now – was circumscribed, varying between 'The Queen walked and drove in the grounds of Windsor Castle' and 'The Queen drove out yesterday afternoon'. The Court Circular informed Delane that on the day the Queen had written him a letter, 'Mr Tidey had the honour of submitting to Her Majesty the Queen his picture in water colours of "The Night of the Betrayal". '

This triptych of much devotional feeling pleased Her Majesty for more than aesthetic reasons; she had bought Henry Tidey's 'The Feast of Roses' as a gift for Albert in 1859. It may have been this human interest touch – not normally associated with *The Times* – which solved Delane's problem. Assuming that no one read the Court Circular, or anything in its immediate vicinity, Delane would remove all identifying marks from the Queen's letter and publish it above the Court Circular – which indeed he did, just seven paragraphs with a heading THE COURT. However, as true identifying marks of the seven paragraphs was their style (as individual as that of a Gibbon, a Macaulay, or a Wodehouse writing a Jeeves and Bertie story), great was the consternation among Ministers. The message 'produced a very painful impression,' wrote Lord Clarendon, 'and is considered very *infra dig* for the Queen.' *The History of The Times* (vol. II, 1939) would be so unsettled that it altered the heading from THE COURT to COURT NEWS, as though fearful of verifying its references.

Modern readers will be intrigued by Delane's omissions when transforming a letter into a *communiqué*. Queen Victoria was a very proper person; if her letters to the King of the Belgians began 'My dear uncle', to the Emperor of the French 'Sire et mon cher frère', and to the widow of the assassinated Lincoln 'Dear Madam' (continuing 'Though a stranger to you . . .'), we may hope that her letter to *The Times* began 'Sir'. But how did it end? what were the words, if any, separating the contents of the letter from 'VICTORIA R'?

Over the years letters to *The Times* have ended in different ways: Yours &c., Yours sincerely, Yours truly, Yours respectfully, Your obedient servant – and the variant I have the honour to be, Sir, your obedient servant, Yours in earnest hope of publication, and Yours affectionately. Bearing in mind what drove Queen Victoria to write to *The Times*, that she was the obedient servant only of the Almighty and of the memory of dear Albert, that she was writing not in the earnest hope of publication but rather in confident expectation, and that she was not truly, sincerely, respectfully or affectionately inclined towards John Thadeus Delane, we may wish Her Majesty had been visited by some premonition and ended with tongue firmly in cheek.

A *Times* leader which begins

'Her Majesty's loyal subjects will be very pleased to hear that their Sovereign is about to break her protracted seclusion' demands a letter with A. P. Herbert's immortal ending,

'I am, Sir, your servant, but, regretfully, not so obedient as usual.'

Queen Victoria never again wrote personally for publication to *The Times*, but her family crops up more than once in *The Third Cuckoo*. The fate of two of her grandsons would not have surprised the Queen: 'Dear Georgie so nice, sensible and truly right-minded' was destined to become a much-loved George V, but another became the subject of an unflattering correspondence in *The Times* ('Extradition of the Kaiser', 1919). Queen Victoria had given many warnings concerning Willy's arrogant behaviour when he was very young.

Queen Victoria was a born letter-writer; so, too, among others who appear in *The Third Cuckoo*, were Admiral of the Fleet Lord Fisher and Bernard Shaw. Whether, at the close of his life, the former's literary style resembled his conversation is not clear; if it did, an hour with Lord Fisher must have been both exhilarating and exhausting – and demanded an extensive knowledge of the Scriptures. Shaw to *The Times* was supreme as a controversialist and also for his sheer readability. The irony implicit in vintage Shaw is that today he could not be fitted to the Letters page, at least not unless willing to reduce his symphonic arguments to the shape of a song. Regular readers of *The Times* will appreciate the difficulty when reminded that the average Shavian letter occupied as many inches as one of Bernard Levin's articles.

Hatching a cuckoo in 1984–85 was even more rewarding than usual. A news item in *The Times*, followed by a flood of correspondence, a leading article, and an outraged nation: 'Hello! we have been here before.' The topic in question concerned honorary degrees for politicians: should dons meet and raise languid hands, approving without thought, or should they – *dare* they – consult among themselves, debate the issue at length, and then vote with the strength of conviction behind them? The hatcher of cuckoos referred to his notes – surely he could find something on a similar theme? He could. Way back in 1926 – the year of a miners' strike – there was much ado about a politician and his proposed honorary degree. Certain dons were outraged by the politician's attitude during the strike. To put the matter in perspective: as a dozen or so degree-awarding institutions have been founded since 1965, there is no reason why a politician of the present or future should not exceed the number of honorary degrees achieved by Sir Winston Churchill.

*The Third Cuckoo* is proud to present letters from other politicians: one who explained why he was giving one-fifth of his own personal fortune to the Treasury, and a gentleman of rare character who felt insulted on receiving a cheque for sitting in the House of Commons. As this 'fee' could have purchased two three-bedroom houses in the home counties, he naturally divided it between local charities. His letter to *The Times* left readers in no doubt as to his meaning: only a cad (or a Labour member) would accept money for doing his duty to the nation. More recently the unemployed were told starkly what to do: get on their bikes. *The Third Cuckoo* adds a footnote to this advice from a politician, or rather warns the unemployed who have grown beards. Should the beard get entangled with a bicycle chain . . .

Should the reader wish to know the colour preferred by moths when they are lunching off a multi-hued coverlet, or what to do with any convenient rat skins, he is here informed. Non-Australians foolish enough to experiment with a boomerang are warned, any descendants of Mrs Grundy advised how to deal with pictures or statues they hold to be improper. Proof is offered of the effect on a Russian court of law when a letter to *The Times* is read aloud; proof is not offered of the fate likely to befall any reader of *The Third Cuckoo* who thinks such letter-reading a good wheeze and makes immediate arrangements to fly eastwards. Better by far to be the father of three or four daughters and, appalled by the cost of three or four weddings, unburden one's anguish to *The Times*. Sound advice is forthcoming – witty if financially unhelpful.

The miners' strike of 1984–85 produced Britain's emotional earthquake of the decade, maybe of the century, judging by the correspondence columns of *The Times*. If the length of the dispute occasionally found readers out of ammunition, it also guaranteed a prolonged exchange of views, and these were often a reflection of views expressed seventy years earlier. The fierce rhetoric of Mr Arthur Scargill on the one hand, and the incoherence of the National Coal Board on the other, did little to clarify the issues. Indeed, there were moments when Mr Scargill appeared to have taken his cue from the greatest of

6

Marxists and was about to sing 'Whatever it is, I'm against it'. (Groucho's garb on that memorable day was an academic gown, mortar-board and leer.) Mr Scargill hailed the miners' strike as part of the class war.

But as any definition of class had changed over sixty, even ten years, the public's understanding of 'class war' was out of focus. And there was no Lord Birkenhead – as there had been after the Great War – to meet the miners' representatives and conclude 'I should call them the stupidest men in England if I had not previously had to deal with the owners.' In 1984–85 neither side was stupid, merely intent on travelling in different directions. To complicate matters further, the miners proceeded some to the north and others to the south. Inevitably letters to *The Times* chose their tangents off which to fly. *The Third Cuckoo* contains a generous selection of the letters in case the recent conflict should prove to be the last of its kind. History will be grateful for a display of present passion, dominated by the past and fearful for the future.

The first letter relating to the miners' strike of 1984–85 is dated long ago, the last was chosen months before the strike ended. Some may even regard it as one of the most momentous letters ever received by *The Times*. Its sender is named in the Index:

Durham, Bishop of . . .

A smirking cuckoo is not a pleasant sight, least of all when preventing the writer from completing an Index entry. But on Thursday, March 28, 1985, a smirking cuckoo intervened with the claim that this was its finest hour. Not only had the Letters page of *The Times* promoted the bird from the customary bottom right-hand corner, it had awarded the cuckoo twelve column inches. Though admitting that these column inches had been shared with bishops, the smirker emphasized the grave truth: the Prime Minister had not likened cuckoos to bishops, but bishops to cuckoos. This, surely, was the greatest compliment ever paid their Spiritual Lordships. Lord North had not attributed the loss of the American colonies to cuckoos in high places, Mr Gladstone made no mention of cuckoos during his Midlothian campaign, Disraeli was unable to inform Queen Victoria he had been hailed by Bismarck as 'der alte Kuckuck'.

As the smirking cuckoo paused for breath, it was gently pointed out that this collection of Letters to *The Times* would include a sequence 'Bird for Britain' wherein readers suggested the name of a bird suitable for adoption as a national emblem. The cuckoo was not chosen. Come to that, neither was the pigeon. During the Second World War the pigeon was a vital

7

part of RAF Bomber Command whose aircraft never carried a cuckoo. Which brings us to the great unanswered question – what happened to the egg?

The letter for July 2, 1941, was referred to the Air Historical Branch of the Ministry of Defence. To discover the targets, and the squadrons concerned, was no trouble at all; one felt that this government department could readily have come up with details of what the station commanders had for lunch. But the egg beat them. They had never heard of the egg, they did not know of its existence. There was a tentative suggestion – soon rejected – that it may have been dropped to augment some bomb load but this was probably against Air Ministry instructions. War cannot be demeaned by the dropping of eggs from a height. The Air Historical Branch wondered if, in due course, some reader of *The Third Cuckoo* might supply the answer. It will be most gratefully received.

## The Court

An erroneous idea seems generally to prevail, and has latterly found frequent expression in the newspapers, that the Queen is about to resume the place in society which she occupied before her great affliction; that is, that she is about again to hold levées and drawing-rooms in person, and to appear as before at Court balls, concerts, &c. This idea cannot be too explicitly contradicted.

The Queen heartily appreciates the desire of her subjects to see her, and whatever she *can* do to gratify them in this loyal and affectionate wish she *will* do. Whenever any real object is to be attained by her appearing on public occasions, any national interest to be promoted, or anything to be encouraged which is for the good of her people, Her Majesty will not shrink, as she has not shrunk, from any personal sacrifice or exertion, however painful.

But there are other and higher duties than those of mere representation which are now thrown upon the Queen, alone and unassisted — duties which she cannot neglect without injury to the public services, which weigh unceasingly upon her, overwhelming her with work and anxiety.

The Queen has laboured conscientiously to discharge these duties till her health and strength, already shaken by the utter and ever-abiding desolation which has taken the place of her former happiness, have been seriously impaired.

To call upon her to undergo, in addition, the fatigue of these mere State ceremonies which can be equally well performed by other members of her family is to ask her to run the risk of entirely disabling herself for the discharge of those other duties which cannot be neglected without serious injury to the public interests.

The Queen will, however, do what she can — in the manner least trying to her health, strength, and spirits — to meet the loyal wishes of her subjects, to afford that support and countenance to society, and to give that encouragement to trade which is desired her.

More the Queen *cannot* do; and more the kindness and good feeling of her people will surely not exact from her.

9

# Cuckoo in the Wind

*Symphony No. 1 (first movement, bars 25–32)*
GUSTAV MAHLER

## Cuckold in the Nest

*From Lord Campbell of Croy*                    *11 April 1983*

Sir,

Your Science Report (March 29) on the almost impossible task of determining the paternity of the progeny of dunnocks (hedge sparrows) did not mention another phenomenon which is surely very relevant. It is the nest of the hedge sparrow, above all, that is chosen by the cuckoo for foster parentage.

May this not be nature's way of preparing the husbands, as well as the paramours, for the grotesque spectacle of a single chick several times larger than any hedge sparrow parent? 'Clearly', they can say to themselves, 'it's not mine'.

Yours faithfully,
CAMPBELL OF CROY

Cuckoos lead Bohemian lives,
They fail as husbands and as wives,
Therefore they cynically disparage
Everybody else's marriage.

*Ogden Nash*

[Folklore insists that disaster is imminent if the nightingale is heard before the cuckoo. In 1952 readers of *The Times* waited anxiously until on April 8 in Surrey a Frensham cuckoo opened up a day before an Ockley nightingale]

## Silent Cuckoo

*From Mr Charles Taylor, MP*                    *16 April 1952*

[Conservative Member for Eastbourne 1935–74; knighted 1954]

Sir,
I have not heard the cuckoo this year. Is this a record? I cannot remember when I heard it last year. Two years ago I never heard it on April 7, possibly because I was in Switzerland. But, then, so many of the clocks are made there.
                I am, Sir, your obedient servant,
CHARLES TAYLOR

[Possibly because the Conservatives were now back in office, the Labour Left reacted in niggardly fashion]

## Unwelcome

*From Mr T. Driberg*                    *21 April 1952*

[Labour MP for Essex (Maldon); Life Peer 1975]

Sir,
    The cuckoo was in full cry at Bradwell-juxta-Mare, Essex, much too early in the morning of Wednesday, April 16.
                Yours truly,
TOM DRIBERG

[Driberg, the original William Hickey of the *Daily Express*, clearly did not share the cuckoo mania of certain other Top People]

# Disturbed

*From Mrs Rosemary Samson*                    *14 June 1983*

Sir,

Last night (June 1), about midnight, shortly before the storm broke, my husband and I, and a friend who lives nearby, distinctly heard the cuckoo. The call came several times, apparently from a bird in flight.

I have never before heard the cuckoo at night. Was the bird disturbed by the impending storm? If so, why did we not hear others?

Yours faithfully,
ROSEMARY SAMSON


# Duettist

*From Dr Pamela Priest*                    *18 June 1983*

Sir,

Mrs Rosemary Samson's letter on the night cuckoo reminds me of my childhood in wartime Somerset, when anti-aircraft guns once set a cuckoo and a nightingale singing together.

Yours faithfully,
PAMELA PRIEST

[The credit shall go to Joseph Cooper who once commanded an anti-aircraft battery in Somerset]


# Willing to Oblige

*From Mr Douglas Vernon*                    *18 June 1983*

Sir,

Is Mrs Rosemary Samson not aware that the *Cuculus Canorus* (the cuckoo) has a marked tendency to behave in an eccentric manner whenever it senses the presence in the neighbourhood of a *Times* correspondence column contributor?

Yours faithfully,
DOUGLAS VERNON

[Perhaps the nightingale preceded the cuckoo in 1984, so presaging domestic disaster in New Printing House Square]

*From Mr Patrick Drysdale*                    *4 September 1984*

Sir,

On some days I think I take *The Times* for the pleasure afforded by the misprints. In today's (August 29) column by John Woodcock, who knows what to do with words, I read, 'Allott bowled one over before giong off'.

While waiting for the opportunity to tell an irritating interlocutor to 'giong off', I find, a few lines lower down, 'England continued to dawdale'. Apart from the fact that it rhymes with my own name, I like the sound of 'dawdale'. It has a measured leisure to it, and I will always associate the summer of '84 with the memory of the England XI, her Majesty's government, and *The Times* proof readers all dawdaling on their way, giong towards imminent disaster.

                                        Yours faithfully,
                                        PATRICK DRYSDALE

[In 1984 England lost all five Tests to West Indies]

*From Mr Gordon Martin*                    *11 September 1984*

Sir,

Whether, like Mr Drysdale, one should take *The Times* only for the pleasure afforded by its misprints is perhaps questionable. But there is no doubt that they can sometimes add to the richness of the language.

Thus, on August 29, I was pleased to see your Labour Correspondent's front-page report of 'confustion' at a Bristol dockers' meeting in support for the coal-miners.

In a situation where combustion is at the heart of the matter, and confusion is so patently widespread, confustion seemed to me a particularly happy, albeit accidental invention by your computer.

                                        Yours sincerely,
                                        GORDON MARTIN

[Before correspondents grow too smug, one must emphasize that *Times* misprints in 1984 did not begin to compare with those in the first editions of the *Manchester Guardian* circa 1950]

*From Mr Fritz Spiegel*                    *30 June 1984*

Sir,

Thank you for helping to revive attractive and apt old English words, e.g. the miners' 'stoggage' (my – early – edition, June 27).

14

On checking with the OED I find that to be 'stogged' means 'to be stuck in the mud, mire, bog or the like'.

Yours faithfully,

FRITZ SPIEGEL

[Two academics now intervened from aery heights]

*From Dr Kieran Flanagan*              *20 September 1984*

[Department of Sociology, University of Bristol]

Sir,

The commentary on the *Alternative Service Book*, 1980, by the Liturgical Commission, tells us that 'in communicating with men, we have to accommodate our audience' according to class, sex and age. Surely this advice has been taken to extremes at the Royal Naval College Chapel, Greenwich, where, according to the service list in *The Times* (September 15) for the Thirteenth Sunday after Trinity, Tye's lovely anthem, 'Laudate Nomen Domini', is to be rendered as 'Laudate Women Domini'.

Is this now to be the anthem of tokenism, the song of incorporation of the Anglican Church adaptable to all social groups as, for instance, 'Laudate Microbiologists Domini'?

I write as a distressed Roman Catholic sociologist with a passing interest in liturgy.

Yours faithfully,

KIERAN FLANAGAN

*From Professor F. M. Fowler*           *29 September 1984*

[Department of German, Queen Mary College, University of London]

Sir,

For a spirited defence of such New Alternative Anthems as 'Laudate Women Domini' Dr Flanagan and others in liturgical distress should contact the splendid la(d)y preacher who, according to your service lists, has − since the introduction of the mini-skirt − most frequently graced the pulpits of London churches. Her name and address: Miss A. Brevis (Palestrina).

Yours neofaithfully,

FRANK M. FOWLER

How long before Ms A. Brevis?

[*The Times*' first issue of 1985 began celebrations of the paper's bicentenary, a facsimile edition of itself (or *The Daily Universal Register* as it then was) for 1 January 1785 being included]

15

# The Great Tradition

*From Mr David Nathan*                    *4 January 1985*

Sir,

Would you kindly draw the attention of your head proof reader to an error in column three, page three, of the facsimile first edition of *The Times*, or *The Daily Universal Register*, as Mr Walter chose to call it.

There, under the heading 'Antiquities', is advertised a collection of 'the most remarkable runs and ancient buildings.'

Surely there is some mistake here. If it is allowed to pass uncorrected there is no knowing where it will end.

Yours faithfully,
DAVID NATHAN

*From Mr John Goodchild*                    *4 January 1985*

Sir,

I hope I am not too late in pointing out an apparent error in your issue of January 1, 1785. You describe the 'Ode for the New Year' as being by Paul Whitehead, though he died in 1774. Could this have been an early example of ghost writing or was it an error for William Whitehead, Poet Laureate, who died in April, 1785?

You may, of course, have printed a correction in the following issue, but I did not see it at the time.

I am, Sir, etc,
J. GOODCHILD

[The following correction appeared in *The Times* of 25 October 1984: 'The words "imported oil" in Woodrow Wyatt's article on Saturday should have read "imported coal" ']

# The Concentration Camps

[In December 1900 Miss Emily Hobhouse left England on behalf of the South African Women and Children Distress Fund. 60,000 Boer women and children were confined in British concentration camps. On 14 June 1901 Sir Henry Campbell-Bannerman spoke at a dinner in London: 'When is a war not a war? When it is carried on by methods of barbarism in South Africa.' At the time of this letter the death rate in the camps was 344 per 1,000 per annum]

*From the Bishop of Hereford*                    *22 October 1901*

[The Rt Rev. John Percival]

Sir,

Every month brings us the dreary record of the enormous death-rate among the children in the South African concentration camps, and to-day you publish one of the worst that we have hitherto received.

According to your tabular statement there are 54,326 white children in these camps, and of these 1,964 died during the month of September. As men read these dreadful figures they cannot but ask, How long is this fearful mortality to be allowed to go on?

Meanwhile, the ladies sent out some months ago to inspect and inquire are, I presume, preparing a report. That report will doubtless testify that almost everything possible under the circumstances is being done by the officers, doctors, nurses, and other humane persons who are working in the camps.

The Government and its friends have constantly reminded us that this is so, and we all believe in their general desire that it should be so. Your Elandsfontein Correspondent, indeed, has the hardihood to assert in your columns to-day that Miss Hobhouse 'has tried her best to foster the supposition that those who have organized these camps are utterly callous as to their welfare,' and that she is thus guilty of 'fostering a base and malicious untruth.' This libellous attack is itself an untruth; we will not call it malicious, because he may have been misinformed, or his pen may have run away with him in South African fashion; but it is certainly mischievous, and not very manly or creditable.

The point, however, for the English public to notice is this. All of us who know the humanity of English officers, doctors, nurses feel assured that they are endeavouring to do everything that personal devotion can do under the circumstances.

This unending death-roll of children is the result. Surely, Sir, we need no other condemnation of the camp system for children.

And these recurring reports, extending over all these dreary and death-laden months, amount to a very strong condemnation of the Government for their supineness in not attempting something better long before this time.

Is no system of distribution possible? Could not all mothers

17

with children and all children without mothers be somehow distributed among the loyalist population of Cape Colony or Natal in healthy situations?

Are we reduced to such a depth of impotence that our Government can do nothing to stop such a holocaust of child-life?

We who ask these questions ask them in no spirit of political controversy; no man would seek to make any political gain out of the sad fate of these little ones.

It is in all sadness and in the name of common human pity that we plead with our authorities here at home — the Cabinet and the responsible heads of the great departments concerned — to do something and to do it speedily.

It is a dismal and hateful thought to multitudes of English men and women, without any distinction of political party, for we are all one in our pity for these little children; and the more truly patriotic we are the more hateful is the thought that England should through the death of these children be blotting out a whole generation, to say nothing of the root of bitterness which must inevitably grow out of their graves.

We also plead for immediate action, because the good name of our country is so deeply involved.

Of all the bitter and humiliating legacies of this war there will be none so bitter, none so sorely felt hereafter, as the untimely death of all these unhappy children.

Moreover, when the Boer exile returns, eager to clasp in his arms the little ones he left, only to find himself a solitary or childless man, is that likely to prove the seed of his future loyalty?

It may be different if the children are kept alive to tell him how tenderly and with what loving kindness they were nursed by English men and English women. It is because those who are now working in these camps are doing their best to save, and yet in spite of all death laughs them in the face as he goes on reaping his ghastly harvest month after month that such camps stand utterly condemned as homes for children.

Therefore the hearts of English fathers and mothers on every side are crying to the Government to bestir themselves and make haste in this saving work, for the love of Christ to make haste.

Your obedient servant,

J. HEREFORD

[*The Oxford History of South Africa* estimates that 25,000 Boer women and children died in the British concentration camps]

18

# Overcrowding on Railways

*From Mr George Kebbell*                    *1 April 1904*

Sir,

Some little time ago, when filling up the usual application for season ticket, I added a stipulation by the company that they would not cause or allow their carriages to be laden with more than the number of passengers such carriages were respectively constructed to carry. The company declined to grant me a ticket on these terms, and further refused my request that they should simply undertake to convey me as a 'human being'.

Now whenever the carriage in which I ride is overcrowded I, on arriving at the barrier, refuse to give up or show my ticket or to supply my name and address, stating distinctly that I do so as a protest against the overcrowding. If these tactics were pretty generally followed by passengers, the companies would soon be brought to their senses.

Your obedient servant,
GEORGE KEBBELL


# The Cuckoo Upstaged

*From Sir Frederick Bridge*                    *11 April 1906*

[organist of Westminster Abbey 1875–1918]

Sir,

It may be of interest to state that this morning at 4.30 I was woken in my quiet house in the Little Cloisters by the loud singing of a thrush. I have lived here over 30 years, and have never heard one in the Abbey grounds until this morning. There was no mistake about it, as I got up and saw the songster perched on the topmost branch of the tree which hangs over the fountain in our little quad. The bird sang beautifully until nearly 6 a.m., when he went off, and I went off to sleep again. I wonder if he will return.

Yours truly,
J. FREDERICK BRIDGE

# Free Meals for School Children

*From Mr Robert F. Horton*     *13 September 1904*

Sir,

Your correspondents who deprecate the application of public money to the provision of meals for unfed children in the schools make out a formidable case; and even those who are not economists can realize the importance of maintaining parental responsibility and the endless demoralization of any attempts on the part of the State to feed its citizens.

But meanwhile here are the 122,000 children in London going to school unfed, and no doctrinaire objections of the economist will compel, or enable, the parents of these hungry children to provide them with meals.

I know that public subscriptions for the object are almost as objectionable as grants from the rates or from the Treasury. The notion that the benevolent heart of the country has undertaken the charge may easily incline heartless parents to leave their children to that heart which is better than their own.

But it occurs to me that there is a way in which temporary help might be given, a way which by its obvious moral significance might neutralize the demoralizing effect of charity. Suppose during this time of stress the great City Companies should voluntarily give up their costly banquets and offer the banquets, in the form of simple and wholesome meals, to the hungriest of the children, would it not be an object-lesson of self-denial and of noble ministry to the suffering, and, indeed, to the whole nation, which would benefit the Companies as well as the children? The guests, no less than the Liverymen of the Companies, would, probably to a man, rejoice in the thought that their self-denial was ministering to hungry children; and the united action of the Companies in trying to meet the crying need of the moment would have a wholesome and quickening effect on the whole community. Under such circumstances, and pending larger and more radical reforms to meet the situation, the gift would not demoralize the children or their parents any more than these noble and costly banquets at present demoralize the guests who sit down to them.

Trusting that your readers will bear in mind that the first consideration is — How can these 122,000 unfed children be fed?

     I am your obedient servant,
       ROBERT F. HORTON

# The Trade Disputes Bill

*From Professor A. V. Dicey*                    *19 November 1906*

[Vinerian Professor of English Law in the University of Oxford]

Sir,

This astounding Bill is now handed on to the House of Lords, and the policy of privilege is revealed to the public in its full enormity. Let me summarize the general effect of a measure which violates the fundamental principles of English law and of common justice.

First. If the Bill becomes an Act, no trade union, whether it consists of workmen or of masters, will be liable to pay damages to any person for any tort or wrong whatever done to the sufferer by the union itself, by its agents, or by its servants. If, to take an obvious example, a union should own a motor-car, and the chauffeur, a servant of the union, should in the course of his employment, through his gross negligence, drive over an innocent wayfarer who has no connexion with any trade dispute whatever, and cripple him for life, the sufferer will not be able to recover a penny of damages from the union, even though it possesses £50,000. All this, I shall be told, is ancient history; we have known for a month or two the effect of the notorious Clause 4. There is, however, more to tell. This clause was at the last moment altered − I cannot bring myself to say amended − so as to protect trade unions not only against actions for damages, but also against injunctions and the payment of costs which such proceedings might involve. A union need no longer fear, whatever be the wrongs it commits, that it will endanger a penny of its funds. It can in no circumstances be called upon to make compensation to any man, woman, or child whom it may injure. It need not fear that it may be checked by an injunction from the notorious commission of wrongful acts. The Attorney-General has surely well earned the thanks of his friends, allies, or masters of the Labour party. To them he has made many sacrifices. He has at last ensured that a trade union may, when carrying out a strike, act on the broad and noble principle 'Do wrong and fear not.' So much for the moment about Clause 4.

Secondly. To persons acting in 'contemplation or in further-ance of a trade dispute,' whom for brevity's sake we may call trade unionists, the Bill will secure three privileges:—

(1) In favour of such trade unionists, and in favour of such trade unionists alone, the penalties imposed on so-called picketing will be relaxed. (Compare Conspiracy, &c., Act, 1875,

21

s. 7 (4), and Trade Disputes Bill, Clause 2). If X, Y, and Z, and 20 more such unionists, with the object of peacefully persuading A, beset his house or the factory where he works or carries on business, they will run no risk of punishment. This is a privilege in the strictest sense of the term. For if with some other object − e.g., with the object of peacefully persuading A to join the Primrose League − X, Y, and Z were to beset his house, &c., they would each run no small risk of being put on their trial and sentenced on conviction to three months' imprisonment with hard labour. The simple truth is that to trade unionists, who have become the favourites of the Government and the House of Commons, the Trade Disputes Bill will concede the right of unlimited picketing so long as the picketing does not involve the use, or the direct threat, of personal violence. This is not the language, but it assuredly is the real effect of Clause 2.

(2) In favour of such trade unionists, and of such trade unionists alone, the law will be relaxed under which a person who induces another to break a contract of employment with a third party is liable to an action for damages. (See Bill, Clause 3.) On the tremendous consequences which may ensue from such an alteration of the law in favour of one particular class of persons I will not to-day dwell. My object at this moment is merely to give the legal effect of the Bill which is tendered to the House of Lords for its acceptance.

(3) In favour of such trade unionists, and in favour of such trade unionists alone, it is in effect declared that no combination shall be actionable as a conspiracy, which is a combination to do an act which would not be actionable if done by any man not acting in concert with others. (Bill, Clause 1, read together with the Conspiracy, &c., Act, 1875, s. 3.)

X, Y, and Z determine to boycott A; they refuse to associate or to work with him; they refuse to work with any man who does work with him; they boycott A's employer; they boycott any man who deals with A's employer; they decline to supply A with the necessaries of life. They, however, take care to do no single act which would be actionable if done by X acting alone and not in concert with others. They thus ruin A and drive him to the workhouse. If the object of X, Y, and Z is to compel A to join the Primrose League, they may, I maintain, be liable to an action for conspiracy and to pay heavy damages. If the aim of X, Y, and Z be to compel A not to work for N − that is, to take part in a strike − they will, if the Trade Disputes Bill becomes law, assuredly incur no legal liability whatever.

Thirdly. The term 'trade dispute' has been at the very last moment given a definition which immensely extends its natural sense, and, indeed, indirectly alters the whole scope of the Act. Every suspicion with regard to this new definition, which is expressed in my last letter, is confirmed by the course of the debates which closed the discussions in the House of Commons. The Bill may include disputes between a landlord and his tenants where they are labourers on his estate. It will assuredly include disputes between a farmer and his labourers as to the terms of their work or the amount of their wages. It will give to labourers' unions all the privileges offered to trade unions of the ordinary kind. It will, therefore, vitally affect the position and rights of persons engaged, not in trade disputes, as that term has been generally understood, but in agrarian disputes — that is to say, in conflicts between landlords and tenants, or between labourers and farmers. Now the Bill extends to Ireland. It practically, though not in so many words, sanctions boycotting: it will certainly, as it now stands, confer new freedom of action upon Land Leagues and other bodies which for the last 25 years have endeavoured, and at times not without success, to override the law of the land. The definition clause of this ill-starred Bill is ominous. It links together the Labour policy and the Irish policy of the Government. The House of Lords is asked to sacrifice individual liberty in England in order thereby to facilitate defiance of the law in Ireland. The Bill, whilst it gives to trade unionists the privilege to commit wrongs, grants to Irish Land Leaguers the legalization of boycotting.

A. V. DICEY

# Lying Clocks

*From Sir John Cockburn*                    *8 January 1908*

Sir,

Surely there should be some censorship as to the time kept by clocks exposed to public view in the streets of London. It is not unusual within a hundred yards to find clocks three or four minutes at variance with each other. Highly desirable as individualism is in many respects, it is out of place in horology. A lying timekeeper is an abomination, and should not be tolerated. A by-law might well be framed requiring clocks in public places to be synchronized with standard time; the penalty for repeated disregard to be removal of the offending dial.

I have the honour to be, Sir, your obedient servant,

JOHN A. COCKBURN

[Underneath this letter Orient Company's Pleasure Cruises announced visits to The Riviera, Greece, Turkey, Palestine, etc. − 30 days for 25 guineas]

## The Cost of Living

*From Mr A. R. Steele*                    *4 September 1911*

Sir,

In the present disputes between capital and labour it has often been stated on behalf of the men that the cost of living has risen in recent years.

It should, I think, be stated what articles have risen in price. Bacon we all know has risen considerably, but I am not aware of anything else, unless it be sugar which rose a halfpenny* a pound some years ago. Bread rose when the price of wheat rose about 12 months ago, but fell again as wheat fell. The great importation of frozen or chilled meat must have put good butcher's meat within reach of many who never tasted it in former days.

The brewers and tobacconists attempted to meet extra taxation by increase of prices, but had to reduce their prices and have restored to a lowering in the quality of both beer and tobacco.

In the towns which I know rents have not risen, notwithstanding the great increase in local rates.

I am, Sir, yours obediently,

A. R. STEELE

[*The halfpenny was about one-fifth of the modern 1p. As late as 1939 a pint of milk cost three-halfpence]

## Chauffeurs' Nocturnal Noises

*From Dr Frederick Needham*                    *10 July 1911*

Sir,

I think that those who live in London should feel great indebtedness to Sir Henry Morris and others who have recently drawn special attention to the inconveniences and dangers of preventible street noises, and to the powerful advocacy of *The Times* in support of that view.

I may perhaps be permitted, as a Commissioner in Lunacy and a physician experienced in the treatment of nervous and mental disorders, to express my strong opinion as to the supreme importance of the subject in the interests of every one of us.

24

I have been long convinced that the noises in our large cities, and especially in London, the largest of them, are a very influential factor in the causation of nervous and mental disorders, and that their suppression or limitation, as far as is practicable, is essential to the health of the community.

Not only do these disturbing influences operate in the prevention of recuperative mental repose by day, but they interfere materially with such sleep as is necessary to preserve the due and healthy relations between mind and body, and bring the nervous system into a condition of irritable instability in which it easily becomes the prey of serious disease.

Moreover, the intermittent sounds which have come in with a new intensity with the 'hooter' in all its varieties of discordance cannot, in my opinion, fail to act as successive shocks which cannot be frequently repeated without the most serious results.

In these circumstances it is greatly to be desired that the County Council and the City authorities should make immediate practical use of the powers which they may possess under their by-laws or otherwise, and, if necessary, seek for fresh powers to enable them to suppress that part at least of the nuisance to which special attention has been recently drawn in *The Times*.

I am, Sir, your obedient servant,

FREDERICK NEEDHAM, M.D.

## The Motor Horn

*From M Nollée de Noduwez*                     *16 September 1911*

Sir,

Le cornet a fait sons temps; supprimons-le. Il n'est pas d'institution légale; il est une simple tolérance. Du moment qu'on en abuse, il devient une intolérable nuisance. Je suis motoriste, et je n'use jamais du cornet; pas plus que je ne mets un sifflet en bouche pour me faire faire place sur les trottoirs quand je suis pressé. Le cornet a été inventé par les cyclistes, qui n'ont jamais demandé d'autorisations. Voilá toute leur origine. Quand on mesure sa vitesse sur le plus ou moins de densité du mouvement des rues (ou routes) on n'a jamais besoin de faire usage du cornet! Le cornet est insolent. Il hurle 'Place! Place! Place!' Nul n'a droit a commander ainsi − sauf pourtant le service d'incendie.

Your obedient servant,

NOLLÉE DE NODUWEZ

# Musical Motor Horns

*From Mr Arthur M. Goodhart*    *3 August 1929*

Sir,

Your amusing leading article upon the subject of motor horns reminds me that about 20 years ago, when some of the horns produced musical sounds of inoffensive quality, I suggested to the makers that an attempt should be made to standardize the combinations employed and to attach some meaning to them. If, for instance, a horn normally produced the chord GBDF, the dominant seventh in the key of C, which could be sustained as long as required, two resolutions would be possible, one indicating 'left,' the other 'right.'

Even unmusical persons might with practice recognize the difference between two notes *p* and four notes *f*. By the omission of G in the first example and G and F sharp in the second, the number of parts could be reduced to three.

Other combinations and resolutions to which a definite meaning was attached could be developed later. Some countries would not be happy unless chords of the 13th and more modern harmonies were employed. This tentative suggestion was politely received, but nothing was done. Is it too late to start educating the man in the street in the rudiments of harmony before he is 'put to sleep' in the key of C?

Your obedient servant,

ARTHUR M. GOODHART

[The summer of 1911 was memorable: a great transport strike with military convoys used to keep essential trains running; the Agadir crisis; Coronation of George V; an Englishman Harold Hilton won both the British Amateur and US Amateur Golf titles; the world's greatest bowler S. F. Barnes played Minor County cricket for Staffordshire; Pavlova and Nijinsky; the Parliament Bill; mutterings in Ulster — and a heatwave.

A Payment of Members Bill, by which MPs would henceforth receive a salary of £400, was regarded by *The Times* as removing the 'last check upon the inrush of mere adventurers'.]

# The Last Straw

*From Mr A. Fell*                              *2 September 1911*

[Conservative Member for Great Yarmouth 1906–22; knighted 1918]

Sir,

I have today received a draft for £94 3s 4d, which is described as the payment for my services as member of Parliament for the quarter ending June 30, 1911, less income-tax at 1s 2d in the pound.

I have never received a payment which has been so repugnant to me as this.

It represents, I calculate, a tax of about 8d on each of the electors in my constituency. I cannot take this money from them of course, so I shall divide the money among the hospitals in the borough.

This cannot, however, wipe out the humiliation I feel at having this money forced upon me to please not more than at the outside 100 out of the 660 members of the House of Commons.

I am your obedient servant,
ARTHUR FELL

# Royal Allowances

*From Mr J. A. Smyth*                           *23 December 1947*

Sir,

Of the 165 members of Parliament who voted to reduce the allowance payable to Princess Elizabeth, can it be stated how many of those members voted to increase their own salaries from £600 to £1,000 a year?

Yours faithfully,
J. A. SMYTH

[A Labour amendment to reduce by £5,000 the proposed additional allowance of £25,000 (making a total of £40,000) to Princess Elizabeth on her marriage to the Duke of Edinburgh had been defeated, though Labour members who voted for the amendment exceeded those who opposed it by 42. Mr Smyth's question was irrelevant.

A *Times* leader on April 3rd 1985 noted that MPs now have a salary of £16,904; with £8,775 a year unchallenged on their car allowance; a maximum of £6,696, in most cases, for staying away from home; and more than £12,000 for secretarial assistance. Little extras include an index-linked pension scheme, travel warrants for wives and children etc. Some wives act as secretaries.]

## The Police and the Poplar strikers

[The Home Secretary had refuted charges that the police behaviour should be condemned]

*From Mr. J. G. Broodbank*                    *19 August 1911*

[acting chairman, Poplar Hospital for Accidents]

Sir,

Our experience on Wednesday week entirely supports Mr Churchill's defence of the police. The scene of the disturbance was immediately in front of this hospital and crowds of people, all more or less excited, thronged the thoroughfares from noon till 11 p.m., yet out of 248 cases (about the normal number) dealt with at this accident hospital on the day in question only one case was connected with the disturbances, viz. that of a man whose leg was bruised by a kick from the horse of a mounted policeman. The staff of the hospital marvelled at the patience shown by the police through the long day.

Yours faithfully,

J. G. BROODBANK

[Parts of London were being protected by 2,000 cavalry and 11,000 infantry sent from Aldershot]

## Sketch of Napoleon

[An original pencil portrait of Napoleon had been discovered in a collection of old papers at the Maidstone museum.

'Sketch of Bonaparte, as laid out on his Austerlitz camp-bed, taken by Captain Marryat, RN, 14 hours after his decease, at the request of Sir Hudson Lowe, May 1821.'

Marryat − later the author of *Mr Midshipman Easy* − was in command of the sloop Beaver.

Correspondents had little to say about this news item, though one did recall an uncle saying in old age that

Napoleon was about 5 foot 6 inches and corpulent, and the possessor of the loudest voice he had ever heard]

*From Colonel Rivett-Carnac*                 *18 September 1911*

[sometime private secretary to the Viceroy, and ADC to the Commander-in-Chief, India; author of *Indian Antiquities*]

Sir,

In relation to the recent correspondence regarding the sketch by Captain Marryat of Napoleon, the following note may interest some of your readers.

Many years ago in India, an officer, then in command of the Fort of Chunan, near Benares, showed me a small oil-sketch of the head of the Emperor on a pillow surrounded by clouds. On the back of the canvas was pasted a piece of paper which had been partially destroyed by white ants, on which could still be deciphered the legend, written in a very fine foreign hand: – 'Esquissé cinq heures après la mort en présence du Général B. . . . . nd.' The history of the painting, related to me by the owner, amounted to this only: – A sergeant of Artillery had said to him, 'Sir, you like old things, and in the bazaar there is an old picture that may suit you.' This was the sketch which was bought for a song. I forget the particular bazaar, but I think it was in Northern India.

It seems possible that the sketch was made by Mme Bertrand, and that it was made in the presence of her husband, the General. I saw it mentioned lately that Mme Bertrand was something of an artist, and that on the Bellerophon she made a sketch of the Emperor which she gave to a naval officer on board.

But how to account for this sketch in an Indian bazaar? Those who years ago amused themselves by hunting for curiosities in the bazaars of Upper India will remember the variety of interesting objects with which the search was occasionally rewarded. I have myself rescued several small objects which told the sad tale of plunder during the Mutiny, and I was able to restore to the family a miniature of a poor lady who was one of many victims. The presence of the Napoleonic relic may possibly be thus explained.

Mr Frazer, the resident at Delhi, who was assassinated there some little time before the Mutiny, was, it was related, a great admirer of Napoleon's. He visited him at St Helena when going home on furlough, and made the prisoner a present of his library. In recognition of this, Napoleon sent Frazer his bust by

Canova, and his Cross of the Legion of Honour. On Frazer's death there came into the possession of his successor, Sir T. Metcalfe (a brother of Lord Metcalfe's, from whom they descended to his son, Sir T. Metcalfe) who was Magistrate of Delhi at the time of the Mutiny, and the story of whose escape will be remembered by some of your readers. After the siege the bust was found in the Metcalfe house at Delhi, and the Cross of the Legion of Honour in a drawer of an old bureau, where it had escaped the notice of the plunderers.

It seems not improbable that the sketch alluded to may have formed part of a Napoleonic collection of Frazer's. The Cross, I may mention, came later into the possession of Lady Clive Bayley, daughter of the T. Metcalfe who was good enough to show it to me on more than one occasion. The purchaser of this picture in the bazaar had a shrewd notion of its value, as he offered it to me at a price far beyond what I was inclined to give.

I am, &tc.,

J. H. RIVETT-CARNAC

## Wall of Death

*From Mr David Le Vay*                    *27 October 1982*

Sir,

One should never overlook the aesthetic factor in disease. Whether Napoleon's death was due to the arsenical content of his wallpaper may be debatable, but perhaps he just didn't like the look of it. After all, it was Oscar Wilde who said on his deathbed: 'This wallpaper is killing me. One of us will have to go.'

Yours faithfully,

DAVID LE VAY

## The Wife of Oscar Wilde

*From Mrs Daisy Swindell*                    *29 April 1976*

Sir,

It would perhaps interest some of your readers to know that whilst in Genoa this Easter, we visited the grave of Constance Lloyd in the English cemetery there.

Constance Lloyd was buried under her maiden name because of the disgrace into which her husband, Oscar Wilde, had fallen. It would now seem that the disgrace is at last absolved, for an

30

additional inscription has been added to the gravestone — 'The wife of Oscar Wilde'.

Incidentally, the burial arcades in this cemetery must surely be one of the most fantastic sights there are to be seen anywhere.

Yours sincerely,

DAISY G. SWINDELL

# Rhodes Scholars on the Track

[Under the will of Cecil Rhodes, 160 scholarships were awarded at Oxford annually — two to students from every state and territory of the USA, three to students from each of 18 British colonies, and 15 to German students selected by Kaiser Wilhelm II. Three facts were to be taken into consideration: scholastic achievements, athletic capacity, and moral force]

*From Mr Anthony Hope*                    *4 November 1913*

[Knighted 1918; *The Times* announced the author of *The Prisoner of Zenda* by his literary name though he signed his letter more modestly]

Sir,

Amidst the stress of greater matters an item of news recently recorded in your columns may have escaped the notice of all except those who take an interest in University athletics. The fact recorded was that all the 'firsts' (and, I think, all the 'seconds' also) at the Oxford Freshmen's sports had been won by Rhodes scholars.

All! Is this merely a remarkable coincidence? It would seem not, if regard be had to the recent history of the Oxford and Cambridge sports. 'We can beat Oxford, but I'm not sure we can beat the British Empire and the United States of America,' I heard a Cambridge man sardonically observe the last time I went to the sports at Queen's Club.

Is it, then, a portent showing the old degeneracy of the youth of these islands? If so, I suppose there is nothing to be done but await, with such faith as we may possess, the progress of eugenics.

But before adopting a conclusion so depressing, I should like to know a little more about the victorious champions. (And may I say that I have no unfriendly feeling about these victories? I have, I trust, all proper sentiments about the Empire overseas, and I have many and strong reasons for friendship with America

31

and her citizens.) It might be material to know their previous records, academic and athletic; it certainly would be material to know the age at which they go up to Oxford; it would even be interesting to follow their subsequent achievements in the schools and in after life.

I do not forget – though I am relying on memory only – that Mr Rhodes desired athletic proficiency to count for something in the award of the scholarships. He desired (so, I think, most people would read his meaning) good, all-round men, the sound mind in the sound body. We should all respectfully agree; but we should all agree also that it would be a great pity if there were ground even for a suspicion that excessive importance were attached to athletic excellence, and truly deplorable if the slightest taint of 'pot-hunting' or if over-specialized and semi-professional athleticism were to creep in. Such a distortion of Mr Rhodes's aims and intentions would amount to something more serious than a mere hardship on Cambridge or some discouragement to native-born Oxford undergraduates – things which could probably be mitigated or wholly removed by fair and sportsmanlike rules governing the entries for University and inter-University sports. As to what these rules should be I, of course, venture on no opinion at present. A careful inquiry would be necessary as a preliminary step.

Motives of delicacy may naturally prevent Cambridge men from raising any questions about this matter in public, but no such reasons exist to hinder an Oxford man from bringing it forward, in the hope that it may receive consideration at the hands of those interested in athletics at Universities and in the future of the scheme from which Mr Rhodes hoped for such great results.

I am, etc.,
ANTHONY H. HAWKINS

[A comment came from a Cambridge man who had represented Great Britain in the 1906 Olympic Games, S. Abrahams: 'The standard of athletics in British public schools is deplorably low.' A younger brother, H. M. Abrahams, won the 100 metres in the 1924 Olympics and, posthumously, lent his person to the film *Chariots of Fire*]

# Rhodes Scholars

[The Rhodes Trustees had decided not to enable Germans once again to come to Oxford]

*From Dr Arnold Toynbee, CH*                    *12 October 1963*

[author of *A Study of History*]

Sir,

In a leading article published on October 5 you honoured the memory of Count Albrecht Bernstorff, who, as Councillor of the German Embassy here under the Weimar regime, did so much for the reestablishment of friendship between Germany and Britain, and who, as you recalled, was afterwards murdered by the Nazis.

One day, between the wars, Count Bernstorff and I got out of the same train from London at Oxford station and walked into the city together. He was looking so happy that I asked him what his obviously pleasant engagement in Oxford was. He told me that he had come to represent his Government at a dinner to celebrate the reestablishment of the German Rhodes scholarships. He added that, to his mind, this was a great day for the cause of Anglo-German friendship, which he had so much at heart.

Events have proved him right. The German Rhodes scholars have had an influence out of proportion to their numbers. They have stood for the best things that are common to the German and British traditions. They have stuck to their principles in adversity, and, as you have reminded your readers, some of them gave their lives for their faith as Bernstorff did.

Experience has thus shown how great a contribution the German Rhodes scholarships can make towards finally closing the unhappy gulf between Germany and other western countries that opened in 1914 and reopened, still wider, when Hitler came into power. President de Gaulle has had the vision to see the importance of reestablishing personal links of friendship with Germany. In Britain we did have the same concern between the wars. It will be sad if we miss our present opportunity of taking the share that we could take in starting a new and happier chapter of European history. May we venture to hope that the Rhodes Trustees will have second thoughts?

Yours, &c.,
ARNOLD TOYNBEE

# The Actress and the Bishop

[On 2 September 1913 *A la Carte* opened at London's Palace Theatre. The star was Gaby Deslys who performed several dances (the style of *The Times* review suggests A. B. Walkley) 'all of them illustrative of the crab-like style she has thought fit, for reasons we cannot understand, to make her own in dancing . . . During the evening Mlle Deslys wore more costumes than we could count.'

Churchwardens were soon hastening to the Palace Theatre, followed by the Bishop of Kensington. His Grace was horrified. Not only did Mlle Deslys appear clad in a dressing gown (over a morning dress), she also lifted her skirt to reveal a stocking-clad leg which she dabbed with a powder puff some nine inches above the ankle. Recognizing vice, the Bishop of Kensington at once warned the editor of *The Times*; *A la Carte* was both 'suggestive' and 'objectionable.' Minor skirmishes took place, then . . .]

*From Mr Bernard Shaw*                    *8 November 1913*

Sir,

May I, as a working playwright, ask the Bishop of Kensington to state his fundamental position clearly? So far, he has begged the question he is dealing with: that is, he has assumed that there can be no possible difference of opinion among good citizens concerning it. He has used the word 'suggestive' without any apparent sense of the fact that the common thoughtless use of it by vulgar people has made it intolerably offensive. And he uses the word 'objectionable' as if there were a general agreement as to what is objectionable and what is not, in spite of the fact that the very entertainment to which he himself objected had proved highly attractive to large numbers of people whose taste is entitled to the same consideration as his own.

On the face of it the Bishop of Kensington is demanding that the plays that he happens to like shall be tolerated and those which he happens not to like shall be banned. He is assuming

35

that what he approves of is right, and what he disapproves of, wrong. Now, I have not seen the particular play which he so much dislikes; but suppose I go to see it tonight, and write a letter to you to-morrow to say that I approve of it, what will the Bishop have to say? He will have either to admit that his epithet of objectionable means simply disliked by the Bishop of Kensington, or he will have to declare boldly that he and I stand in the relation of God and the Devil. And, however his courtesy and his modesty may recoil from this extremity, when it is stated in plain English, I think he has got there without noticing it. At all events, he is clearly proceeding on the assumption that his conscience is more enlightened than that of the people who go to the Palace Theatre and enjoy what they see there. If the Bishop may shut up the Palace Theatre on this assumption, then the Nonconformist patrons of the Palace Theatre (and it has many of them) may shut up the Church of England by turning the assumption inside out. The sword of persecution always has two edges.

By 'suggestive' the Bishop means suggestive of sexual emotion. Now a Bishop who goes into a theatre and declares that the performances there must not suggest sexual emotion is in the position of a playwright going into a church and declaring that the services there must not suggest religious emotion. The suggestion, gratification, and education of sexual emotion is one of the main uses and glories of the theatre. It shares that function with all the fine arts. The sculpture courts of the Victoria and Albert Museum in the Bishop's diocese are crowded with naked figures of extraordinary beauty, placed there expressly that they may associate the appeal of the body with such beauty, refinement, and expression of the higher human qualities that our young people, contemplating them, will find baser objects of desire repulsive. In the National Gallery body and soul are impartially catered for: men have worshipped Venuses and fallen in love with Virgins. There is a voluptuous side to religious ecstasy and a religious side to voluptuous ecstasy; and the notion that one is less sacred than the other is the opportunity of the psychiatrist who seeks to discredit the saints by showing that the passion which exalted them was in its abuse capable also of degrading sinners. The so-called Song of Solomon, which we now know to be an erotic poem, was mistaken by the translators of the 17th century for a canticle of Christ to His Church, and is to this day so labelled in our Bibles.

Now let us turn to the results of cutting off young people — not to mention old ones — from voluptuous art. We have families who bring up their children in the belief that an undraped statue is an abomination; that a girl or a youth who looks at a picture by Paul Veronese is corrupted for ever; that the theatre in which *Tristan and Isolde* or *Romeo and Juliet* is performed is the gate of hell; and that the contemplation of a figure attractively dressed or revealing more of its outline than a Chinaman's dress does is an act of the most profligate indecency. Of Chinese sex morality I must not write in the pages of *The Times*. Of the English and Scottish sex morality that is produced by this starvation and blasphemous vilification of vital emotions I will say only this: that it is so morbid and abominable, so hatefully obsessed by the things that tempt it, so merciless in its persecution of all the divine grace which grows in the soil of our sex instincts when they are not deliberately perverted and poisoned, that if it could be imposed, as some people would impose it if they could, on the whole community for a single generation, the Bishop, even at the risk of martyrdom, would reopen the Palace Theatre with his episcopal benediction, and implore the lady to whose performances he now objects to return to the stage even at the sacrifice of the last rag of her clothing.

I venture to suggest that when the Bishop heard that there was an objectionable (to him) entertainment at the Palace Theatre, the simple and natural course for him was not to have gone there. That is how sensible people act. And the result is that if a manager offers a widely objectionable entertainment to the public he very soon finds out his mistake and withdraws it. It is my own custom as a playwright to make my plays 'suggestive' of religious emotion. This makes them extremely objectionable to irreligious people. But they have the remedy in their own hands. They stay away. The Bishop will be glad to hear that there are not many of them; but it is a significant fact that they frequently express a wish that the Censor would suppress religious plays, and that he occasionally complies. In short, the Bishop and his friends are not alone in proposing their own tastes and convictions as the measure of what is permissible in the theatre. But if such individual and sectarian standards were tolerated we should have no plays at all, for there never yet was a play that did not offend somebody's taste.

I must remind the Bishop that if the taste for voluptuous entertainment is sometimes morbid, the taste for religious edification is open to precisely the same objection. If I had a neurotic daughter I would much rather risk taking her to the Palace Theatre than to a revival meeting. Nobody has yet counted the homes and characters wrecked by intemperance in religious emotion. When we begin to keep such statistics the chapel may find its attitude of moral superiority to the theatre, and even to the publichouse, hard to maintain, and may learn a little needed charity. We all need to be reminded of the need for temperance and toleration in religious emotion and in political emotion, as well as in sexual emotion. But the Bishop must not conclude that I want to close up all places of worship: on the contrary, I preach in them. I do not even clamour for the suppression of political party meetings, though nothing more foolish and demoralizing exists in England to-day. I live and let live. As long as I am not compelled to attend revival meetings, or party meetings, or theatres at which the sexual emotions are ignored or reviled, I am prepared to tolerate them on reciprocal terms; for though I am unable to conceive any good coming to any human being as a set-off to their hysteria, their rancorous bigotry, and their dullness and falsehood, I know that those who like them are equally unable to conceive any good coming of the sort of assemblies I frequent; so I mind my own business and obey the old precept — 'He that is unrighteous, let him do unrighteousness still; and he that is filthy let him be made filthy still; and he that is righteous let him do righteousness still; and he that is holy let him be made holy still.' For none of us can feel quite sure in which category the final judgment may place us; and in the meantime Miss Gaby Deslys is as much entitled to the benefit of the doubt as the Bishop of Kensington.

Yours truly,

G. BERNARD SHAW

*Reproduced by courtesy of The Society of Authors, for the Bernard Shaw Estate.*

[In the column adjoining Shaw's letter were details of the imminent arrival at Windsor Castle of the Archduke Francis [*sic*] Ferdinand of Austria and his wife, the Duchess of Hohenberg. Little more than seven months later, the couple visited Sarajevo. Bernard Shaw's attitude towards the war increased his unpopularity]

## Top of the Top Pops

*From Mr David Chesterman*                    *6 November 1962*

Sir,

Your Music Critic rightly deplores the lack of adventure in London's current musical life. It would not be so bad if some attempt were made to avoid repeated performances of a particular symphony within a few days, but this is continually happening.

I have analysed all the symphonies scheduled for performance in the Festival Hall during 1962. Taking Beethoven, there are no less than 10 Eroicas, while Nos 1 and 2 get one performance each. Is this sensible? And during 1961 there were 13 Brahms symphonies, yet not a single appearance of No. 3.

For the record the Top Ten in 1962 are:

| Beethoven | 44 | Haydn | 12 |
|---|---|---|---|
| Mozart | 26 | Schubert | 9 |
| Tchaikovsky | 19 | Berlioz | 8 |
| Dvorak | 14 | Mahler | 6 |
| Brahms | 13 | Bruckner | 5 |

Yours faithfully,
DAVID CHESTERMAN

[By 1971 Mr Chesterman had apparently installed a computer in his attic. 'To Mahler's basic 14 I must add 1/5 + 1/6 + 1/6 (the *Adagio* only from No. 10, and two appearances at Ernest Read Children's Concerts of What the wild flowers tell me from No. 3). *Das Lied von der Erde* is scheduled twice, but should it be counted? It is not a numbered symphony . . .' A cry of pain was heard]

*From Mr J. P. Jackson*                    *3 November 1971*

Sir,
It seems pointless to judge the popularity of composers by the number of times their symphonies have been performed at the Royal Festival Hall. Indeed, it is totally meaningless. J. S. Bach wrote no symphonies, as did Monteverdi, Purcell, Debussy, Ravel and goodness knows how many more. Haydn wrote 104, Roussel 4, Elgar 2. So what? What is Mr Chesterman trying to prove? Let him tell us the *playing time* devoted to each composer. That would be interesting, even if limited to the Festival Hall.

Yours faithfully,
J. P. JACKSON

*From Mr David Chesterman*                    *November 1971*

Sir,
Mr J. P. Jackson chides me for confining my musical statistics to symphonies, and asks for the *playing time* devoted to *all* the orchestral compositions of the Top Ten at the Royal Festival Hall during 1971. Here are the figures in minutes, calculated from S. Aronowsky's 'Performing Times of Orchestral Works':

| Beethoven | 1,922 | Tchaikovsky | 1,012 |
| Mozart | 1,696 | Bruckner | 691 |
| Brahms | 1,488 | Haydn | 519 |
| Bach | 1,320 | Shostakovich | 507 |
| Mahler | 1,172 | Schubert | 429 |

In other words, the audience could have heard all the Beethoven at a sitting if they took their seats at 8 p.m. on a Monday evening and rose at 4.02 a.m. on the following Wednesday morning (excluding the time necessary for tuning up).

Bach, who never appeared in my symphonic statistics, is fourth by this reckoning and Sibelius, who was tenth, disappears, with only 391 minutes to his credit. There are slight differences of order, but the rest of the Top Ten remain in the picture.

Yours faithfully,
DAVID CHESTERMAN

[Mr Chesterman omitted to give a plug to the RFH's catering department: 8 p.m. on Monday to 4.02 a.m. on Wednesday covers one breakfast, one lunch, one tea, one dinner, and two late suppers − plus stimulants for the orchestra. If Aronowsky's 'performing times' are faster than those of, say, a Klemperer, we may add another breakfast.

The years brought complications. A 'finished' version of Schubert's 'Unfinished' Symphony prompted the thought that normal versions should each be reduced to ½. In 1980 Mozart recorded 39 8/924 performances − a false start to No 41 when the conductor noticed after eight bars that a wind player was missing.

Chesterman 1978 encouraged the *Sunday Times* to join the act. Foreign correspondents reported that Beethoven was champion in Paris, Berlin, Rome and Moscow as well as in London, New York dissenting in the shape of Schubert. Stravinsky ranked high in Paris and Berlin, Schumann and Richard Strauss in Rome. Moscow admitted Mozart and Brahms but otherwise concentrated mainly on home products. Meanwhile Chesterman had extended the scope of his investigations]

*From Mr David Chesterman*                    *9 January 1985*

Sir,

Analysis of all symphonies played in London's Barbican, Royal Albert, Festival and Queen Elizabeth halls and at St

John's Smith Square during 1984 shows that Mozart, with 70, has retained the lead for the second year, but only by a whisker.

Beethoven scores 69½, to which must be added an incalculable fraction representing chunks of the 'Eroica' included in Carl Davis's score for the silent film *Napoleon*, given at the Barbican on December 29 by the Wren Orchestra. Even straining a point, these chunks do not amount to half a symphony.

Tchaikovsky is third with 35½.

Haydn and Schubert appear to be equal with 33¼ each, but Haydn claims priority. At a Robert Mayer concert, in which the first movement only of No. 99 was scheduled, the conductor decided to give the children an idea of the second movement and played six bars of it.

Dvorak has 24, Brahms 22¼, Sibelius 15, Mahler 13¼ and Mendelssohn 13, achieving a place in the top ten for the first time.

Beethoven No. 3 was most frequently played — 14 plus the incalculable fraction.

Yours faithfully,<br>DAVID CHESTERMAN

[The most frequently played symphonies, 1962–84, were Beethoven Nos 3, 5, 7 and 9; Schubert No. 9; and Dvorak No. 9]

## Prince Louis of Battenberg

*From Mr J. H. Thomas, MP*                    *4 November 1914*

[Labour Member for Derby; future General Secretary of the NUR, and Cabinet minister]

Sir,

It is very seldom that I trouble your readers with a communication, but as a Labour leader I desire to express my extreme regret at the announcement that Prince Louis of Battenberg has, by his resignation, pandered to the most mean and contemptible slander I have ever known.

When addressing recruiting meetings in all parts of the country I was simply astounded to hear the base suggestions and rumours current, and I am afraid that his action will simply be looked upon as a triumph for the mean and miserable section of people who, at a time of national trial, is ever ready to pass a foul lie from lip to lip without a tittle of evidence.

I know nothing of Prince Louis except that I have never met any one, either in Parliament or connected with the Navy, but who spoke in the highest terms of his great ability and usefulness in our Navy; and if a man's honour is to be impugned in the manner and method as adopted in this case, then it will indeed be difficult for public men to endeavour to serve their country in a manner we have a right to expect.

I am yours faithfully,

J. H. THOMAS

[Prince Louis was forced to resign the office of First Sea Lord – 29 October 1914 – on account of his German origins. His younger son was the future Admiral of the Fleet, Earl Mountbatten of Burma]

# 1815–1915

*From Canon W. Wood*                    *15 January 1915*

Sir,

May I add another illustration to those which have already appeared in your columns, showing how near two lives can bring together events which seem so far apart? I remember my father telling me how, when he was attending a country grammar school in 1805, one day the master came in, full of a strange excitement, and exclaimed, 'Boys, we've won a great victory!' Then he stopped, burst into tears, and added, 'But Nelson – Nelson is killed!' When I was myself a boy Waterloo was a recent event, and even 'the '45' was remembered and talked about.

In a few weeks I shall be 85, but can still ride my bicycle.

WILLIAM WOOD, DD

## Racing in Wartime

*From Lord Rosebery*                    *5 March 1915*

[Between 1883 and 1923 the winner of the Derby twice (when Prime Minister 1894–95), the One Thousand Guineas three times, the Two Thousand Guineas, the Oaks and the St Leger]

Sir,

I am afraid I cannot follow your reasoning with regard to Epsom and Ascot as set forth in your brief leading article to-day. I put aside the remarks about the affair of the Epsom Grand Stand, as to which there has been both misstatement and misapprehension, which I should have thought the matter-of-fact statement of the Stewards of the Jockey Club would have finally cleared away.

But that is a side, and I may add a false, issue. You say that our Allies 'cannot understand how Englishmen can go to race meetings when their country is engaged in a life and death struggle.' With all submission I think our Allies understand us better than this. They know that Englishmen do not think it necessary to put up the shutters whenever they are engaged in war. They know that we are paying two millions a day for this war, and do not think that we shall add the sacrifice of our thoroughbred horses, which are so invaluable for the future of our Army. For, make no mistake, if our races are to cease our thoroughbred horses must disappear. No man can afford to keep bloodstock for the mere pleasure of looking at them in the stable. You hope that there will be no attempt to hold meetings at Epsom, and, 'above all,' at Ascot this year. Of what nature, may I ask, is the original sin attaching to these meetings? You record races of a very inferior character almost daily in your columns, sometimes in impressive print. Why do you sanction these and select for special reprobation the two noblest exhibitions of the thoroughbred in the world?

But you say our Allies will misunderstand us. There are many, however, of our French allies who will remember that the winner of the Derby was announced in General Orders during the Crimean War.

Why, indeed, should we embark on the unprecedented course which you indicate, and condemn all our historical practice? Once before our country has been 'engaged in a life and death struggle,' at least as strenuous and desperate as this; I mean that against the French Revolution and Napoleon. All through that score of bloody years the Epsom and Ascot Meetings were regularly held, nor indeed does it seem to have occurred to our forefathers that it was guilty to witness races while we were at war. I remember asking the late Lord Stradbroke which was the most interesting race that he had ever witnessed for the Ascot Cup. He replied (I am almost sure, though it is outside my argument) that for 1815, which was run on June 8, eight days before Quatre Bras, 10 days before Waterloo, when Napoleon and Wellington were confronting each other to contend for the championship of the world.

I am and desire to remain remote from controversy, but am anxious to remind you of our history and tradition with regard to this question, and to ask you to pause before you condemn not merely Epsom and 'above all' Ascot, but also the principles and practice of ancestors not less chivalrous and humane than ourselves.

ROSEBERY

## A Field for Lord Derby

[In the autumn of 1915 Lord Derby was told to organize a scheme whereby men of military age 'attested' their willingness to serve when called upon. The hope was to avoid conscription]

*From Sir Frederick Milner*                    *19 October 1915*

[Conservative member for Bassetlaw, 1890–1906; a recreation was 'stalking']

Sir,

I would suggest to Lord Derby that he may find Newmarket Heath, during Cambridgeshire week, a fruitful ground for his new recruiting scheme. I am told that during the past week swarms of able-bodied slackers were to be found daily at Newmarket. They can hardly plead they are rendering useful service to the State by betting and gambling. Every one of them should be plainly told they have got to come in, or will be fetched.

I remain very truly yours,<br>FREDERICK MILNER

## Starched Linen

*From Lady Selborne*                    *17 February 1916*

Sir,

I should be much obliged if anyone would tell me why the authorities have not forbidden the wearing of starched linen. If there is a scarcity of bread-stuffs it is surely the height of folly to permit a large quantity of rice or maize to be used in obedience to a not very sensible fashion for the personal adornment of the male sex. Fortunately, for the moment, women's fashions do not demand starched collars, and the cruel custom of starching little children's frocks is a memory of Victorian times. Surely it is not a great demand on the patriotism of our husbands and fathers that they should forgo this adjunct to their appearance.

Let them reflect that what they lose in beauty they will gain in comfort, and if every man wears a flannel or canvas shirt no one will feel any embarrassment at doing so. The bread ration decreed by the Food Controller is ample for the upper and middle class households, who can eat a variety of other foods. It is not enough for labourers' families. One of the chief substitutes they can use is rice. It is within their means, and the children can be fed on it. In these circumstances it does seem to me that it ought to be used with economy, and not to be wasted in an employment which is certainly not of national importance.

I am your obedient servant,

MAUD SELBORNE

## The Ideals of Brahms

[Robert von Mendelssohn, banker and brilliant amateur cellist, had died in Berlin]

*From Sir David Hunter-Blair*            *29 August 1917*

[OSB; (titular) Abbot of Dunfermline]

Sir,

The writer of your little obituary notice of Robert von Mendelssohn, who had, we are told, nothing German about him except his name, describes him as 'the friend of so many of Germany's best – Clara Schumann, Joachim, and Brahms – none of whom, happily, lived to see the wreck of their ideals.'

With regard to Brahms, one would rather like to know what ideal of his has been wrecked by the present policy, attitude, and action of Germany, which is presumably what the writer refers to. Brahms was a great musician and a German (though not a Prussian). His music is eternal, and independent of the limits of place and time. But his personal ideals were German through and through, and his dislike and contempt for England were notorious and invincible all through his life, which almost coincided with the long reign of Queen Victoria. He never set foot in England; he twice refused a degree from an English university, and his letter declining to write a work for a great English festival, though sometimes cited as humorous, was simply offensive. Brahms's English biographers have almost entirely glossed over his hatred of England, one of the best known of them naively stating that he would not visit us because he dreaded being lionized and made much of. And I remember at a university musical club meeting much indignation being wasted on a member who objected to an English club

45

contributing to a memorial to a man, however eminent, who detested England and all her works.

Once more, what 'ideal' cherished by Brahms has been wrecked in the present upheaval of Europe? One would really like to hear.

Your obedient servant,
DAVID HUNTER-BLAIR

[Below this letter was notice of a Memorial service at St Nicholas Church, Liverpool, for Captain Noel Godfrey Chavasse, RAMC. This officer had recently been awarded a Bar to his Victoria Cross, posthumously]

*From Sir Charles Stanford*                    *1 September 1917*

[His friends included Brahms, Joachim, von Bülow and Saint-Saëns, his pupils Vaughan Williams, Holst, Ireland, Bridge (Britten's master) and Howells]

Sir,

Sir David Hunter-Blair had not, as far as I am aware, the only direct means of ascertaining Brahms's attitude to this country – personal knowledge of the man. I am one of the few left who had that privilege. I state positively that Sir David Hunter-Blair and his University Club friend are entirely wrong, and, from ignorance of course, took a wholly false view of his opinions. I know why Brahms did not come for an English degree, and have his letter (written in very different terms from what Sir David imagines) in my possession now. I also know the reasons why he wrote the letter to a 'great English Festival', which, so far as being offensive, was a model of well-deserved and subtle irony; but I refrain from specifying the reasons for it, because to do so would involve personal matters which are none too creditable to ourselves and are best left buried with the protagonists.

The *naïveté* to which Sir David alludes is so obviously intended for me that I feel compelled to reply thus: – He may consider the dislike of social publicity *naïf*, but it still happily exists in some men who are too big to care for it, and Brahms was one of these. He shared with Beethoven an admiration for this country, which like Beethoven, he never could face the journey to see. His scathing condemnation of Prussian policy at the time of the Chino-Japanese war, expressed in no measured terms at a Grand Ducal State Dinner, is on record. He loved his country, but to hazard the guess that he despised and detested ours is to cast an unwarrantable slur both upon his memory and upon his judgment.

Yours faithfully,
CHARLES V. STANFORD

# A Poltergeist

[On 8 August 1919 explosions shook Swanton Novers Rectory, near Melton Constable, Norfolk. Soon oil began to pour from the ceilings and gush from the floors. The week ending 30 August saw various spurts: Monday water, Tuesday petrol, Wednesday pure paraffin, Thursday petrol and paraffin, Friday water. 'Inexplicable,' said the experts]

*From Sir Sydney Olivier*                    *3 September 1919*

[Civil servant; Fabian; as Baron Olivier Secretary for India in MacDonald's first Labour government 1924; uncle of Laurence Olivier]

Sir,

These manifestations of unction at Swanton Rectory have all the characteristics of a case of *Poltergeisterei*. In such cases, as the records of the SPR [Society for Psychical Research] bear witness, there may almost invariably be found 'a little 15-year-old girl' about the place, or sometimes an equally ostensibly innocent boy. It seems that such young creatures serve the Poltergeist as a *nidus* or *point d'appui* for his (or her) diversions. It is therefore probable that if the 'little girl' mentioned is removed from the Manse the energies of the mysterious agent of these exudations may languish and shortly cease.

Yours faithfully,
SYDNEY OLIVIER

[In Noel Coward's *Blithe Spirit* (1941) there was found a little 18-year-old (?), the maid Edith. Admirers of the Master's sublime farcical masterpiece will not need to be reminded of:

MADAME ARCATI: That cuckoo is very angry.
CHARLES: How can you tell?
MADAME ARCATI: *Timbre.*]


# Richesse Oblige

[This letter was delivered to *The Times* by hand, its bearer (J. C. Davidson) explaining to the editor the identity of the writer]

*24 June 1919*

Sir,

It is now a truism to say that in August 1914, the nation was face to face with the greatest crisis in her history. She was saved by the free will offerings of her people. The best of her men rushed to the colours; the best of her women left their homes to spend and be spent; the best of her older men worked as they had never worked before, to a common end, and with a sense of unity and fellowship as new as it was exhilarating. It may be that in four and half years the ideals of many became dim, but the spiritual impetus of those early days carried the country through to the end.

Today on the eve of peace, we are faced with another crisis, less obvious but none the less searching. The whole country is exhausted. By natural reaction, not unlike that which led to the excesses of the Restoration after the reign of the Puritans, all classes are in danger of being submerged on a wave of extravagance and materialism. It is so easy to live on borrowed money; so difficult to realise that you are doing so.

It is so easy to play; so hard to learn that you cannot play for long without work. A fool's paradise is only the ante-room to a fool's hell.

How can a nation be made to understand the gravity of the financial situation; that love of country is better than love of money?

This can only be done by example and the wealthy classes have today an opportunity of service which can never recur.

They know the danger of the present debt; they know the weight of it in the years to come. They know the practical difficulties of a universal statutory capital levy. Let them impose upon themselves, each as he is able, a voluntary levy. It should be possible to pay to the Exchequer within twelve months such a sum as would save the tax payer 50 millions a year.

I have been considering this matter for nearly two years, but my mind moves slowly; I dislike publicity, and I had hoped that somebody else might lead the way. I have made as accurate an estimate as I am able of the value of my own estate, and have arrived at a total of about £580,000. I have decided to realize 20% of that amount or say £120,000 which will purchase £150,000 of the new War Loan, and present it to the Government for cancellation.

I give this portion of my estate as a thank-offering in the firm conviction that never again shall we have such a chance of giving our country that form of help which is so vital at the present time.

Yours, etc.,

F.S.T.

48

[The initials F.S.T. stood for Financial Secretary to the Treasury – Stanley Baldwin.

Although a *Times* leader described his letter as 'noble,' the future prime minister's idea does not appear to have caught on]


# The German Prisoners

*From Mr J. D. Rees*                                  *3 September 1919*

Sir,

May I try to answer Lord Selborne's question of yesterday? As Director of the Prisoners of War Information Bureau, I have visited large numbers of the camps, and as I am not responsible in any way for the discipline maintained therein, I am at least an impartial and independent witness. Each prisoner has his fixed, and admittedly ample, ration. This he distributes over the day as he pleases, and he does please very often, too often, to take out with him for his work in the field a very small proportion of the whole allowance. The farmer, for instance, sees a prisoner produce a few biscuits, or a lean luncheon of the like character, and he says, 'No man shall work for me on an empty stomach,' and gives the wily foreigner a square meal. The latter on return to camp finds his day's ration only slightly diminished, and dines at large, rejoicing in his guile. To prevent this exploitation of the employer, some commandants of camps, wisely, as it seems to me, have insisted on the provision of a suitable proportion for the mid-day meal.

At any rate, the total ration has proved quite sufficient, and it has been necessary, in view of charges of indiscipline and of intercommunication which have been made, and of the necessity for maintaining the status of prisoner, to forbid the receipt of food, money, or letters by the occupants of the camps, when they are out at farms, or in quarries, or engaged in other occupations. The opportunity should not be lost of explaining that the employers of prisoners of war always pay the full local market rate for their labour to Government, which credits the taxpayer with the difference between that amount and the far smaller sum which the prisoners are actually paid. Nor, while doing justice to the War Office and the Government should less be done for the prisoners of war, who have, for the most part, worked well and made no complaints of the *dura ilia* of their captors.

I am, Sir, your obedient servant,

J. D. REES

49

# Baths for Prisoners

*From Mr L. Sandeman Allen*                    6 June 1946

Sir,

About five months ago, on being demobilized, I bought a derelict farm in Devon which I and my wife and daughter are struggling to reclaim. We have for some time employed two German prisoners of war daily. A little while ago we were told that unless we could accommodate these prisoners of war we would not be able to have them. Our farm house is in a state of semi-reconstruction, we have done all our cooking on primus stoves, and in spite of all permits are still not possessed of a bath. We managed, however, to clear a room for two men to live as family.

The military inspector arrived subsequently. He declared the place was in a bit of a muddle; perhaps if the men came in a fortnight's time we might be able to get it a little straighter; and as we had no bath we should of course drive the prisoners of war to their camp eight miles away each Sunday evening. Presumably as we are only decadent democrats we may, without comment, bath in a tin bath and cook on a primus stove while spending our hard-earned Sunday evening's rest taking men of the master race to a bath eight miles away, using our basic petrol ration for the purpose. It goes without saying that the Germans get the agricultural cheese ration, the owner of the farm does not.

> Yours faithfully,
> L. SANDEMAN ALLEN

# Mr Weller's Watch

*From Mr William Canon Smith*                    12 September 1919

Sir,

I am the fortunate owner of a watch which, I believe, once belonged to Mr Weller, senior. The watch is a pound in weight, within a fraction of an ounce. It is a verge, double-cased watch, by Edward Manley, London, No 17,394. I have had the date verified as about 1830, five or six years, anyway, before the publication of *Pickwick*. The watch is of silver, with proper Hall marks, which of course give the date. On the back of the outer case is inscribed 'Mr Weller, Senr.'

The watch was left to me by a Mr George Parker, deceased, an Uppingham and Oxford man, who told me that the watch was given to him by a lady, who told him that she had often seen Charles Dickens riding on the box-seat of the Bath and Bristol coach with Mr Weller, senior. Any further remarks about the watch are the result of my own surmise. I imagine that the watch was made for a show watch in the shop window. It is too heavy for wear, and I suggest that the watch was bought and presented to Mr Weller, senior, by some jovial friends and admirers. Any further information about the watch would be of interest to me and, I think, to the public.

Yours, &c.,
WILLIAM CANON SMITH

*From Mr T. Sturge Cotterell*      *16 September 1919*

Sir,

The letter of Mr William Canon Smith, of Liverpool, in your recent issue is of great interest to the comparatively few readers and admirers in these days of the *Pickwick Papers* but whether the watch referred to was ever the property of Mr Weller, senior, of Bath, it is difficult to say with any certainty. The Weller family were well known in the early part of the last century in Bath, and particularly by the coaching fraternity. Old 'Daniel Weller' possessed many characteristics of the 'old 'un.' He was a hostler, and daily busily engaged in tending the coach-horses stabled at the York House mews. Daniel was a widower, and adjoining the mews was the 'York House Tap,' kept by a widow; it was a favourite resort of old Daniel, who spent many a pleasant evening in the 'snuggery,' and thinking in time that a quieter life would suit his constitution, proposed to the widow and married her.

Daniel congratulated himself on having made a good bargain. The prospect held out to him of a comfortable competence in congenial surroundings in his declining days led him to be particularly generous on his wedding day; but no sooner had the marriage taken place and he had installed himself as the landlord of the 'tap' than the widow whom he had married was found by him to be head over ears in debt, and all the romance of his marriage was rudely dispelled. He had his work cut out to keep himself out of a debtors' prison.

It is probable that Dickens heard his story first hand when in Bath in 1835, but it is highly improbable that Daniel ever drove a coach; he may have driven one of the two horse omnibuses that plied between Bath and Bristol. This singular watch may have been a wedding gift from his many friends on the occasion of his second and unfortunate marriage. His eldest son John, who died in 1893 at the age of 76, possessed many of the characteristics of the original 'Samivel.' In his early days John went to London, eventually rose to be a coachman; subsequently he returned to Bath. He was an amusing and instructive little man, popular with his class and excellent at repartee, and was a well-known character in the city of Bath.

T. STURGE COTTERELL

*From Canon William Smith*         *September 1919*

Sir,

Mr Cotterell evidently knows all that is to be known about the Weller family. He acknowledges that the watch is 'singular' and of great interest, but is dubious about its ever being in the possession of Mr Weller, senior. Well, Sir, I headed my letter modestly as 'A Dickens' Relic,' and you yourself, Sir, altered the heading to 'Mr Weller's Watch,' and, of course, I think you are right, and am grateful for the alteration. Whoever Mr Weller, senior, was, I think that there are three very good proofs that he owned this watch. There is the date of manufacture, 1830. There is the date of the first edition of *Pickwick*, 1837. There is the inscription on the back, 'Mr Weller, Senr.' Could anything be clearer? It is highly probable, as Mr Cotterell says, that it was a wedding present. A word about the definition of my poor self, to prevent further confusion. I am a Catholic priest and a Canon of the Catholic Archdiocese of Liverpool.

Yours, &c.,

WILLIAM SMITH (Canon)

## All Must Work

*From Admiral of the Fleet Lord Fisher, OM*    *5 January 1920*

[During the 14 months prior to his death in July 1920, the greatest British sailor since Nelson had 36 letters in *The Times*. Their style was unique]

Sir,

A friend tells me in Canada a policeman can ask any saunterer, even in a glossy silk hat and white spats, if he is idle, and can hale him there and then before authority to be made to work. My friend may be lying, but it's a righteous lie. Elisha lied to the hosts of the Syrians and said: – 'This is not the way, neither is this the city – follow me, and I will bring you to the man whom ye seek' (being himself!). By the way, I've never read any episcopal or ecclesiastical remonstrance about Elisha's lie – I suppose it's the origin of 'All is fair in love and war'!

To resume: – The only escape from national ruin is by *increased production*, and to this end the object of these few words is not to saddle the 'working man' alone with this vital necessity, but to lay that vital necessity on the whole nation. A huge co-operation of all classes is imperative. 'Co-operation in profits' being the first article in the new Magna Charta. Some have brains, some have money, some have physical aptitude. All lend a hand. This is the only way to get rid of class antagonism, nationalization, and all the other funny systems of getting something out of nothing, or 'eating your cake and drinking it' (as someone said I said – another Elisha lie!).

According to recently disclosed departmental facts (I own also these may be lies) the United States dollar is scooping us out, and the United States mercantile marine (at zero before the war) possesses now 12 million tons of shipping, as against our corresponding 18 millions – not that I think England will succumb – *she never does* – but *Production is the one word*. The artisan must be encouraged and be made free by becoming a partner. That's the way out. To be a *flaneur* in Bond-street does us no good in production. Such must 'pay up' for that luxury or go to prison (as in Canada). *Every one must work*.

Yours,

FISHER

P.S. Soon it may be once more 'too late'. Read Ludendorff's epilogue that 'Workmen's Councils' brought about the Revolution and the Revolution stopped the war. I don't agree. That same bevy who won the war for Elisha (when he lied) won the war for us. We prayed – the others didn't! Kitchener said to Lord Roberts at the Marne, 'Someone has been praying'! There was no other way of accounting for the miracle.

[Bond Street is an 8-iron from the east side of Dover Street which houses The Drones]

## Aviation Spells Salvation

*From Admiral of the Fleet Lord Fisher, OM   8 January 1920*

Sir,

Justly described as the most distinguished of living poets, he writes me that Thor's Hammer is urgently required to beat into the British mind that Aviation spells Salvation. Even Macaulay's Schoolboy knows that it's not war aviation that's at stake! Civil aircraft are capable of the war job. They are depicted leaving their peaceful avocations (I take this from a war lecture) and arriving in their thousands of thousands (darkening the heavens in their flight), and without a declaration of war appearing unexpectedly over London and pouring down cascades of lethal gas (the humane describer adds there is a good deal to be said for a gas which kills without torturing).

Terror is no argument, least of all in our nation. When our blood is up we are equal to any fate. Nevertheless, the Germans are going ahead of us in aviation-structure and aviation-engines. Intellect, imagination, push, money − all are pleading − yet the Air Service, under a Sub-Secretary, is relegated to the War Office − bad enough if it had been relegated to the Admiralty, for, after all, that good Admiral was right (all Admirals ain't good) who told Mr Pitt that the business of the Admiralty was to prevent oversea invasion, and that it wasn't a military business. We must appeal unto Caesar (Caesar has had a good look in at the Spen Valley). Over four hundred millions sterling for probably more conscription if we are going to take on Russia, and a hundred and fifty millions for the Admiralty to buy 'bows and arrows' when a fraction of all this wanton waste spent in aviation would keep us in the forefront of the world, both in commerce and in war. All this is what no fellow can understand! Caesar shortly will Sack the Lot!

Yours,

FISHER

P.S. I've quoted from a lecture on the next war. Every fool knows that every war begins where the last war left off. Every airman knows that when the last war left off such a bombing had been arranged for Berlin (and was kept from starting) that would have made that city dust and ashes. Some people say the German nation at large still believe it wasn't beaten. There is a good deal to be said for this atmosphere that pervades Germany. Yet one does admire Foch, even if he saved but one widow. It is computed that by agreeing to the Armistice when he did Foch saved two hundred thousand Allied casualties alone. The Germans would have been mown down (or bombed) in masses.

[At the recent Spen Valley by-election, the prime minister, Lloyd George, had received a rebuff. Sponsoring a Coalition Liberal against an Independent Liberal, he had seen his candidate come third, and the seat won by Labour.

54

The identity of Lord Fisher's 'most distinguished of living poets' escapes the Cuckoo. Robert Bridges perhaps? Or had Thomas Hardy entered the Admiral's orbit? More likely the poet was Sir William Watson who, four days after the above letter was published, had some verse in *The Times*:

FISHER
Foreseer renowned! . . .
The anger of the sea is in your lips,
The laughter of the sea is in your eye.]


## Extradition of the Kaiser

*From Mr Walter B. Woodgate*                    *27 January 1920*

[barrister; member of the winning Oxford crews 1862–63]

Sir,

The refusal of Holland to extradite the Kaiser appears to be founded on a contention that diplomacy must not recognize *ex post facto* legislation as regards crime, and that certain acts of the Kaiser now alleged by the Allies to be criminal were not — by any international 'statute' — crimes when the late war began.

Now, 'statute' law only comes into existence in situations where pre-existing *lex non scripta* (common law) is deficient. But ever since the era of establishment of diplomacy, with embassies and legations, acts of brigandage or piracy have been held — by *lex non scripta* — to outlaw those who practise them, and, *a fortiori*, when involving wholesale slaughter of unarmed civilians of both sexes, with rape and robbery thrown in as concomitants.

Civilization and diplomacy have long ago differentiated belligerency and its regulations from brigandage and piracy. The indictment against the Kaiser (and divers of his henchmen) would be that they have in certain situations acted as brigands and pirates, and not as belligerents.

Surely it would be internationally immoral to rule that the role of leader of a Kelly gang of bushrangers or of train robbers in the Rockies, or of a skipper under the black flag with plank walk for victims, can become venial and 'privileged' when expanded and adapted as the function of a State under the ordinances of its sovereign, whether monarchical or presidential?

WALTER B. WOODGATE

[On 17 June 1940 – the day on which Pétain asked the Germans for an armistice – the exiled Kaiser sent from Doorn, in occupied Holland, a telegram of congratulations to Hitler.

'Under the deeply moving impression of the capitulation of France I congratulate you and the whole German Wehrmacht on the mighty victory granted by God, in the words of the Emperor Wilhelm the Great in 1870: "What a turn of events brought about by divine dispensation."

In all German hearts there echoes the Leuthen chorale sung by the victors of Leuthen, the soldiers of the Great King: "Now thank we all our God!" '

William L. Shirer, *The Rise and Fall of the Third Reich* (1959)

Kaiser Wilhelm II died at Doorn on 4 June 1941]

# What Bird for Britain?

*From Lord Hurcomb*            *18 October 1960*

[Chairman, British Section, The International Council for Bird Preservation]

Sir,

The International Council for Bird Preservation has invited all its member countries to name one of its birds as a national emblem. In some countries – for example, Denmark, which has chosen the skylark and Germany which has chosen the white stork – this has already been done. For us the choice will not be altogether an easy one. We are, of course, consulting the representative scientific and other bodies interested in the protection of birds, but I think the selection will have a wider interest. It will undoubtedly be felt that the choice is not one to be made primarily by taxonomists or specialists of any kind but should reflect, so far as possible, the views and indeed the sentiments of all lovers of the countryside.

The views of your readers would be a valuable indication of the choice of species which would find most favour and the British Section of the International Council would, I am sure, be greatly helped if, through your columns or by direct communication with us, we could be made aware of their preferences.

I am, &c.,

HURCOMB

*From Mr L. R. Conisbee*          *20 October 1960*

Sir,

Lord Hurcomb's request in your columns today, for the name of a bird best suited as a national emblem, should produce an interesting and close debate. The chaffinch is generally accepted as the most abundant bird and in the countryside the rook is probably the most noticeable, but the first has little traditional background and the second lacks attractiveness. The ubiquitous house sparrow and starling are too commonplace, without any appealing attributes.

Probably the robin, the blackbird, and the song thrush would get the most votes. All are familiar throughout the year, likeable, and long known in national story and song. The robin is easily the most popular bird, but that popularity extends to a number of other countries, and so, unfortunately, it may have to be eliminated for our present purpose.

There remain 'the ousel and the throstle-cock, chief music of our May.' A personal choice would be for the blackbird, because of its handsome appearance, its intimate association with English gardens and homesteads, and the mellow beauty of its song; but many others, especially Scots, with equally good reasons, would plump for the mavis, throstle, or song thrush.

Yours faithfully,

L. R. CONISBEE

*From Mr E. C. H. Jones*                    *20 October 1960*

Sir,

A few years ago the answer to Lord Hurcomb's query today 'What Bird for Britain?' would have been the falcon. That, undoubtedly, was the most admired bird and therefore we find it enshrined in the heraldry of the period in many disguises. For somewhat similar reasons one might select today the pheasant, or possibly the grouse.

Another approach to the question brings us to the robin or the wren, which are universally protected because, as the old country rhyme puts it: 'The robin and the wren are God Almighty's cock and hen.'

For myself I would like to put in a plea for some of the loveliest of our birds which unhappily are being persecuted to the point of extinction; such as, for example, the goldfinch, because it looks pretty in a cage, or the bullfinch, because it eats fruit buds, or the wood pigeon, because authority has decreed its extermination. The elevation of any one of these outcasts to the status of a national symbol might help to preserve it for the enjoyment of future generations.

Yours faithfully,

E. C. H. JONES

*From Mr Hockley Clarke*                    *20 October 1960*
[Founder and Editor, *Birds and Country Magazine.*]

Sir,

The letter from Lord Hurcomb, in your issue today, is of special interest to me and I hope that I may be allowed to comment upon it. When *Birds and Country* was founded in 1948 I had to search for a bird of general appeal, suitable to reproduce as an emblem and a permanent decoration in the magazine.

Eventually, from the wide choice available, the rook was chosen as having the most solid claims on the grounds that it is a common resident species, its close association with the land from times immemorial, its sociable disposition and liking for building rookeries near man's dwellings, often near the village church; and its early nesting activities in the leafless trees are for many the most impressive evidence of the coming of spring in Britain.

I am, Sir, yours faithfully,

HOCKLEY CLARKE

*From Mr E. C. Davis*                    *20 October 1960*

Sir,

Our emblem has already been chosen for us but with the disappearance of the farthing we are likely to lose it again.

I suggest therefore that 'Jenny Wren' be retained as our national emblem.

Yours faithfully,

E. C. DAVIS

*From Mr Anthony Buxton*                    *21 October 1960*

Sir,

I suggest a robin – well known, well liked, and apparently in this country liking human beings, although robins on the continent seem to hide themselves in the depths of woods.

Yours faithfully,

ANTHONY BUXTON

*From Mr Roger Perry*                    *21 October 1960*

Sir,

Why not a bird with character and one that is truly British, the Red Grouse?

I am, Sir, your obedient servant,

ROGER PERRY

*From Mr L. G. Duke*                    *21 October 1960*

Sir,

It is elegantly dressed: 'rich not gaudy'. It has perhaps the most beautiful flight of any British bird. Its call is romantic and is heard in 'the deep heart's core' of many a countryman in town. It is a farmer's friend. Now that it has been intelligently protected for some years past it is again widespread throughout the British Isles and is familiar to everyone in the countryside. Large numbers stay with us all the year round, and many come to visit us.

59

It is true that to lunch off its delicious and protected eggs renders the gourmet an accessory to a misdemeanour, but the eggs of the black-headed gull are just as good: a gourmet who is not an ornithologist does not know the difference.

In short, the lapwing (or peewit) is both beautiful and good, and deserves to be our bird.

Yours faithfully,

L. G. DUKE

*From Mr Harold Paulley*                    *21 October 1960*

Sir,

Sparrow, and not define it any further.

Yours faithfully,

HAROLD PAULLEY

*From Mr Gerald W. Henderson*                *21 October 1960*

Sir,

Let the indomitable British raven croak for Britain — a splendid bird, whose species have been honoured and officially cared-for inhabitants of the Tower of London for many centuries.

He has been respected in these islands a thousand years and more and in consequence is one of the earliest birds known in heraldry.

I am, Sir, your obedient servant,

GERALD W. HENDERSON

*From Mr David Garnett*                      *22 October 1960*

Sir,

Whatever may be the result of a popular vote, the red grouse is the British bird *par excellence*. It is the only species not found outside the British Isles. But *Lagopus scoticus* has other claims which make it peculiarly representative of our national ethos.

Its very name, though perhaps not linked etymologically with the Norman-French *groucer*, i.e., to grumble, recalls the spirit of the British soldier since Agincourt while its cry, 'Go-back, Go-back', expresses our innermost longings. That South African bird, the ostrich, burying its head in the sands is not for us.

We fly straight forward to the butts, where doom may await us, but with nostalgia for the past in our hearts.

Yours faithfully,

DAVID GARNETT

*From Mr Geoffrey Law*                22 October 1960

Sir,

The Curlew might well be our choice of emblem for the International Council for the Preservation of Birds (*The Times* of today). Its joy song and its wilder notes are an everlasting memory for those who, in their leisure, may visit the wilder parts of these islands.

There can never be too many.

Yours faithfully,
GEOFFREY LAW

*From Miss Charlotte Stephenson*          22 October 1960

Sir,

The bird should represent the main features of the British tradition and future. How about a colonizing seabird, black and white, reserved with strangers and rather pompous; in short, the Puffin?

Yours faithfully,
CHARLOTTE STEPHENSON

*From Miss Barbara Keith-Roach*          22 October 1960

Sir,

May I suggest the black headed gull as a suitable emblem for Britain? We are above all a seaminded nation, and this very decorative bird, owing to its habit of coming inland, is well known even in the middle of our enormous cities.

Yours truly,
BARBARA KEITH-ROACH

*From Mr Leslie Farmer*                22 October 1960

Sir,

The most popular bird in Britain today is the budgerigar.

Yours sincerely,
LESLIE FARMER

*From Sir Henry Bashford*                24 October 1960

Sir,

Nobody knows better than my friend Cyril Hurcomb, whose letter you printed on October 18, that I am not an ornithologist. But I am rather surprised that none of your correspondents seems to have suggested the owl as Britain's emblem.

Lovable and intelligent as is the robin − two or three generally have tea with me in the summer − surely he lacks the *gravitas*, not to say the stature, desirable for a national emblem.

61

These the owl possesses, together with a legendary repute for wisdom and a characteristic dislike for exhibitionism. What is more dignified than his leisurely and unobtrusive flight round the edges of a water-meadow in a June dusk? What is more comforting, even if a trifle ominous to some possible prey, than his watchman's cry of 'All's well' on a winter night?

Yours faithfully,<br>H. H. BASHFORD

*From Colonel E. R. M. Bowerman*         *24 October 1960*

Sir,

Bullfinch, without doubt – red, white and blue – John Bull – sadly maligned – generally misunderstood and persecuted.

Yours faithfully,<br>E. R. M. BOWERMAN

*From Mr Ernest C. Hetherington*         *24 October 1960*

Sir,

The fabulous, the heraldic-historic, the elegant swan.

Yours faithfully,<br>ERNEST C. HETHERINGTON

*From Mrs Ethel Kelleway*         *25 October 1960*

Sir,

Most of us have never even *seen* a Red Grouse.

Yours truly,<br>ETHEL KELLEWAY

*From Mr F. W. Stoddart*         *25 October 1960*

Sir,

The most obvious choice seems to have been overlooked. What about the bittern? (I quote) 'A shy, secretive bird . . . when disturbed it points its bill to the sky. . . . The boom is uttered only by males.'

The slogan 'The Bittern for Britain' would be both alliterative and euphonious.

Yours faithfully,<br>F. W. STODDART

*From Miss Elizabeth Goble*         *25 October 1960*

Sir,

As a bird emblem for Britain we should choose a less cautious character than the red grouse which says 'Go back, go back' and which is anyway only a familiar sight in Scotland. One would so much prefer a bird that everyone knows and can admire, and which is not a helpless target for guns.

The lapwing or green plover is known all over Britain and loved by farmers, is beautiful, brave, and hardly to be matched for endurance on the wing. Tradition also places it first on the list as a bird of sagacity, as Edward Fitzgerald's fine translation from the Persian clearly shows. In this poem, 'The Parliament of Birds', the lapwing after much interesting debate is chosen by the bird assembly because of his wisdom and stamina to be their leader on the long and perilous journey to Paradise.

I am, Sir, yours truly,

ELIZABETH GOBLE

*From Mr E. J. Pryor*                    *25 October 1960*

Sir,

The starling seems symbolic. It crowds and messes up civic centres at night, yarping unmelodiously. The fledglings are boorish, and bully their industrious parents unless food is actually lifted from before them and put in their mouths. Yet behind this spivvery of the breed a lot of solid and useful work is done by these birds all round the countryside.

Yours faithfully,

E. J. PRYOR

*From Mr Lawrence E. Tanner*                    *26 October 1960*

Sir,

May I put in a plea for 'the temple haunting martlet', so intimately connected heraldically with St Edward the Confessor, once the Patron Saint of England until superseded by St George in the fourteenth century?

In the reign of Richard II St Edward's 'Cross patonce between five martlets' was impaled with the Arms of England. The coat appears many times in sculpture and glass in Westminster Abbey, and to this day forms part of the Collegiate Coat of Arms.

The martlets and cross also appear in the Arms of two Oxford colleges (University and Worcester), while the Valence martlets are prominent in the Arms of Pembroke College, Cambridge.

I am, Sir, &c.,

LAWRENCE E. TANNER

*From Mrs Ruby D. Goldberg*                    *26 October 1960*

Sir,

I wonder why your correspondents have included the missel-thrush and omitted the song-thrush, ornament of every garden.

And why put the red grouse at the top of the list except for its peculiarity in preferring Britain to the rest of the globe? Like the woodpecker it is often heard but seldom seen, especially by southerners.

Yours truly,
RUBY D. GOLDBERG

*From Air Marshal Sir Victor Goddard*        *27 October 1960*

Sir,

You and your bird-fancying correspondents do not seem to be aware that the competition to be Britain's Bird was decided over a century ago with − to judge from contemporary official portraits − the full approval of *Britannia* herself. (Have you never studied your 1860 penny-pieces, Sir?)

Britain's Bird must have − and *has* − truly Britannic wave-ruling capabilities. Indeed, the only bird you are ever likely to see, with or without *Britannia*, demonstrating supreme and serene ridership of the ocean waves is that noble, majestic, nautical and essentially British bird − the Albatross (British, because of the spelling).

And if that, Sir, is not enough for you, please recall that the Albatross has ever been the emblem bird of the Royal Naval Air Service and of the Royal Air Force, and so is not competing in your popularity poll: it has its pride.

I am, Sir, your obedient servant,
VICTOR GODDARD

*From Mr Eric Sutton*        *27 October 1960*

Sir,

Why not the kingfisher? A regal name, symbolic of a nation whose fishing fleets have for so long been in the forefront of our trade and commerce. Not forgetting the thousands of anglers who watch this beautiful bird in free competition with themselves.

Yours faithfully,
ERIC SUTTON

*From Mr L. H. Oliver*        *27 October 1960*

Sir,

Why not let some modern artist draw a bird, which could then be taken equally to be any one of the 20 or more kinds suggested by your correspondents, and thus satisfy them all?

Yours faithfully,
L. H. OLIVER

Sir,

I suppose the support given to the grouse as Britain's bird is humorous. For the grouse has no sanctity and is popularly considered not as an individual but as a brace: the rich man's target and dish.

The goldcrest wren is the 'king of all birds' in English folklore as well as in the Ancient Greek and Latin. (Aesop has a fable about it.) The female, according to John Skelton, Henry VIII's Poet Laureate, was popularly known as 'Our Lady's hen'.

The Druids used wren and raven as their chief prophetic birds, perhaps because both were sacred to Bran, whose oracular head was said to have been buried on Tower Hill to protect Britain from invasion.

The robin, as the bird of Bran's twin Beli, has a counterclaim to sovereignty with the wren and is similarly protected by a taboo: 'Who touches the eggs of robin or wren, Will never see his mother again.' But the red breast in British legend is a mark of his murderous disposition, not, as the monks later claimed, of his devout presence at the Crucifixion.

Yours faithfully,

ROBERT GRAVES

Sir,

Colonel Bowerman's reasons for the bullfinch in his letter yesterday will never do. Superficially, no doubt, he looks more like John Bull than any of us, but are we by implication to accept his drab grey wife? As for national characteristics, what about the lapwing – attractive, beneficent, and widespread?

If distinctiveness is a merit the lapwing's claims are doubly great. With his upright crest on the ground and in flight, he makes an excellent silhouette.

I am, Sir, yours faithfully,

H. S. DEIGHTON

Sir,

Handsome rather than ornamental; powerful on the wing; dignified and stately in stride; unafraid, but by no means domesticated; social in domestic matters; enterprising and courageous in solitary expeditions – the heron is as good a candidate as we are likely to find.

Yours faithfully,

J. E. ASHFORD

*From Professor A. J. E. Cave*                    *28 October 1960*

[former Professor of Anatomy, St Bartholomew's Hospital]

Sir,

Lord Hurcomb's appeal, in your issue of October 18, for the name of a bird suitable for adoption as a national emblem has initiated an expected variety of suggestions. The particular aspect of Britain and British life which the chosen bird is intended to represent remains, however, obscure.

An increasingly industrialized and urbanized society might be not unfairly portrayed by the ubiquitous house sparrow, a handsome enough fellow when clean-plumaged despite his detractors. Others, however, may be of opinion that, under present conditions of penal taxation, our most appropriate avian emblem were a chicken — well and truly pluck'd.

Yours faithfully,

A. J. E. CAVE

.   The final table of principal preferences is:—

|                        | Per cent |
|------------------------|----------|
| Robin                  | 17       |
| Grouse                 | 11       |
| (Red Grouse, 6)        |          |
| Wren (various)         | 7        |
| Plover (various)       | 6        |
| (Lapwing, 5)           |          |
| Gull (various)         | 5        |
| Bullfinch              | 4        |
| Chickens, &c.          | 4        |
| Blackbird              | 3        |
| Owl (various)          | 3        |
| Skylark                | 3        |
| Sparrow (various)      | 3        |
| Cuckoo                 | 2        |
| Ostrich                | 2        |
| Raven                  | 2        |
| Rook                   | 2        |
| Swan                   | 2        |

*From Lord Hurcomb*                    *15 December 1960*

Sir,

The British Section of the International Council for Bird Preservation gratefully acknowledges the assistance they have received from readers of *The Times* in selecting a bird representative of Britain. The question has no scientific or statutory significance, but the response to the inquiry permitted through your columns amply confirms the Council's view that the adoption of a favourite bird as a national symbol ornithologically may help to stimulate and sustain general interest in bird protection.

After taking account of the analysis of your correspondence and of suggestions from other individuals and sources, the Section is left in no doubt that, in spite of strong claims of several rivals, the right choice for us is the Robin, for the evidence of its popularity from all sections of the community is overwhelming.

In addition to slight differences of plumage, the British race of the Robin is also distinguished from continental races by its open and exceptionally friendly behaviour to human beings in both town and country.

I am, Sir, your obedient servant,

HURCOMB

## Use for Rat Skins

*From Mr G. L. Moore*                           *28 January 1920*

Sir,

Is it not possible in these times of a world shortage of raw material (especially leather) for such serviceable articles as rat skins to be put to some useful purpose? It will be generally conceded that if a market can be found or created for such skins it will be an incentive for the destruction of these noxious rodents, which is so essential. It is possible there are at present a few buyers, but so far I have been unable to discover them. Any information on this point will be appreciated. For some one with enterprise and imagination rat skins should be a sound commercial proposition – they would make excellent leather purses and gloves.

Yours faithfully,

GEO. L. MOORE

## Cookery by Sunlight

*From Mr J. E. E. Craster*                           *2 February 1922*

Sir,

Perhaps the following notes may be of interest. Some years ago I made a modified parabolic mirror, and measured the heat produced at the focal line by the sun's rays. I found that a square foot of mirror surface produced 17½ therms per hour, in latitude 54° 30′ north, at midday. The declination of the sun was then 15° north. No special precautions were taken to prevent loss of heat by draughts of cold air, or by convection currents, so that I think the above figure might easily be increased.

In the tropics parabolic mirrors have been used for some time to heat the boilers of steam engines. I believe it is usual to provide 100 square feet of mirror for each horse power. The cost of my mirror worked out at almost 30s per square foot of mirror surface. No doubt the cost would be less for larger mirrors.

Yours faithfully,

J. E. E. CRASTER

## The Cuckoo in March

[Coincidentally with a correspondent's assertion that since 1917 the Bolshevists had executed 1,766,118 persons including 28 Bishops, came news of a cuckoo in Epping Forest on 15 March]

*From Mr A. B. Clarke*                    *25 March 1922*

Sir,

I was quietly walking between Melksham and Holt, in Wiltshire, on Thursday last, the 16th inst., and distinctly heard the cuckoo call three times in succession. Knowing that he had arrived exceptionally early, I asked a girl who was passing on a bicycle if she had heard him. Her answer was, 'Yes, Sir, I heard him quite plain.' Therefore I do not think there is much doubt about his arrival, although with this easterly wind, I am sorry for him.

Yours faithfully,

A. B. CLARKE

[As news of a fall in the cost of living revived readers, a correspondent asked what was a cuckoo without hairy caterpillars]

## 'Ça Passe'

[A leading article had discussed Emile Coué whose clinic at Nancy had become a place of pilgrimage for those in search of cure by auto-suggestion; his other formula was 'Every day, in every way, I am better, and better, and better'.]

[now engaged on his translation of Proust's *A la recherche
du temps perdu*]

Sir,

The Nancy formula which you commend in a leading article
this morning is not without a precedent, 10 or 12 centuries old,
in our own tongue. Our earliest lyric poet, whose name was, he
tells us, Deor, bases his one surviving work (a poem which
would extend to 42 lines were not some of them dismissed as
suspect by modern scholarship) upon the same two words. As
Theocritus, at the end of his Third Idyll, makes the goat-herd
envy three of the fortunate ones of the past, Hippomenes,
Melampus, and Adonis, and resolve to die, so, conversely, Deor
recalls the classic examples of misfortune and suffering,
comparable to his own, and resolves to live, ending each verse
with the simple refrain: —

> '*thaes ofereode, thisses swa mæg'

Which may be interpreted, in modern French, *ça passe*.

I am, Sir, your obedient servant,

CHARLES SCOTT MONCRIEFF

[*That was surmounted, so may this be]


## 'Probable' Time-Tables

Sir,

1923 — April Bradshaw, p. 924:

'11 am train from Victoria. Note Z — Will probably leave at
10.10 from April 5th to 21st inclusive, if Summer Time begins
earlier in France than in England.'

What would our fathers have thought of Governments which
allowed 'probable' time-tables? I suppose it has something
to do with Einstein, or space of five dimensions, quite easily
understood by every elementary school child, but incomprehensible to old fogies, who dislike the Oriental plan of going to
a railway station like a Hindoo, to squat until it pleases
Providence or the railway company to provide a train.

This astonishing advertisement has led me to look back a
little, and to compare our communications between England
and France, 1923, with those of twenty-five summers ago. Much
to my surprise, I find that in summer 1898, there were at least

two more boat and train services each way by the short sea routes (Dover – Folkestone – Calais – Boulogne) than today, between England and France, and the fares were so much less than today that it is roughly true to say that the fare from London to Paris in 1898 was the same as from London to Boulogne today.

|  | First Single | Third Single |
|---|---|---|
| 1898 London to Paris (*via* Boulogne) | £2 12 0 | £1 2 9 |
| *1923 London to Boulogne | £2 7 11 | £1 2 4 |

*These fares vary with 'exchange' but the ones I give are from the published Continental Handbook, winter service 1922–23.

If it be true, as Adam Smith says, that the first need of civilization and peace is quick and cheap intercourse, it hardly looks as if we had been very successful in this respect with our nearest Continental neighbour during the last quarter of a century. How does our new 'Southern Railway' propose to give to its generation as good and cheap a proportionate service as our fathers did to our generation, since I read recently that the number of passengers 'transported across the Channel at Easter by the short sea routes largely exceeded the pre-war figures'?

Yours faithfully,

FARRER

[The General Manager Southern Railway (South-East and Chatham Section) explained that 'probable' time-tables were all the fault of the French.

The Chancellor of the Exchequer is sometimes asked for the real value of £100 at each year since 1920 in terms of comparable purchasing power. His answer includes such years as 1933 (£178), 1946 (£94) and 1975 (£21).

Asked to work backwards from 1920, he would answer 1914 (£248) and 1900 (£290)]

# Nuts in May

*From the Principal of King's College, London*     *9 May 1923*

Sir,

I remember that, when I read the Classics, I had always a liking for the reading of the manuscript and a distaste for emendations. It is probably the same instinct which leads me to think that 'nuts in May' are really nuts. (But I remember that, when I joined in the chant some forty years ago, we used to say 'nutsimay', and I liked the mysterious sound, and wondered what 'nutsimay' was.) If nuts do not grow upon trees in May, I conceive it to be possible that they grow in the ground. Certainly one of my pleasantest memories is that of hunting for nuts in the ground (a long time ago) somewhere about the month of May. They were to be found on a little bank, overshadowed by trees, that overhung a disused quarry. You knew their presence by the tender green shoots which grew from them; and when you saw those shoots, you took your knife, made a small excavation, and had a succulent reward. I have consulted the *New English Dictionary* (my general refuge in all mental perplexities), and I have found there, s.v. groundnut, the admirable entry which awakens a pleased reminiscence and rumination. '*Bunium flexuosum*: Culpepper, *English Physitian*, 64; they are called earth-nuts, earth-chestnuts, groundnuts.'

What I cannot really remember is whether we actually gathered *Bunia flexuosa* in May. But while I cannot prove it (except by the obvious device of consulting some scientific work of reference), I flatter myself that it is extremely probable. In any case, there was some real fun in gathering this sort of nut. It was elusive; it was succulent; it was neither so obvious, nor so unsatisfactory, as your hazel nut.

But it pains me to think of these things. They belong to the Arcadia of a vanished youth. *Où sont les neiges d'antan?* Where are the nuts of yesteryear?

Yours obediently,

ERNEST BARKER

## Back to Methuselah

['It is a world classic or it is nothing,' wrote Shaw of his 'metabiological pentateuch' in 1944. Twenty years earlier it had been presented by the Birmingham Repertory Company at London's Court Theatre when the players included Gwen Ffrangcon-Davies (Edith Evans had also appeared in the Birmingham production), Cedric Hardwicke and Leo G. Carroll, who ended his career in television's *The Man from U.N.C.L.E.*

The two principal characters in Part II – circa 1920 – were Joyce Burge and Henry Hopkins Lubin. The former, 'a well-fed man turned fifty, with broad forehead, and grey hair which, his neck being short, falls almost to his

71

collar', was clearly Lloyd George; the latter, 'a man at the
end of his sixties, a Yorkshireman with the last traces of
Scandinavian flax still in his white hair . . . and taking his
simple dignity for granted, but wonderfully comfortable
and quite self-assured', Asquith.

The drama critic of *The Times* was Arthur Bingham
Walkley, a friend of Shaw's, to whom had been dedicated
*Man and Superman*]

*From Mr Edward Marsh*                    *22 February 1924*

[classical scholar; civil servant; sometime private secretary
to Winston Churchill; friend of poetry; knighted 1937]

Sir,
Many of your readers will have welcomed the trouncing given
by your Drama Critic this morning to Mr Bernard Shaw for the
personal allusions which disfigure the second part of *Back to
Methuselah*. The most painful of these to Mr Shaw's admirers
was the passage in which (without any disguise of the persons
aimed at) he pours his special scorn on the 'Politician' who
actually allowed his own son to get killed in the war. At this
point Mr Shaw seems to part company not only with decency but
with sense; for somebody must be killed in a war, and surely the
statesman who allows his own son to sacrifice himself is more,
and not less, admirable than one who saves his family at the
expense of others.

I am, Sir, your obedient servant,

EDWARD MARSH

[Asquith's son Raymond had been killed in September
1916]

*From Mr Bernard Shaw*                    *25 February 1924*

Sir,
I am very reluctant to make any comment on the expressions
of irritation which my play at the Court Theatre must inevitably
provoke from the short-lived, but Mr Edward Marsh, whose
sensibilities I have every personal reason for respecting, must
not accuse me of 'pouring scorn on a politician, who actually
allowed his own son to be killed in the war.' In what sense did
any man 'allow' his son to be killed in the war? Would any man
have allowed such a thing if he could have prevented it? Many
men who were more or less responsible for the war had that
responsibility brought home by the loss of a well-beloved son,
but they will hardly, I think, regard that as a fact to be
suppressed as shameful, or deny the son his right to his record

and his share in the moral of the greatest tragedy of his time. Does Mr Marsh really believe that his delicacy is greater and more consoling than mine when he dismisses the son with the remark that 'somebody must be killed in a war,' and treats his fate as a mere personal episode in which a father 'allows his own child to sacrifice himself,' and is to be contrasted with 'one who saves his family at the expense of others'? In the framework of my play such phrases would be heartless nonsense; the case is bigger and deeper than that.

As to 'pouring scorn' on anyone, what I have done is to exhibit our Parliamentary politics in contrast with politics *sub specie aeternitatis*. If under this test they shrink to a ridiculous smallness and reveal a disastrous inadequacy, that is not a reason why the exposure should be spared; it is a most urgent reason for submitting them to it ruthlessly. And as the dramatic method requires that the politics should be expounded by politicians, and the test can be valid only if the politicians are recognizably true to historic fact, the politicians must to some extent share the fate of the politics. This inevitable effect may scandalize critics who, being innocent of political life, imagine that statesmen approach elections with their minds wholly preoccupied with abstract principles, oblivious of the existence of such persons as voters, and most undemocratically indifferent to their likes and dislikes. Such critics imagine that in representing two ex-Premiers, on the eve of a General Election, as keenly alive to such considerations, and only too bitterly aware of our electoral ignorance, folly, and gullibility, I am representing them as unprincipled scoundrels; but I can hardly be expected to defer to a judgment so ludicrously uninstructed. My play, as far as it goes outside the public history of public men, contains not a word against the private honour of any living person; and if I do not share the delicacy as to equally public and politically active women which restrained Silas Wegg from going into details concerning the Decline and Fall of the Roman Empire, I can only say that my blue pencil is at the service of any lady who can find a single reference to herself which is not within the privilege of the friendliest good humour.

I have been accused in your columns of 'shouting scandal from the housetops.' Is it scandal to say of one statesman [Burge – Lloyd George] that he is happily married? or of another [Lubin – Asquith] who has an almost embarrassingly clever and famous wife, and two daughters whose achievements in politics and literature threaten to eclipse his own, that he is in this fortunate condition? Surely my apology is due to these ladies for having given them minor and even mute parts in a

73

drama in which they actually played much more important ones, and not to your critic, who grudges them any mention at all.

It is true that in stage fiction many marriages are scandalous, and most of them triangular. The critic's mind becomes at last like the dyer's hand: the wedding ring suggests nothing to him but the Divorce Court. But my plays are not theatrical plays in that sense; and I hope an honest woman may be mentioned in them without a stain on her character.

Finally, as Miss Eileen Beldon [Zoo in Part IV – *Tragedy of an Elderly Gentleman*] has been accused by your critic of mispronouncing the word 'isolate' (perhaps he rhymes it, as many do, to 'why so late'), may I ask how he pronounces it himself? I once asked Thomas Hardy how he pronounced The Dynasts. He replied that he called it 'The Dinnasts' but that so many people knew no better than to call it The Die-nasts that he was getting shy about it, and preferred not to mention it at all. I appeal to your critic not to make Miss Beldon shy, and, after consulting the pronouncing dictionaries, to send her a suitable apology.

Yours truly,<br>BERNARD SHAW

[Walkley responded to Shaw over 'isolate', then Shaw to Walkley: 'He dares refer me to Murray, knowing well that Murray gives issolate as a received pronunciation, though he has the bad taste to prefer eye-solate. Webster gives issolate, Ogilvie gives issolate, the invaluable Chambers, compared to whom and to the others Murray is the merest upstart, gives issolate and izzolate. . . .'

Walkley had summed up *Back to Methuselah* thus: 'the work of a remarkable mind. We have been irritated, we have been bored, we have been stimulated, and, more often than not, we have been, in the best sense of the term, amused.'

*Back to Methuselah* was revived by the National Theatre in 1969]

## Outbreak of the Russian Revolution

*From the Reverend B. S. Lombard*                    *9 March 1925*

[late British Chaplain at Petrograd]

Sir,

Saturday was the anniversary of the outbreak of the Russian Revolution. No one who was present in Petrograd at the time is likely to forget it. During the morning and early afternoon, sullen crowds thronged all the main streets. Mounted police moved quietly among them. There was no disorder, all seemed to be waiting for something; they might have been workmen outside the gates of a factory before opening time. Nevertheless one felt instinctively that the atmosphere was charged. It reminded one of the strange, gloomy silence that so often comes before a storm.

I boarded a tramway car to visit some people near the Nikolai Station. It was very crowded, but I was able to stand in front near the driver. As we proceeded up the Nevsky Prospect I became aware that a lady I knew was a fellow-traveller. I suggested that she should stay with the friend she was on her way to visit, and not attempt to return, as I felt there was going to be trouble.

I had hardly spoken the words when there rose a dull murmur, and one caught snatches of 'Give us bread, we are hungry.' The tramway car was not travelling fast owing to the crowds. A university student jumped on to the footboard, said something to the driver, and then turned to the control lever, and the car came to a standstill. This held up all the rest, so my friend and I got off and walked. I took her to her destination, and begged her friends to keep her for the night, and then returned to Nevsky.

There I found everything changed. The placid dullness of these sullen crowds was replaced by alertness and excitement. As I neared the statue of Alexander III, a workman ascended to the plinth, and began to address the people. A policeman approached and remonstrated. The speaker refused either to get down or stop talking, whereupon the policeman drew his revolver, and shot him. It was the match to the fire; the smouldering fuse had reached the powder, and it went off. The Revolution had begun. In 20 minutes there was hardly a vestige of that unfortunate policeman left. Men, women, and even children fell upon him and literally tore him to pieces. One could hardly believe that those sad, silent people of half an hour before could have been suddenly transformed into such savages, lusting for the blood of the wretched man.

After this the crowd moved down Nevsky in one solid mass, were met by police, and were fired on. Every one knows the rest: innocent and guilty alike were shot down until the troops joined the people, and the so-called 'bloodless Revolution' began.

I am, etc.,

B. S. LOMBARD

# Letter from Rome

[*The Times* had criticised the Duce]

*From Signor Mussolini*                                       *26 June 1925*

Sir,

I am very sensible of the fact that your most important paper attentively follows my political and polemical manifestations. Allow me, however, to rectify some statements contained in your last editorial.

It does not correspond with facts that the last Bills voted by the Italian Chamber are against the most elementary liberties, whereof you will be convinced by carefully considering the article of the aforesaid laws. It is not true that patriots are discontented. On the contrary, the truth is that the opposition is carried on by a small dispossessed group, while the enormous majority of the Italian people works and lives quietly, as foreigners sojourning in my country may daily ascertain. Please note also that Fascism counts 3,000,000 adherents, whereof 2,000,000 are Syndicalist workmen and peasants, these representing the politically organized majority of the nation. Even the Italian Opposition now recognizes the great historical importance of the Fascist experiment, which has to be firmly continued in order not to fail in its task of morally and materially elevating the Italian people, and also in the interest of European civilization. Please accept my thanks and regards.

I am, &c.,

MUSSOLINI

[There is no record of Hitler or Stalin writing to *The Times*]

# Loin-cloths for Horses

*From General Sir Charles Warren*                          *29 January 1925*

[Variously in charge of excavations at Jerusalem, High Commissioner for laying down the boundary line between Griqualand West and Orange Free State, and Commissioner of the Metropolitan Police.]

Sir,

My experience over a great many years with horses in the open and kept under cover is:

(1) Horses kept wholly out in the open without stabling do

not require loin-cloths provided they can seek their own shelter; but, when tied up in line, a loin-cloth is desirable in very inclement weather if it can be kept close to the horse's flanks.

(2) The danger of a loin-cloth in inclement weather is that at the most critical moment (when the cold wind is fiercest) the flap is forced up on one side, and the warm flank of the horse is suddenly exposed to a very cold blast and the horse gets a chill.

(3) When horses are kept in warm stables and they are taken out and left exposed to cold blasts, a loin-cloth is necessary, provided it cannot be turned up by the wind. If it can be turned over when the wind is at its highest the use of the loin-cloth ensures a chill to the horse. If loin-cloths are used they must be securely fixed down or constantly looked after.

Your obedient servant,<br>CHARLES WARREN

## From Dogs to Watches

*From Mr H. B. Hemming*        *10 November 1925*

Sir,

I have just lost my fifth watch on my way between Paddington and Lincoln's Inn. I know by experience that it is useless to apply to the police and that it is practically useless to offer a reward, which may also result in compounding a felony. Yet I suppose that no man in his senses would hesitate to recover his watch if he could at the price of letting the thief go when he knows that the only alternative is that the thief will almost certainly escape and keep the watch into the bargain.

I suppose I am abnormally careless, but I find it difficult to acquire the habit of looking upon my neighbour as a potential thief. Nine times out of ten when I enter a tube lift I button up my coat or put my finger round my watch chain, but on the tenth I forget, and then I am apt to find myself minus my watch. Forty years ago I lost a couple of dogs in London under suspicious circumstances and it was a judge of the High Court who told me how to recover them. I followed his advice and in a week's time my dogs returned safe and sound. Would that some distinguished luminary would tell me how best to recover a lost watch! The tube lift is naturally a happy hunting ground for the pickpocket and my only object in writing is to add one more warning to the public of the danger which they run.

H. B. HEMMING

# The Servant Problem

*From Mr J. T. K. Tarpey*           *7 April 1926*

Sir,

Some of your readers may be interested in a solution of the servant problem that has been found successful by several friends of mine. It is especially suited to the household employing only one maid, or to the week-end cottage where someone must be left in charge of pets or live stock during the week. I allude to the very large numbers of young mothers with babies who are willing to go into service if they can keep their children with them.

For some unknown reason the number of desertions has increased greatly during the last few years. I know personally of three cases of young educated women whose husbands have left them to earn a living for themselves and their children as best they can. In addition, there are many cases of unmarried mothers deserving of sympathy and help. In fact this is the only source of domestic help I know of in which the supply far exceeds the demand. If any of your readers desire further information I shall be happy to give it.

Yours faithfully,

J. T. KINGSLEY TARPEY

# Mrs Grundy at Hampton Court

[Grundy. 1798. The surname of an imaginary personage (*Mrs Grundy*), proverbially referred to as a personification of the tyranny of social opinion in matters of conventional propriety.

*Shorter Oxford Dictionary*]

*From Mr Ernest Law*           *7 June 1926*

[barrister; designer of gardens; author of numerous books on Hampton Court]

Sir,

In reference to your article on Tuesday last on 'Mrs Grundy,' that lady was, as a fact, embodied in the Housekeeper of that name at Hampton Court Palace in the late forties and early fifties of last century. Her fame is perpetuated in a dark space – one of the mystery chambers of the Palace – the door of which is rarely opened, and which is still known as 'Mrs Grundy's Gallery.' Here she impounded any picture or sculpture which she considered unfit for exhibition in the State Rooms: and here she kept them under lock and key, in defiance of the authority and protests of the Queen's Surveyor of Pictures. No entreaty, no persuasion would ever induce Mrs Grundy to let any one so much as peep into her Gallery, still less penetrate into it.

The story goes that on one occasion the First Commissioner of Works on a visit of inspection, noticing a closed door, asked what it led to. 'That is Mrs Grundy's Gallery, sir,' replied the Clerk of the Works in awe-stricken tones, and he had no key to admit him. So Mrs Grundy was sent for. In answer to the First Commissioner's request, she declined to open the door for him. 'But I am one of her Majesty's Ministers, and I have authority over the structure of the Palace.' 'I cannot help that, sir,' replied Mrs Grundy, 'only on an order signed by his Lordship the Lord Chamberlain of her Majesty's Household can I allow anybody to enter my Gallery.' That is the sort of thing that 'Mrs Grundy would say.'

History does not record the eventual result; though he did not get in on that occasion. But in the century-old struggle between the Office of Works and the Lord Chamberlain's Department, some 40 years after her death the First Commissioner succeeded in having the occupation of 'Mrs Grundy's Gallery' transferred to his Department, to be used for stores. Some 15 years afterwards its treasures were gradually brought forth, and the pictures hung in the State Rooms, notably Cariani's beautiful 'Venus Recumbent,' No. 88 in the Second Presence Chamber, identified three years ago by Mr Tancred Borenius as having belonged to the famous Venetian collector, Andrea Vandramin, from a drawing in his catalogue of 1627. It was not until 20 years ago that a leaden statue of Venus, which had been sent from Windsor and was stored in 'Mrs Grundy's Gallery,' was brought forth to adorn Henry VIII's Pond Garden. 'What *would* Mrs Grundy say?'

ERNEST LAW

[Hampton Court Palace, the home of kings and queens of England in centuries past and now one of Britain's top tourist attractions, could soon become the home of Arab oil sheikhs − *The Times*, March 1, 1985]

# A Day of Loyalty

[The general strike had ended on May 12, 1926]

*From Mr Allan Fea*                                    *28 May 1926*

Sir,

Now that the thundercloud which so recently has over-shadowed the Old Country has passed away, the 20th of this month should be celebrated as of yore as a symbol of loyalty to the Throne. By oak-leaf decorations of villages and towns on 'Restoration Day,' staunch British allegiance to Monarchy, law, and order would be manifested; a demonstration of the power and pre-eminence of his Majesty's loyal subjects; a protest against any form of republicanism.

If the 20th century May Day heralds in universal turmoil and trouble, why not, then, let 'Restoration Day,' or 'Oak Apple Day,' have full fling and take over the festive responsibilities which in past times were allotted to the always somewhat premature date (and temperature) for 'going a-maying'?

Your obedient servant,

ALLAN FEA

# Fragile Eggshells

*From Mrs Stella Palmer*                    *7 April 1977*

Sir,

How reassuring to be told by the Poultry Research Centre that the shells of modern eggs are as good as they were 40 years ago! (report by your Agricultural Correspondent on Saturday, April 2). The reason they break so easily is that they are too fresh when we buy them.

Yet I am old enough to remember when the farmer's wife brought baskets of eggs to market travelling in a jolting cart over unmade roads. The baskets were at least 10 to twelve inches deep and the pressure of weight on the bottom layer must have been considerable. Some of the eggs were probably a week old but some would have been collected that morning.

With all respect to the scientists, the results of their 10 years' research only confirms me in my admiration for the old-fashioned hen.

I am, Sir, yours truly,
STELLA F. PALMER

*From Major A. E. Sturdy*                    *12 April 1977*

Sir,

I cannot entirely agree with the finding of the scientists that the shells of eggs laid by factory bred hens are not inferior to those of their free range sisters. I sometimes find that the former crumble between the fingers even before boiling. I contend that they are inferior because the layers receive no grit in their diet, whereas the grit picked up by free range hens is generally supplemented by ground oyster shell.

Incidentally, it is only in old age that I have at last discovered that the tops of boiled eggs should be sliced off at the thin end, to avoid spilling the yolk. A difference of opinion on this subject was, if I remember correctly, the cause of the war in Thackeray's *The Rose and the Ring*, the delight of which is, I fear, unknown to modern generations of science fiction-fed children.

Yours faithfully,
A. E. STURDY

Sir,

I am glad that the Poultry Research Centre has, after 10 years' investigation, been able to solve the worrying problem of modern hens' eggs splitting during boiling. People who have been worried lest food quality should be changed by technology will be reassured to know the fault lies with the housewife, not the hen. May I offer some simple advice, known to all husbands who have learnt to boil an egg, that a small pin prick made in the egg's rounded end will let expanding air escape from the air sac and save the shell from splitting?

Yours faithfully,<br>G. F. Brookes

*From Mrs Curtis Dean*                    *14 April 1977*

Sir,

The Major is quite right, the modern hen lacks grit.

For several hilarious months during the War I was responsible for a large number of hens kept to provide fresh eggs for the officers' mess. My ignorance of poultry rearing was total so I was dismayed when the eggshells turned soft. I was told that oyster shells were needed in the diet – quite unobtainable in wartime – but luckily the sea was near so I spent many tedious hours collecting and crushing shells found on the beach and feeding them to the hens. And, hey-presto! It worked.

By the time I was posted, the catering officer had been persuaded to provide official RAF transport and once a month Operation Seashell set off, with many volunteers, for a day by the sea. And the officers were again enjoying their new-laid, hard-shelled breakfast eggs.

Thus was the War won.

Yours faithfully,<br>Curtis Dean

*From Miss Jennifer Fellows*                    *16 April 1977*

Sir,

Major Sturdy does not, I fear, 'remember correctly' that a dispute as to the end at which an egg should properly be broken was the cause of a war in *The Rose and the Ring*: it is in *Gulliver's Travels* that such an incident occurs – the disputants being the Lilliputians and the Blefuscans, and eleven thousand people being prepared to lay down their lives for their beliefs on this subject.

I entirely agree with Major Sturdy as to the comparative

fragility of the shells of battery-produced eggs. The best means of preventing an egg from cracking when boiled is to prick the shell at the *larger* end – if the smaller end is pierced, the egg-white tends to escape during cooking. I have not found other suggested preventive measures – such as the addition of salt or vinegar to the water – comparable in efficacy to this.

Yours faithfully,
JENNIFER FELLOWS

*From Mrs E. M. Selby-Boothroyd*          *23 April 1977*

Sir,

At risk of sounding pedantic I would like to correct terms used in the recent letters about fragile eggshells. All hens have to have grit – not as part of their diet but to be stored in the gizzard to churn up their food.

The oyster shells Mrs Curtis Dean fed to the hens were adding the extra calcium to harden the shells.

Yours faithfully,
E. M. SELBY-BOOTHROYD

*From Dr T. C. Carter*          *25 April 1977*

[writing from the Agricultural Research Council's Poultry Research Centre]

Sir,

Mrs Stella Palmer is right to admire the old-fashioned hen, which was a remarkably efficient converter of animal feed into human food. But she should admire even more the modern hen, which is yet more efficient, and modern egg producers and distributors, most of whom try hard to ensure that eggs are of good quality when they reach the housewife.

Forty years ago when my mother made a cake or omelette she broke every egg into a cup, for fear of spoiling the mixture by adding an egg that was rotten. Rotting was commonly a consequence of shell cracking, which allowed spoilage organisms to get in. My wife has not been sold a rotten egg since 1954.

Yours faithfully,
T. C. CARTER

*From Mr D. Livermore*          *25 April 1977*

Sir,

Would the poultry experts now investigate the reduction in thickness of Easter Eggs?

Yours sincerely,
D. LIVERMORE

# Honorary Degrees for Politicians

[The University of Cambridge had considered conferring
an honorary degree on Ramsay MacDonald, leader of the
Labour party and prime minister in 1924, only to learn that
there would be opposition from some dons who had served
in the Great War (which MacDonald opposed), and others
who held he had been party to an illegal act in bringing
about the general strike of 1926, and its consequences.

On June 2 the Vice-Chancellor informed the Senate that
MacDonald had intimated he did not desire to receive a
degree conferred on him by the votes of a majority]

*From Dr G. G. Coulton*                            *8 June 1926*

[Fellow of St John's College, Cambridge]

Sir,

Since the recent unfortunate occurrence may easily be
misinterpreted outside, or even inside, this University, may I
express what I know to be the feeling of others also, from the
point of view of one who has twice voted for Mr MacDonald's
party at General Elections, but who would probably have
abstained from voting either way on the question of his degree?

A memorial has been circulated in Cambridge deploring that
this incident will embarrass, or even destroy, the convention of
offering honorary degrees to politicians as such, apart from any
direct services which they may have rendered to learning, letters,
or art. Some of us, on the other hand, while deeply regretting
this incident on other grounds, would welcome that result, and
rejoice that some good, at least, had emerged from the present
evil. Many, even among Mr MacDonald's political opponents,
have the greatest admiration for what he did, as Foreign
Minister, in the cause of this country and of world-peace. They
heartily regret that, practice in these matters having been what
it has been, the first break in that practice during the last few
years should seem to imply personal discourtesy to Mr
MacDonald. But they cannot agree with the memorialists in
branding the small group of determined opponents as persons
whose political intolerance humiliates this University; they feel
that this would come perilously near to denying the right of
conscientious objection to all persons whose objections we
ourselves do not happen to share.

Is there any real way out of this difficulty, so long as
universities are in the habit of offering Doctorates in Law to
politicians or soldiers *as such*? It is argued that the honour is

here offered not to the politician but to the distinguished servant of the Crown, *ex officio*. If that were clearly understood on all sides; if it were generally known that the Prime Minister is thus to be honoured automatically, while others must take their chance of an adverse vote, this would certainly remove the misgivings felt by many at the present moment. Although an honour is certainly somewhat lessened by being automatic, yet such a clear understanding would relieve us from our present attempt to fly in the face of nature, and to combine the advantages of free will with those of absolute obedience to rule. We should be a very dead University if there were not strong differences of political opinion, accentuated by the present crisis.

Is it not a contradiction in terms to say that we offer degrees to politicians *qua* politicians, yet without reference to their politics? At least, this is contrary both to reason and to practice in normal cases, where the scholar, the *littérateur*, and the artist are chosen with the directest and most explicit reference to the value of their performances in scholarship, literature, or art. There are men here who joined in a similar public protest against Lord Randolph Churchill's degree; this did not prevent Lord Randolph from receiving his degree on a majority vote. It is as certain as anything can be that Mr MacDonald would have had a sweeping majority; to doubt this would be to suggest, by that very doubt, the strongest possible justification for the opposers' action. In the absense of absolutely clear understandings and precedents, this matter could not possibly have been emptied of all political significance. Some people (as things are at this moment) would have found political significance in the unopposed grant of a degree; even more will find political significance in the fact that it was opposed. Therefore (to repeat my earliest question in a different form), must not a politician be always ready to face a politician's chances?

If universities deliberately intend that a certain studied gesture, when made to a politician, should mean something essentially different from that identical gesture towards a scientist, then ought it not to be understood beforehand, beyond any possibility of misconception, that this offer of a degree is simply an automatic sequel to the King's offer of the Premiership?

Yours, &c.,

G. G. COULTON

[ In the tenth month of the miners' strike − on January 28, 1985 − Oxford University Congregation voted by 738 to

319 not to confer an honorary degree on the prime
minister, Mrs Margaret Thatcher. A *Times* leader condemned the decision]

*From Sir Ian Percival, QC, MP*                    *1 February 1985*
[Conservative Member for Southport; Solicitor General
1979–83]

Sir,

Can there ever have been such reason to feel ashamed of one
of our great institutions?

The world knows that Margaret Thatcher is one of the very
finest people who has ever passed through any university.
Oxford could and should be justly and immensely proud to
honour her as their own. And all credit to those of its leaders
who wished to do so in the traditional way.

But what shame on those who have thwarted that wish. Such
bigotry is beyond belief. The discourtesy defies description.
That so many should so behave for political purposes – men
and women who no doubt pride themselves on practising and
protecting the freedom to differ – is surely deplorable.

None of this will do our Prime Minister any harm. And she
is too big a person to allow the very real personal hurt which she
must feel to interrupt her endeavours or colour her approach.
But what a terrible reflection it is on the university. What harm
it may do to Oxford.

So many of its leaders have shown themselves to be such small
people swimming in a pond which seems too big for them. It is
as sad as it is anger-making to find that so many of those to
whom the achievements and glories of Oxford over the centuries
have been entrusted are not up to that trust – and that so many
of our young people should be at risk of indoctrination by them.

A sad day indeed for the Oxford of which all of us, of
whatever university, or of none, have always been so proud.

Yours etc.,

IAN PERCIVAL

*From Professor Emeritus Bernard Crick*          *1 February 1985*

[formerly Professor of Politics, Birkbeck College, London
University]

Sir,

It is never easy to know why people vote. Your remarkable
editorial, 'Sale of honours' (January 30) suggests that the
campaign against giving Mrs Thatcher an honorary degree was
got up by 'militantly left-wing dons' and 'Marxist dons' who

gained 'more respectable support' from those who object to the Government's policies in higher education.

Your assumption is questionable. The vote was very large and very decisive, 738 to 319. Few Oxford dons are either militant or Marxist (are you joking?); overwhelmingly they are of a conservative disposition, very unlikely to reject either a 'customary civility' or a Conservative prime minister; and certainly very few Oxford dons, except leading scientists, have much knowledge of or care for the higher education system outside Oxford. Oxford has been cut the least.

Many of the votes cast must have been from Conservatives wishing to show that they think that she has *uniquely* divided and polarized the country. No one else has so broken from Baldwin's conciliatory tradition except Edward Heath in his brief 'Selsdon' phase.

This vote shows once again that some of the most important political divisions are *within* the two main parties, not just between them. You are very sensitive to divisions in the Labour Party, perhaps a bit less so among Conservatives.

Yours sincerely,
BERNARD CRICK

*From Countess Badeni*                    *1 February 1985*

Sir,

When the Beatles were given the MBE some members of the order sent their medals back.

Now that Oxford University has devalued its honorary degree by refusing it to one of our greatest prime ministers, will those who have it feel it worth keeping?

Yours faithfully,
JUNE BADENI

*From Mr R. G. Opie*                    *2 February 1985*

[Fellow of New College, Oxford]

Sir,

In a friendly effort to help you to use the English language more accurately in your bicentennial year, may I refer to your editorial phrase (in 'Sale of honours', January 30), 'the Marxist dons who spearheaded this campaign'?

To the best of my knowledge, no such person was among us.

Yours faithfully,
R. G. OPIE

[MacDonald received honorary degrees from Glasgow, Edinburgh, Wales, McGill – and Oxford]

# Kitchener's Army

*From Sir Arthur Conan Doyle*                    *15 February 1927*

Sir,

One could not read the last paragraphs of Mr Winston Churchill's accounts of the Somme Battles, as given in your issue of February 12, without rejoicing that Kitchener's Army has at last received a worthy panegyric. Personally, I have long recognized that Winston Churchill had the finest prose style of any contemporary, and it is indeed a splendid thing that he should use it to do that which seemed impossible – namely, to give an adequate appreciation of that glorious Army of patriotic volunteers who gave themselves so ungrudgingly to their country's service.

Yours faithfully,
ARTHUR CONAN DOYLE

[The last sentence referred to by Doyle in *The World Crisis* ran: 'Unconquerable, except by death, which they had conquered, they have set up a monument of native virtue which will command the wonder, the reverence, and the gratitude of our island people as long as we endure as a nation among men.']

# Traffic by Old Buildings

*From the Dean of Lincoln*                    *22 February 1929*

Sir,

Suffer me to urge on Parliament to pass a short 'suspensory Bill' to compel local authorities to submit all road and bridge proposals to the control of the Ministry of Transport, in the neighbourhood of precious memorials of the past. Otherwise we shall have fresh and irremediable calamities forced on us; and resistance will come too late.

Your obedient servant,
T. C. FRY

# 'Keep Off the Grass'

*From Sir David Hunter-Blair*                 *19 August 1930*

Sir,

In one of the loveliest gardens in the West of Scotland, opened freely on certain days to a vast public from Glasgow and the neighbourhood, courteous notices everywhere intimated that 'Visitors are requested not to pick the flowers without leave.' A waggish tourist went round with a paint brush, adding an 's' to the word 'leave,' with the deplorable result that not only were flowers plucked, but whole plants – flowers, leaves, and roots – were excavated and carried off.

Yours, &c.,
DAVID HUNTER-BLAIR

# The Tithe Sausage

[Trouble at Demen in Mecklenburg-Schwerin, where the church claimed every year 130lb of sausage (*Mettwurst*) but where the tithepayers withheld their dues. Compelled by law to pay, they delivered (so the church insisted) an inferior article]

*From Baroness Ladenburg*                *10 February 1931*

Sir,

With reference to the article in your issue of yesterday entitled 'The Tithe Sausage', it may interest your readers to know that in many parishes in Mecklenburg-Schwerin it was customary for the tithepayers to deliver to their incumbent *Mettwurst* measured by the ell. The parishioners used to express their liking for their pastor in the size of the diameter of the sausage; on the other hand, if he was unpopular the unfortunate man was the recipient of the right length, but the sausage was of the smallest circumference.

I am, Sir, yours, etc.,
ASTER LADENBURG

*From the Reverend Cecil Holmes*       *11 February 1931*

Sir,

You speak of 130lb of sausage as being 'an idea so massive as to oppress the imagination of all but a hungry school-boy.' I do not know about that, but when I was a 'Bush-Brother' at Cunnamulla, in the West of Queensland, the horse-boy at Calwarro managed 11ft 6in of sausage for breakfast one morning. He had been out early for horses, and they had been hard to find. On his return to the homestead the Chinaman cook had just finished making his batch for the week and had retired to his hut. Into the frying-pan they all went, and Jack did not even leave one in ten for the parson.

Yours truly,

CECIL HOLMES

[In Mecklenburg-Schwerin 130lb of sausage would provide a family, children and servants with breakfasts, lunches and suppers for a whole year]


# A Full Dress Parade

*From Mr L. E. Jones*                    *26 March 1931*

[Sir Lawrence Evelyn Jones, Bart., was later the author of two enchanting volumes of reminiscence, *An Edwardian Youth* and *Georgian Afternoon*]

Sir,

After to-day's Levée, a brigadier, who is also A.D.C. to the King, was good enough to visit my bed of sickness. In cocked hat, scarlet tunic, and gold lace, he was, like Mrs Ewing's Lancer, 'beautiful to behold.'

Now, if a *blasé* business man of 46 can be gladdened and enlivened by the aspect of one brigadier, what might not be the happy effect if a *posse* of admirals and generals should, after leaving a levée, pass through the wards of some of our children's hospitals? Even if only one man in 10 will be unselfconscious enough to do it without a painful effort, surely the other nine, fortified by their medals, will be gallant enough to make that effort? No speeches would be expected — but they must be prepared to turn themselves round and, if required, to draw their swords. It might help to break the ice if the hospitals would take the initiative by extending an invitation.

I am, Sir, your obedient servant,

L. E. JONES

# Mrs Beeton

[An article on the former Isabella Mary Mayson, who later achieved fame as the author of *Mrs Beeton's Cookery Book*, had described the book as 'the work of a young, beautiful, highly talented woman doomed to early death.']

*From Mrs Smiles*                                  *6 February 1932*

Sir,
   I feel compelled to add to your notice of my sister, Mrs Beeton, in *The Times* of February 3 that she was an accomplished pianist, educated in Heidelberg, and later was a pupil of Sir Julius Benedict. She was also very charitable. I was staying with her at her home at Pinner during a severe winter, I think about 1859, and she was busy making soup for the poor, and the children used to call with their cans regularly to be refilled.

Believe me yours truly,

LUCY SMILES

# Plus a Little Something

*From Mr Walter B. Harris*                            *1 February 1933*

[Commander of the Ouissam Alaouite of Morocco; correspondent of *The Times* in Morocco]

Sir,
   A Berber chieftain who has installed a radio set in his castle in the Atlas Mountains asks me to obtain through *The Times*, which he describes as 'the origin and source of all knowledge,' the following information.
   He is anxious to know where he can obtain one of those small and inexpensive machines, to be affixed to the loud-speaker, which interpret into Arabic all air communications that are received from abroad in foreign languages. Perhaps some reader of *The Times* would kindly let me know.

I am, Sir, your obedient servant,

WALTER B. HARRIS

# Sighting at Billiards

[A winning hazard entails the potting of the object ball, as distinct from a losing hazard when the striker's ball is pocketed after contact with another]

91

Sir,

The 1933 season of billiards will be remembered with the names of two great British players standing out − J. Davis and Sidney Lee, professional and amateur. They are both great winning-hazard players, the most difficult shot. Davis, I think, the best in the world, and Lee not far behind him.

They are the only two professionals or amateurs that I have seen − and I have seen most of them − that are right-handed and left-eyed. Where aiming is required, as in rifle shooting or billiards, only one eye can be used. All the right-handed and right-eyed players play with the cue under the right eye − *i.e.*, about an inch or so to the right or outside their chin. Davis and Lee play with the cue about the same distance to the left of or inside their chin, to bring their left eye over the cue. This brings the right hand about 4 in. nearer the body, the right arm from elbow to shoulder in the same line as the cue. Is it not possible that this helps to keep the cue swing absolutely true, and may it not be that this fact enables these two players to make winning hazards at any strength with wonderful certainty?

I am yours, &c.,

DOUGLAS CARNEGIE

[Joe Davis's mastery of the winning hazard explains why he has never been surpassed in the game of snooker]

## George III's Bathing Machine

*From Mr L. G. Wickham Legg*     *29 June 1933*

[Fellow of New College, Oxford]

Sir,

In regard to your recent article, entitled 'Sea Bathing,' it may be worth while to put on record that the bathing machine reputed to have been used by King George III at Weymouth was in regular use down to the summer of 1914, when I saw it in its accustomed place of honour on the extreme right of the line of bathing machines.

It differed from the others in its octagonal shape, which gave it of necessity a pyramidal roof surmounted by a small staff, whereas the other machines were oblong in plan with gabled roofs. Further, above the door the Royal Arms, similar in design to those now on your front page, were placed in summer on a strut and removed in winter when the machines were drawn to

Lodmoor, where the royal machine retained its pride of place. The last time I saw it was some 10 years ago, when, owing to the popular disfavour which had fallen upon bathing machines, it had been removed from its wheels, and, along with its fellows, had been degraded to some mean use, apparently a tool shed, which I was sorry to see, for I thought Weymouth would have had more regard for this relic of its royal patron.

Your obedient servant,

L. G. WICKHAM LEGG

## High Tea at Six

['In a recent announcement on the front page of *The Times* an advertiser begged his friends to abstain from asking him to sherry and cocktail parties at six pm, because, he said, he could not endure them.' — Leading article, 23 June 1933]

*From Mr Edward Cadogan, MP*                    *30 June 1933*

[Conservative Member for Finchley; knighted 1939]

Sir,

With many others I have been much intrigued by the third leading article in *The Times* of June 23. Since the War there has been so great a revolution in the habits and customs of the English people in all other respects, it is indeed surprising that our meals have been so immune from the innovators. The late Victorians, as I can testify, conformed with a rigid orthodoxy to both the time and the nature of their meals prescribed for them by tradition. For instance, I was brought up to believe that tea could not be served at any other hour but 5 o'clock, and that its somewhat unsufficing and unattractive fare was as immutable as the laws of the Medes and Persians. I remember that, at a certain house in the highlands of Scotland, where I used to visit, weary sportsmen who returned home at 5 o'clock were allowed tea, but if they came in at a later hour they found the table as bare as the cupboard of the nursery rhyme. I should have thought that the later they came home the more they would have needed and the more they would have deserved refreshment, but my hostess could not bring herself to break with the Victorian tradition. Sherry, cocktails, chipolata, or tea at 6 o'clock would have been right outside her philosophy.

So far as meals are concerned I am a Bolshevist of the deepest dye. Nothing is more palatable to me than the right thing at the wrong meal. Although the sausage, according to all Victorian rules, belongs to the morning, I protest that it tastes far more delicious at any other time of day. The many evening expeditions I am called upon to make to my constituency necessitate for myself an anomalous meal too late for tea and too early for supper, but it is none the less agreeable in that it breaks away from tradition.

Why is it that the right thing tastes so much better at the wrong meal? It may be that the palate undergoes a physical or even a psychological change in the course of the day's work, but I am disposed to believe that the fact that you are doing something which is prohibited by all nice people adds a special flavour which no well-advertised sauce could produce.

For all I care then, let the new generation of epicures rise up and call our meals anachronistic and unsuitable to modern ways and means. Let them exercise to the full their ingenuity to devise meals which in time, place, and substance are at once more convenient and more suitable to our changed and changing needs.

Yours faithfully,
EDWARD CADOGAN


## 'Alcoholic Hyenas'

*From Mr. Cyril Asquith, KC*                    *19 June 1937*

[fourth son of H.H. Asquith; later Judge of the High Court of Justice]

Sir,

Distinguished correspondents of yours have lately deprecated the practice of 'lecturing' Signor Mussolini.

In an article in the *Populo d'Italia* ( = Signor Mussolini) the leaders of the British Press — including, I suppose, yourself — are described, rather to my surprise, as alcoholic hyenas. I hope that no one need incur the charge of 'lecturing' who calls attention to the confusion both of metaphor and zoology involved in this accusation.

'These hyenas in human form,' says the Duce or his newspaper, 'threw themselves on the pure blood of Italian youth as if it were whisky, without a trace of shame . . .'

The implication that a hyena is not safe if there is a bottle of whisky about, and is, if anything, disappointed to find that the

94

beverage is, in fact merely blood, will come as a surprise both to distillers and naturalists, and does, I feel, some injustice to a strictly temperate quadruped. The real offence of the hyena is not that it drinks, but that it laughs.

I am, dear hyena, yours, etc.,

CYRIL ASQUITH

## Typical Bloody Pom

*From Mr W. E. Lane*                          *4 July 1933*

Sir,

I can assure Mr William Mabane from personal and painful experience that a boomerang can be quite accurately described as a weapon 'which may recoil with catastrophic effect.' In the hands of an expert it will behave even as he says; but if thrown unskilfully let the thrower beware! During a visit to Australia a few years ago we spent a long day in the Gippsland bush, where we came across an interesting, nondescript, wandering individual who proceeded to give us a thrilling exhibition of the art of boomerang throwing.

Wishing to try my hand, and my friends having discreetly taken cover, I made several attempts, and finally threw one that skimmed far away and was lost to sight in the gathering twilight, presently reappearing at close range and striking me square in the forehead, fortunately at the end of its flight, but nevertheless inflicting a wound which has left an indelible scar. It is now a trophy in my hall. So it is that policies and measures must be not only sound in themselves but skilfully applied, else they 'may recoil with catastrophic effect.'

Yours obediently,

W. E. LANE

## The Times — and an English Hat

*From Mr F. S. Joelson*                          *1 January 1934*

[editor, *East Africa*]

Sir,

I wonder if you know and feel certain that the vast majority of your readers do not know that *The Times* is today used by some foreign visitors to Germany to declare their foreign identity, in order that they may not be subject to the assault and battery which might otherwise be their lot.

I have just heard from a business man of obvious Jewish appearance who has done a great deal of travelling in Germany for some years past that he attributes his escape from molestation to two things only: – (a) The wearing of so English a hat that it seems a little incongruous in a German street; and (b) the fact that he carries at all times of the day in a very conspicuous way a copy of the latest available issue of *The Times*.

Yours faithfully,

F. S. JOELSON

*From Mr Michael Fry*                                          *9 January 1934*

Sir,

What constitutes an English hat? This question occurs to me after reading Mr Joelson's letter, published in your columns, in which he explains that a friend of his was able to escape molestation in Nazi Germany by wearing an English hat and carrying a copy of *The Times* 'at all times of the day in a very conspicuous way.'

I grant Mr Joelson that a copy of *The Times* is indubitably English – no one could possibly mistake it for the *Petit Parisien* or *Der Angriff* – but what sort of hat did Mr Joelson's friend wear which immediately made belligerent Storm Troopers exclaim, 'That is an English hat'?

It could not have been a bowler, for that particularly uncomfortable form of headgear is international. Panamas and straw boaters are the hall-mark of the American. Homburgs are much favoured by Germans and Austrians. Soft felt hats known as 'Trilby' hats vary very little from one country to another. It seems, therefore, that it could not have been any of these.

Could it have been a cricket cap? Worn with an ordinary lounge suit it might easily have seemed 'a little incongruous in a German street.' Was it a London policeman's helmet? Was it an English postman's hat? None of these offer an adequate solution to the problem. From my own knowledge of foreign forms of headgear I can only suggest that a truly British hat would be a deerstalker cap, as worn by the immortal Sherlock Holmes. For centuries foreign cartoonists have depicted John Bull wearing a cap of this sort.

During my stay in Germany a few weeks ago it never occurred to me to dress in an obviously English manner to avoid persecution. I admit that I frequently carried *The Times*, but this was merely done with the object of eventually reading it. Although my appearance is not, like that of Mr Joelson's friend, obviously Jewish, I fully offset it by my journalistic inquisitiveness, which must have been a source of annoyance to the authorities. Despite that, I do not remember one single unpleasant incident either with Government officials or with Storm Troopers. I frequently gave the Nazi salute as a matter of elementary courtesy, just as I would expect a German to take his 'German' hat off to the Union Jack. No pressure was brought to bear on me in that respect.

It is unfortunate that all the readers of *The Times* are unable to go to Germany and see conditions for themselves. Apart from furthering international cordiality it would, if they all adopted Mr Joelson's suggestions, considerably stimulate the 'English' hat trade.

I am, Sir, yours faithfully,<br>MICHAEL FRY


## From Olympus

*From Sir Buckston Browne*                    *2 January 1935*

[an eminent surgeon]

Sir,

For many years I have divided my friends into two classes, those who read *The Times* and those who do not. I have always felt sorry for the latter.

I am, Sir, your obedient servant,<br>BUCKSTON BROWNE


## Hint to the Kremlin

[In his later years Count Leo Tolstoy prepared an anthology, *The Circle of Reading*, which sold freely until his death in 1910. Thereupon the book was seized and the publisher Posadov Gorbunov prosecuted. On 5 February 1912 a devastating letter from Mr Charles Hagberg Wright appeared in *The Times*]

[Secretary and Librarian, the London Library]

Sir,

On February 5, 1912, a letter appeared in *The Times* condemning in strong terms the prosecution of Mr Posadov Gorbunov, the Russian publisher of Tolstoy's popular stories.

In 1928 I was at a public meeting in Russia during the Tolstoy centenary celebrations, where I again met Mr Posadov Gorbunov, and found him full of vigour and ready to issue a new series of tales for the people.

He related how in 1912 he was condemned to twelve years of exile by the Appeal Court in Petrograd, when a Senator named Michael Stahkovich rushed into Court flourishing a copy of *The Times*. Holding it up before the Judges, he exclaimed:

'Your Excellencies, you cannot convict Mr Gorbunov; listen to what *The Times* says.'

'You must not interrupt the proceedings, Mr Senator, the sentence has been pronounced and it is final.'

But the Senator, undaunted, read out loud an extract from *The Times*, which was heard in silence.

When he had finished there was a brief consultation between the Judges, after which the President of the Court declared that they could not revoke the sentence, but a rider would be added that it was not to be carried out. Mr Gorbunov was set free.

> I am, etc.,
> C. HAGBERG WRIGHT

# The King at the Microphone

Sir,

It may interest you to know that as Lord Lieutenant of the county, to mark the Jubilee, I am presenting to all schools in the county, including Dollar Academy, a framed copy of *The Times* portrait of the King at the microphone.

> I am yours faithfully,
> MAR AND KELLIE

[Does that 'including Dollar Academy' suggest the existence of a Stuart cell?]

# Toscanini and Elgar

*From Sir Landon Ronald*        *3 June 1935*

Sir,

I have been constantly told that Elgar's music is so English in character and feeling that it could only be really understood and interpreted by one of his own countrymen. I have always strenuously denied this.

Last Monday's magnificent performance of the 'Enigma' Variations by Toscanini has, I lay claim, proved me to be correct. This great conductor rendered the work exactly as Elgar intended, and the composer's idiom obviously has no secret for Toscanini. Some of the best performances I have ever heard were from the composer himself, but this one on Monday night last excelled, because Toscanini has a genius for conducting and Elgar had not.

Elgar knew exactly how he wished his music interpreted, and the result was often magnificent. However, this was due, in my opinion, not so much to his powers as a conductor, as to the love and respect he inspired in the orchestra, both as a great musician and a lovable man.

We had the 'Variations' from Toscanini exactly as Elgar wished them played, plus the genius of a great master of the orchestra. I maintain that Elgar did not write English music – whatever that may be; he wrote great music. On Monday last a great foreign conductor proved this.

Yours faithfully,<br>LANDON RONALD

[Sir Landon was the dedicatee of Elgar's *Falstaff*. 'Never could make head or tail of the piece, my dear boy,' he said to the young John Barbirolli]

## Celebrations of the Nineteenth Century

[King George V's Jubilee had just been celebrated]

*From Mr G. Wilson Burn*        *3 June 1935*

Sir,

As I am just completing my eighty-eighth year, more than the first half of which was lived in London, a few incidents in public rejoicings which have occurred in my experience may interest your readers.

Let me say at once that I have heard very many cheering

crowds, but never before have I heard anything like the stentorian roar of welcome that I listened to on the wireless on Jubilee Monday. My father sufficiently often referred to the following reminiscence to make it seem to be my own.

On the occasion of Queen Victoria's first visit to the theatre (Drury Lane) in state after her marriage my father, after strenuously struggling in a crowd for two hours, succeeded in getting into the vestibule in front of the pit doors and was congratulating himself on the prospect of getting in when they put up a notice 'Pit full.'

My own experience begins with the Duke of Wellington. We used to watch my father put on his Wellington boots on Sunday morning, but on one occasion he returned from the office to put them on, and we were told it was to go to the funeral of the Duke of Wellington, which we thought quite appropriate! When a little more than seven years old I was taken by my grandmother to see a display of fireworks which formed an item in the peace rejoicing after the Crimean War. Some years later I walked across London to Ludgate Hill and stood there from 10 a.m. to 3 p.m. to see the Princess Alexandra come into London; but just as she passed a great burly fellow who stood beside me put his hand on my shoulder in order to lever himself up, and all I saw was the tops of the whips! Some months afterwards my brother and I walked from London to Windsor to view St. George's Chapel, where the marriage took place, and there took part in a mild kind of scrimmage in order to kneel down before the altar in the same place that the Princess had knelt.

Among the various public illuminations which took place during the next period, when I was living in Fleet Street, the following stands out prominently. From late afternoon till 1 o'clock in the morning a constant stream of people occupying the whole of the roadway was passing from east to west to see the illuminations. It was like a flowing river, and the noise was not the tramp of soldiers but a more diffused roar. To go from west to east was only possible on the pavements.

Now for Thanksgiving Day, 1872. I was in the crowd at the east of Temple Bar accompanied by a lady when the tragedy occurred, but fortunately we were close to a big man with a broad back, so by placing my hands on his back and pushing with all my might I was able to relieve the pressure a little from my companion. The trouble was caused by every one as they came through the bottle-neck of Temple Bar trying to follow the Royal example and knock at the door. As soon as they had passed the Bar they came against the stream of people coming from Chancery Lane. Three incidents are worth mentioning in connexion with this public rejoicing: – (1) One of the victims of the tragedy was an old lady over 70 who had, unknown to her people, come up to London from Lincolnshire by herself to see the illuminations; (2) one of the casualties treated at Charing Cross Hospital was a dislocated jaw caused by intense yawning while waiting in the crowd; (3) a good many people, our own friends among them, chartered a conveyance to take them along the principal route of illumination, but on attempting to enter from a side street they were stopped, and as they were unable to turn the vehicle round were compelled to sit there for several hours seeing nothing.

Yours faithfully,<br>
G. Wilson Burn

## Means Test

*From the Master of Balliol College, Oxford 14 February 1935*

[later Lord Lindsay of Birker]

Sir,

May I plead for a reconsideration of that part of the means test which at present arouses more resentment than any other, inflicts much social injury by breaking up families, and is, I submit, in principle unjust? That is the provision which, by taking account of the earnings of relations in considering an applicant's means, imposes on these relations an obligation to maintain him.

The assumption underlying such a provision is that a man on transitional payments is an applicant for charity, and the consequence is drawn that he has a claim on the charity of his relations before he has a claim on the charity of the community – *i.e.*, his fellow citizens. If the assumption is granted, and it is often taken for granted, the consequence is rightly drawn. But it is this assumption which is bitterly and justly resented.

We now realize that most men who are on transitional payments are unemployed through no fault of their own, but because of the defective working of our industrial system. They bear in their persons the imperfections of our social machinery. That they should be supported by the rest of us, no doubt in such a way as not to involve injustice on those who are employed, is therefore the community's obligation. While a claim to charity falls primarily on a man's family and not on us all, this obligation falls primarily on us all and not on a man's family. To assume that a man who is unemployed through no fault of his own ought to be supported by his relations who are earning is to shift on to them the obligation of the community.

I realize that the detailed provisions of any means test involve complicated problems, but I cannot believe that if the above distinction had been recognized and clearly kept in mind the provisions of this part of the means test could have been what they are.

Yours sincerely,

A. D. LINDSAY

## 'Pax Britannica'

[George V had died on 20 January 1936]

*From Mr G. H. Stevenson*                 *3 February 1936*

[Fellow of University College, Oxford]

Sir,

May a student of the Roman Empire be permitted to record briefly a thought suggested to him by the tributes of veneration and affection paid to our late Sovereign by every country of the world? The Empire which maintained for centuries the peace of the civilized world derived its strength and stability from the person of the Emperor, for the republican system was doomed when once the power of Rome extended beyond quite narrow limits. The Emperor symbolized the system of government which united under one rule Gauls and Syrians, Britons and Egyptians. His prestige was not derived from his personal qualities, but from the fact that he bore the name of Caesar.

The British Commonwealth of Nations provides the nearest parallel in history to the Empire of Rome. Like the Romans, we are no devotees of rigid uniformity, and, like them, we interfere as little as possible with established customs and traditions. The only thing on which we insist is that the *pax Britannica* should not be broken. Is it too much to hope that some day the British Empire may be able to extend its limits so as to include all States which are genuinely inspired by the ideals of peace and of international cooperation? Such a Commonwealth of Nations would possess in the historic British monarchy a bond of union which it would take centuries for any League of Nations to create.

Yours, &c.,

G. H. STEVENSON

# Playing Cricket

[England beat Australia in the first two Tests of 1936–37, then lost the last three. D. G. Bradman's first five innings totalled 133 runs, his last four 677. The famous ex-cricketer referred to below sounds like C. B. Fry who accompanied the MCC party to Australia.]

*From Mr Reginald Grenfell*                    *5 March 1937*

Sir,

It is interesting to read that a famous ex-cricketer and present journalist has suggested that the reason England lost the Test Matches was not so much because they failed to get Bradman out as because they ever attempted to do so. He suggests that a more methodical strategy would be to try to deprive Bradman of the strike by placing a field which would make it very easy for him to score a single early in the over and exceedingly difficult for him to score a two or a four. The English bowlers would then be able to concentrate on the other batsman. The writer states that it may be argued that this would not get Bradman out, but 'it would, however, reduce his rate of scoring annoyingly and materially.'

With due respect to this famous cricketer, I would humbly suggest that the mistake in this policy is that it would allow Bradman to score at all. Would it not be more advisable, whenever Bradman got the strike, to bowl him a very slow underarm ball that never left the ground at all? The field could then be so placed that he could never score, and this policy would have the added advantage that the bowlers would not waste any energy in bowling at him and would always remain fresh for attacking his partner. In like manner I would suggest that in limitless time matches, if, with the adoption of this policy, it were found that the other batsmen were still making too many runs, the correct procedure would then be to bowl these same 'grubs' from both ends, and to postpone trying to get out the opponents until the right day arrived when a good downpour of rain had rendered the wicket difficult.

It seems a pity that the captains of English teams do not pay sufficient notice to these important sides of the game. For instance, in the golf matches against America it would be advisable to study the idiosyncrasies of the opponents. If it were found that an opponent disliked being forced to play a slow round, it would seem common sense to train his opponent to take all the time he was allowed. He might, for example, take a shooting stick out with him and sit down for five minutes between each stroke. Such a policy could not do any harm and it might always put the opponent off his game.

I beg to inform you, Sir, that the employment of simple tactics of this nature has resulted in the Rugby football fifteen which I coach having had a most successful season. The scheme which I adopted was as follows: —

As soon as any member of my team obtained the ball he was immediately surrounded by the remainder of his side, who then marched slowly, but in perfect order, over the opponents' back line. The fact that it is against the rules to tackle a player who is not in possession of the ball rendered it impossible to prevent the scoring of a try. Having scored a try, the only difficulty was once more to obtain possession of the ball. As soon as this had been accomplished the team would then once more encircle the player, who would then simply stand still and smoke a cigarette for the remainder of the game.

I am, Sir, your obedient servant,<br>REGINALD GRENFELL

[In the 5th Test at Melbourne, Bradman had hit only seven boundaries in reaching 100 in 125 minutes, scoring mainly in 1s and 2s.

The Rugby team coached by Mr Grenfell seems also to have employed him as referee — the off-side laws in obeyance. Stephen Potter's *The Theory and Practice of Gamesmanship* appeared in 1947.]

## Beards and Bicycle Chains

*From Mr N. R. Davis*                                    *5 May 1937*

Sir,

It is curious that there should be a (Reuter) news paragraph in your issue of April 29 about a man at Holsted who caught his beard in a bicycle chain while adjusting the mechanism, for when I was there in the spring of '92 there was a very popular rhyme which went something like this:

> At Holsted an elderly Dane
> Caught his beard in a bicycle chain.
> It's hoped if it grows
> Till it reaches his toes,
> He'll be able to cycle again.

Yours, &c.,<br>N. R. DAVIS

# Britannia's Teeth

[The Coronation of George VI would take place on 12 May 1937]

*From the Reverend H. A. Wilson*                    *5 May 1937*

Sir,

East London is as busy as West preparing for May 12, and perhaps more original. Hoxton streets are already roofed by the flags of all nations and the flags of no nation at all; Shoreditch High Street is decking itself with silvered poles, streamers, and electric light festoons: though I have yet to see in these parts the slogan painted at the Jubilee across a South London street, 'Lousy But Loyal.' But the *chef d'œuvre* at the moment appears to be the four-foot figure of Britannia that stands above the main entrance of a Dalston publichouse. Only a few are aware that this arresting effigy is composed of a dressmaker's dummy swathed in sheets and topped by a repainted Guy Fawkes mask; that the trident is a gilded toasting-fork; that, thanks to a customer who has recently been shingled, the flowing tresses are human; and that the teeth of this emblem of our Empire are the upper and lower dentures of a false set.

Yours truly,

H. A. WILSON

# Germany and the Press

[*Der Angriff* had been founded by Josef Goebbels; *Der Stürmer*, an anti-Semitic weekly, was edited by Julius Streicher]

*From Mr C. W. Robinson*                    *20 August 1937*

Sir,

May I congratulate you on the leading article in your issue of yesterday dealing with the recent attitude of the German press towards foreign journalists? The picture which your Correspondents paint of conditions in Germany resembles very closely that which has been formed in my own mind during the six months I have lived in Germany, using every opportunity for conversation, travel, and reading the newspapers.

One cannot live for long among the German people without gaining a very sincere regard for a large proportion of those one meets. For that reason one is glad that *The Times* gives publicity (erring, however, on the side of kindness) to the extravagances of those Nazi propaganda measures that are nauseating and probably pernicious to all educated German people. How often I am told that the *Stürmer* is not intended for foreigners to read. Most certainly it is not. Mercifully for Anglo-German relations your Correspondents do not give the publicity to its crudities that they deserve, considering that it is published in a country where the Press is 'controlled.' When one of your Correspondents comments on articles appearing in *Angriff* he does it with a tone of moderation which it would be refreshing to find in that journal itself. I admire and am impressed by the generosity with which you allow space in your columns to Germans writing in favour of the Nazi system of government.

Like many others who live or have lived in Germany, I would welcome an opportunity of working for the improvement of British relations with the German people, to whom I am indebted for unlimited friendliness and hospitality. To many of the Nazi propaganda measures, however, I am indebted only for their attempt to graft intolerance into the character of the people. One is constantly and at the cost of great disappointment coming up against the brick wall of Nazi intolerance, which one cannot identify with the spirit of the people. I believe that the finest qualities of the German nation will survive the rude assaults of Nazi propaganda. Your discrimination in permitting attacks only on the spirit which is inimical to a better Anglo-German understanding and not on the German nation must be a matter of thankfulness to all those who place a high hope on Anglo-German friendship.

Yours faithfully,
C. W. ROBINSON

*From Mr Charles W. Robinson*          *18 January 1985*

Sir,

In Mr Roy Jenkins's contribution to your bicentenary booklet there is an italicized reference (p. 33) to the expulsion of your Berlin Correspondent, Norman Ebbutt, from Germany on August 19, 1937.

On the day before that event I wrote from my lodgings in Germany supporting the valuable contributions which your correspondents within Germany were making at that time. *The Times* printed my letter August 20, and the immediate, but not unforeseen, result was my own expulsion from that country.

Yours sincerely,
CHARLES W. ROBINSON

# In Praise of Archery

*From Captain Clive Temperley*                    *7 February 1938*

Sir,

In your columns to-day you refer to the growth of popularity of archery in America, where there are said to be 1,500,000 archers. The Americans are not nit-wits and there must be a reason for this. There is! The long bow is an intriguing and temperamental weapon – far more intriguing and temperamental than any golf club in the bag. Every bow and every arrow has individual characteristics to be mastered. Part by a hairbreadth from the correct shooting style and the shot is affected: A beginner who once takes a bow in his hand is lost. He may score for his first round a few dozen points where an expert will score 500 or 600. He has a vast field ahead of him for improvement, experiment, and emulation.

And exercise? The principal archery round is the York round, in which 144 arrows are shot at distances varying from 60 yards to 100 yards. Drawing a bow is a strenuous affair, so that only three arrows are shot at a time and after each three a trip to the target is necessary. Consequently the York round takes anything up to three hours to complete – all exercise and walking, the latter some 2½ miles. The bow is drawn 144 times and each time a force corresponding to a weight of perhaps 50lb. has to be borne by the arms and shoulders and held while the aim is completed. This is roughly the same as lifting three tons of packing cases from the floor to a shelf 2ft. high.

During the summer what can a business man of the City of London do between leaving the office and sitting down to dinner? Golf courses are too far away; tennis is too strenuous. Archery provides an ideal solution. He need not change his clothes. He can start as late and stop as early as he wishes. He is in the open, in pleasant company, and taking part in a sport which is good for his health and his soul and one, moreover, which has a longer and more world-wide history than all the rest put together – a history measured not in decades nor in centuries, but in millennia.

Yours faithfully,
CLIVE TEMPERLEY

# Lack of Labour

*From Mr Malcolm Brereton*                    *15 March 1939*

Sir,

In his quiet corner and with his customary restraint, your Agricultural Correspondent on March 6 told us something which one hopes will be read not merely by his agricultural readers.

The R.A.F. have lured away a shepherd of 20 years' standing to be a waiter at an aerodrome for, it is reported, 70s. a week. If a shepherd earning 40s. can turn waiter and earn 70s., then no one who is not a shepherd can criticize the individual concerned for his decision to desert his calling and his sheep. But the taxpayer who finds the 70s. may well be appalled at the Government's idea of spending his money. This truly egregious loss of one shepherd must outweigh an infinite number of volunteers attracted to less vital departments of national service. The aerodrome itself has selected a curious method of defending ourselves, our flocks and our herds, and from the point of view even of its own supplies shows little foresight in bribing the shepherd to carry to our feasting aeronauts the lamb he should be tending. Soon they will have devoured his flock, and all will be waiters at last.

Yours faithfully,
MALCOLM BRERETON

[During the Battle of Britain a sergeant pilot's pay was 94s. 6d. per week.]

# Eighteenth-Century Neckwear

*From Mr Kenneth W. Sanderson*                    *15 March 1939*

[Hon. Curator of Costume, City Art Gallery, Leeds]

Sir,

I am frequently asked when lecturing what would be the correct neckwear which should be worn with an eighteenth-century costume. Historical films and plays have familiarized many people with the costume of the eighteenth century, but in almost all cases the so-called jabot consisting of a bunch of lace hanging over the chest is still believed to be the correct neckwear for this period. This fashion has no foundation of historical fact. It arose in the first half of the nineteenth century when the ruffled shirt went out of vogue. The shirt had sewn on both sides of the breast opening a gathered frill of fine linen or muslin which showed between the unbuttoned waistcoat top, or low cut front of the waistcoat and the coat.

This was the true jabot, and with it was worn a cravat wrapped round the neck several times. Instead of the jabot being attached to the shirt it was sewn to a linen band which fastened behind the neck with the frill hanging over the chest. This type of neckwear was worn as a part of eighteenth-century costume by all actors during the past 100 years. Actually the jabot, consisting of a double frill of lace, lawn, or muslin, was worn on all shirts from the time of Charles II to George IV with a long cravat up to 1728, and a gathered stock after this period to the end of the century. Only three eighteenth-century shirts are known in this country, at Westminster Abbey and at Nottingham and Leeds Art Galleries. The original stocks have also been preserved.

Yours faithfully,
KENNETH W. SANDERSON

## 'Literally Speaking'

*From Mr B. W. M. Young*                    *18 April 1949*

Sir,

Your recent report that a rackets player 'literally blasted his opponent out of the court' suggests that gamesmanship is becoming less subtle. Is not the use of dynamite as out of place in a first-class match as, for instance, the word 'literally' in a metaphor?

Yours truly,
B. W. M. YOUNG

*From Mr E. W. Fordham*                    *20 April 1949*

Sir,

Perhaps the most picturesque use of 'literally' was that of a writer who asserted that 'for five years Mr Gladstone was literally glued to the Treasury Bench.'

Yours faithfully,
E. W. FORDHAM

*From Mr G. Millington*                    *22 April 1949*

Sir,

The story recalled by Mr E. W. Fordham about Mr Gladstone being literally glued to the Treasury Bench is incomplete without the comment that appeared in *Punch*: 'That's torn it,' said the grand old man as he literally wrenched himself away to dinner.

Yours faithfully,

G. MILLINGTON

*From Mr Gerald Barry*                                    *22 April 1949*

[Director-General Festival of Britain, and knighted 1951]

Sir,

My own favourite for the 'Literal Stakes' is the biographer who wrote of his subject that 'he literally died in harness.'

Yours faithfully,

GERALD BARRY

*From Mr Philip Jordan*                                   *22 April 1949*

Sir,

My small collection of 'literallys' was bombed in the war; but two I recall. Writing of a horse, it was, Sir, your own Racing Correspondent who said that it 'literally ran away with the Two Thousand Guineas.' My second appeared in the gossip column of an evening paper, which wrote of a naval officer that he 'literally won his spurs at the Battle of Jutland.' It was, I recall as I write, that same paper which said that 'Clemenceau literally exploded' during an argument.

Yours faithfully,

PHILIP JORDAN

*From Lady Eileen Orde*                                   *23 April 1949*

Sir,

Last summer a BBC commentator describing an easy victory in the ladies' singles at Wimbledon, said: 'Miss so and so literally wiped the court with her opponent.'

Yours faithfully,

EILEEN ORDE

*From Mr Edward Evans, MP*                                *23 April 1949*

[Labour member for Lowestoft]

Sir,

I submit the following, long and lovingly remembered from my 'penny dreadful' days: 'Dick, hotly pursued by the scalp-hunter, turned in his saddle, fired, and literally decimated the Indian.'

Yours faithfully,

EDWARD EVANS

*From Miss I. Davison*                    *25 April 1949*

Sir,

When I was assistant editor of the *Saturday Review* in the
early 1920s, during a temporary absence of the editor I allowed
a reviewer to declare in those august pages that his heart was
literally in his boots.

Yours faithfully,
IVY DAVISON

*From Mr F. J. B. Watson*                 *25 April 1949*

Sir,

A widely-read pre-war guide to Greece used to describe the
inhabitants of that country as so interested in politics as to be
visible daily 'in cafés and restaurants literally devouring their
newspapers.'

Yours faithfully,
F. J. B. WATSON

*From Miss E. M. Bullock*                 *26 April 1949*

Sir,

The over-large vicarage of a Westmorland parish was
described at a local meeting as 'literally a white elephant round
the neck of the incumbent.'

Yours faithfully,
E. M. BULLOCK

*From Mr L. A. Impey*                     *29 April 1949*

Sir,

The author of Printers' Imp is correct. The phrase 'literally
devouring a book' should be removed from the index of square
adverbs in round holes. An Eton tutor once wrote of a boy who
nibbled the edges of his Virgil while construing that 'he
devoured the classics without digesting them.'

Yours, etc.,
L. A. IMPEY

*From Mr Compton Mackenzie*               *2 May 1949*

[Knighted 1952]

Sir,

For over 20 years Lord Samuel and I have been exchanging
'literallys' for our respective collections. We have between us
most of those recorded by your correspondents, but that
decimated Indian is a new gem. Here are a few more chosen at

111

random. From a book about Isadora Duncan: 'Our eyes were literally pinned to the curtain till it went up.' From a newspaper report of Highland Games: 'Literally yards of brawny beef and red hair assembled to toss cabers.' From a speech in the House of Commons in 1932: 'Our industries will be literally poleaxed.'

Your obedient servant,

COMPTON MACKENZIE

[For the correct use of 'literally', see letter for 9 March 1925.]

# Addressing Air Marshals

---

*From Marshal of the Royal Air Force Sir John Slessor*
*7 March 1953*

[Chief of the Air Staff 1950–52]

Sir,

A dignitary of the Church, who was a welcome visitor during the war to some squadrons armed with the 20-millimetre weapon, was known affectionately by the pilots as 'the 20-millimetre job.' Actually he was a canon – not a cannon. If this had gone on for 30 years, the pristine freshness of the jest might have worn thin. It is now rather longer than that since King George V decreed that his Air officers of ranks corresponding to Major-General and above should bear the titles of Air Vice-Marshal and so on up to Marshal of the Royal Air Force. Yet, more often than not, they are still addressed in other than official correspondence as Air Vice Marshall, &c.

We recognize that up to a point this is natural. The name 'Marshall' is in more common use. There is the Marshall plan. There is the famous emporium that couples that name with the other of Snelgrove. We are a law-abiding people and, even in these days when some form of military service is an almost universal experience, few have more than a nodding acquaintance with the Provost Marshal. Time was when we felt there was something pleasantly traditional and seventeenth century about it – 'the King's Generall' &c. But, Sir, we are beginning to get a little bored with it. We are modest enough to realize that it is not a matter of earth-shaking importance, but we do sometimes envy our brother officers of the older Services who are not nowadays addressed as Admirall or Generall.

While I am on the subject, may I remind your readers that officers of the rank of Air Vice-Marshal and Air Chief Marshal can be referred to in conversation and introduced as Air Marshal, without undue flattery in the one case or fear of offence in the other. We do not bother to wind our tongues round the full dignity of 'Lieutenant-General Bramble' or 'Vice Admiral Hornblower.' It is equally unnecessary to do so when

113

introducing Air officers. Marshals of the Royal Air Force may not inappropriately be introduced as Marshal, but that hurdle can usually be avoided by referring to them by the titles by which they are known to Messrs Burke and Debrett − *cf*. Lord Fixe or Sir Percy Prune.

Yours faithfully,<br>J. C. SLESSOR

*From Lady Cynthia Colville*            *10 March 1953*

[Woman of the Bedchamber to Queen Mary 1923–53]

Sir,

Is not the thoughtless addressing of your distinguished correspondent Sir John Slessor as Marshall of the Royal Air Force just another symptom of that distressing disregard for accuracy that is so prevalent to-day? If, for instance, your Christian name is Philip, you may be certain that nine times out of 10 you will be addressed as Phillip, oblivious of the fact that this 'Apostolic' name is never so spelt except when used as a surname. If one sends a parcel to Lisbon from a famous London store, it may well be dispatched to Spain; and, indeed, the Portuguese are now inured to this roundabout postal route.

Personally, I seldom receive a letter from correspondents, whose education ranges from primary school to university, that does not contain two or three glaring mistakes in spelling, punctuation, misquotation, &c. (and I am not thinking of the constitutional bad-speller). Perhaps the old-fashioned concern for these things, to which, I believe, educational authorities attach little importance nowadays, was justified by inducing a greater consideration for what was careful and exact.

Obviously, we all make mistakes from time to time, but constant slovenliness of thought does seem to be growing on us as a nation, and one cannot escape the conclusion that habitual inaccuracy leads on by degrees to insincerity of mind. As a famous Frenchman said: ' "A peu près" really will not do!'

Yours faithfully,<br>CYNTHIA COLVILLE

*From Professor G. R. Driver*            *11 March 1953*

[Professor of Semitic Philology in the University of Oxford 1938–62; knighted 1968]

Sir,

Sorry as I am for the distinguished Marshal of the Royal Air Force who so greatly dislikes being addressed as 'Marshall' (in spite of the goodly company of persons so named), I am equally sorry for myself. During the war I waged a losing battle with typists in the Army and in various Ministries who would address me as 'Proffesor'; and only yesterday I had a letter addressed to me on the envelope as 'Proffessor' − and that from a lady, my own cousin!

I can only offer your correspondent the dubious consolation of consulting Mr Follick and asking him for a simplified (!) phonetic spelling of his title; but will anyone then recognize his rank or my title? I have some difficulty in believing that illiterate persons of this decadent age who cannot learn one alphabet will ever become masters of two.

I am, Sir, &c.,

G. R. DRIVER

[Mont Follick − Labour member for Loughborough 1945–55 − was an advocate of English spelling reform and Decimal Currency]

*From Prebendary J. H. Powell*　　　　　　　*12 March 1953*

Sir,

Air Marshals are not the only victims of popular ignorance. What about the far more ancient and, it is to be hoped, equally honourable Prebendaries of the 'Cathedrals of the old foundation' (*e.g.,* York, Exeter, St. Paul's, Wells) who, when not, as is usual, addressed as Preb., Prev., Prep., are as likely as not to be Prependaries?

Air Marshals do not, as yet, suffer the added indignity of mispronunciation of their rank, whereas prebendaries are not infrequently called prebéndaries, and that by people who really should know better. When Air Marshals become 'Airms,' Admirals (whether 'of the Fleet,' 'Rear,' or 'Vice') 'Ads,' Generals (of sorts) 'Gens,' then they also will have something to grumble about. Merely to enumerate the various forms of address thought applicable to a rural dean would take up too much of your space.

I am, Sir, your obedient servant,

J. H. POWELL

*From Mr John Macadam*　　　　　　　*13 March 1953*

Sir,

Junior Royal Air Force officers had their embarrassments as well as the Marshals. Serving in an Anglo-American command with the rank of flight lieutenant, I was invariably addressed by the G.I.s as plain 'Loo-tenant.' I used to speculate idly on what they would do if I were promoted. I was, eventually, and

115

speculation ended. The G.I.s addressed me invariably as 'Squad Leader.'

Yours faithfully,<br>JOHN MACADAM

*From Mr John Harris*                        *14 March 1953*

Sir,

During the 1914–18 war I had the honour of accompanying the late Lord Coleridge more than once on circuit as his marshal. He always insisted that the proper spelling of the word, when applied to that office, was 'marshall' – not 'marshal.' The Judge was a master of the English language and must, I think, have had some authority for his spelling. Possibly he was influenced by Pepys's 'so to the office in the evening to marshall my papers.'

I am, Sir, your obedient servant,<br>JOHN HARRIS

*From the Reverend A. G. C. Langford*          *14 March 1953*

Sir,

Perhaps I fall into the class of the sloppy-minded against which Sir John Slessor and Dr Driver inveigh. But during my service in the Royal Air Force I was gratified rather than annoyed when I saw myself (as I did often enough) described in daily routine orders and on envelopes emanating from the orderly room as 'The Station Chaplin.' The only person who seemed to take my designation amiss was the entertainments officer.

Yours faithfully,<br>A. G. C. LANGFORD

[Sir John Slessor's mention of Fixe and Prune is a reminder of the official Air Ministry Training Memorandum, *Tee Emm*, in which Squadron Leader Anthony Armstrong Willis (Anthony Armstrong the playwright) and Corporal W. J. Hooper (the cartoonist 'Raff') delighted thousands with the inanities of Fixe and Prune. The demobilization of both Willis and Hooper in March 1946 brought forth a *Times* leader and . . .]

# P.O. Prune Protests

*From P.O. Prune*                                                   *7 March 1946*

Sir,

Your issue of March 4.

What, Sir, are you talking about in your last leading article about me? You accuse me, Sir, of having a 'long flowing moustache.' I've never had a moustache in my life, not even when I was a child.

Yours, etc.,

P. PRUNE, P.O.

I agree.

ANTHONY ARMSTRONG

. . Apologies are due to P.O. Prune. The moustache should have been affixed to his comrade in arms, Flying Officer Fixe.


# Plain English

*From Mr G. H. Palmer*                                              *2 August 1939*

Sir,

At the foot of the menu in use in the restaurant cars of our most up-to-date railway we read that: 'A supplementary portion of any dish will be served on request.' I suppose the first six words mean 'second helpings.' Why not say so?

I am, &c.,

G. H. PALMER

*From Mr A. P. Herbert, MP*                                         *3 August 1939*

[Independent Member for Oxford University; knighted 1945; Companion of Honour 1970]

Sir,

Your correspondent Mr G. H. Palmer should read *Punch*, in which (on March 8, 1939) the official answer to his question was recorded.

A lady wrote to the manager of a railway refreshment department asking as he does, 'Why not second helping?' The manager made this disarming answer: –

'I . . . have great respect for the English language but, knowing the public so well, I feel sure, for the few who do

117

not understand the meaning of "supplementary" there would be many who would accuse us of uneducated crudity if we quoted the phrase in such plain verbiage as you suggest.

I fully agree we should all be the better for expressing ourselves in simple terms, but in official printed documents it is "not done," and I will confess I fear to make myself look odd by being different from others.'

It is for the same sweet reason, no doubt, that almost all politicians and papers now say 'anticipate' when they mean no more than 'expect,' 'as to whether' instead of 'whether,' 'following' instead of 'after,' and 'emergency' when they mean 'war.' One might also mention such recent recoils from 'plain verbiage' as 'deratization,' 'redecontamination,' and 'self-evacuating persons.'

It is almost unfair to blame a refreshment department when Government Departments set such an example. And, alas, the strong silent Services have been corrupted, too. If Nelson had to repeat his famous signal today it would probably run thus: —

England anticipates that as regards the current emergency personnel will face up to the issues and exercise appropriately the functions allocated to their respective occupation-groups.

I am, Sir, your obedient servant,

A. P. HERBERT

## Miss Sitwell and Dr Goebbels

*From Miss Edith Sitwell*                    *11 October 1939*

[DBE 1954]

Sir,

Some weeks before the present war broke out Dr Goebbels, in a diatribe against Britain addressed to Commander King-Hall, was good enough to drag in my name as a witness to the truth of his accusations.

Dr Goebbels quotes me as having written: — 'Unhappily, side by side with this increasing enlightenment on the part of the governing classes, grew a wish to interfere with all nations possessing a different pigmentation of the skin — purely, of course, for their own good and because Britain had been appointed to this work by Heaven.' This quotation is correct:

but he omits to say that I was writing of the years that ran between 1833 and 1843.

It is understandable that Dr Goebbels finds it difficult to believe that a nation can improve, and can become more humane, in 100 years. But it is a fact. All nations have, I am afraid, been guilty of great cruelties and injustices in the past (some of the deeds in the years of which I wrote are indefensible); but I am unable to agree with Dr Goebbels that this makes it right and advisable that any nation should commit cruelties and injustices in this age.

Dr Goebbels is shocked, I presume (one can do no more than guess at his meaning, owing to his rather turgid and over-emotional style of expression), at the idea that, in the benighted years of which I wrote, the British should have wished to 'interfere' with other nations. Let me point out to him that side by side with this 'interference' has come a great amelioration of conditions among the people interfered with. Can the German Minister of Propaganda claim that the German 'interference' with people of another race, the wretched, stricken Jews, has resulted in any amelioration of their conditions?

It must astonish Dr Goebbels that when this war was forced upon us, the Indian native rulers, without one exception, made offers of help and of treasure to the King Emperor. It must astonish Dr Goebbels that the whole of the Empire, and the Dominions, have declared themselves as standing by our side. But this may no doubt be the result of the horrible cruelties and persecutions to which they are subjected by Britain. Just as the rising of the valiant Czecho-Slovak nation against their German 'protectors' may be a tribute to one year's experience of the gentle loving kindness of these.

I am, Sir, yours faithfully,

EDITH SITWELL

P.S. This letter will, of course, be represented as part of a new Jewish plot, although I am 100 per cent Aryan; or else as an attempt to encircle Dr Goebbels and the Beloved Leader.


## Three Little Pigs

*From Mrs M. Barrow-Dowling*                 *9 October 1939*

Sir,

I am enclosing a letter from a Kenya native which you may consider worth publishing. It is a charming — and not unusual — example of loyalty. The letter, which was addressed to the

District Commissioner, South Nyeri, was first published in the native paper which we are issuing now in order that the natives shall know exactly what is going on in Europe.

Yours faithfully,<br>MINNA BARROW-DOWLING

Dear Sir,

I beg you to accept me to offer my three pigs to Government, to be used in the war. I have kept three pigs only and I am in wanting them to be in the work of your Crown according my love and power, like other fellows who have given up their lives in order to defend other people's lives. I felt heartedly as I have no knowledge, or experience of any work, except these pigs which I decided that I must give them to Government, exactly as I would give up my life for our Kingdom to remain just to us as it has forever.

In measuring my pigs, they are four feet in length, etc.

Now, sir, I would be very much pleased to hear from you what you have decided for that question of these offerings.

Your obediently servant,<br>KANOGA S/O NIEGA

### 'Evacuees'

*From the Reverend F. H. J. Newton*          *14 October 1939*

Sir,

If ordinary English usage counts for anything, an evacuee is a person who has been evacuated, whatever that may be, as a trustee is one who has been trusted; for 'evacuee' cannot be thought of as a feminine French form, as 'employee' is by some.

Where are we going to stop if 'evacuee' is accepted as good English? Is a terrible time coming in which a woman, much dominated by her husband, will be called a dominee? Will she often be made a humiliee by his rough behaviour and sometimes prostree with grief after an unsought quarrel?

Must sensitive people suffer the mutilation of their language until they die and are ready to become cremees?

I am, Sir, your obedient servant,<br>F. H. J. NEWTON

# How to Use the Telephone

[On 19 May 1940 General Gort was preparing a retreat to the sea which would save the British army. At home, too, things were taken seriously]

*From Professor A. Lloyd James*                    *20 May 1940*

[Professor of Phonetics, School of Oriental and African Studies; linguistic adviser to the BBC]

Sir,

There is one important duty that may fall to the lot of any of us at this time; it is the simple duty of passing an important message by telephone. Long experience has persuaded me that knowledge of the factors which determine the recognition of electrically transmitted speech is essential to all of us, whether in the fighting Services or in civil life.

The first thing to be remembered is that all speech suffers distortion in telephony. There are sounds which, no matter how carefully they are made, will not emerge in a recognizable form when transmitted by ordinary telephones. However well the speaker makes his signal, he can be sure that a certain percentage of it will be lost in transit. The moral is obvious: the more carefully the signal is made the better are its chances of emerging in a recognizable form.

Here, in brief, is a word of advice. Don't shout; don't lose your head; don't lose your breath; and be brief. Speak slowly; keep the pitch of your voice as even as possible. Above all, try to preserve the normal rhythm of your speech, even though the tempo is slower. Rhythm is not distorted in transmission, and is always an invaluable clue to recognition. Don't let the unaccented syllables be lost.

Remember that the intelligibility of transmitted speech depends upon knowledge of the general context. Place names will figure in messages, and they are usually lacking in context. Staines is likely to be heard as Hayes, Grays, Thame, Base, or what not. Recognition here depends upon a critical examination of the phonetic details of the signal, which, as we have seen, are imperfect. Therefore be certain that your listener has got the right place in his mind before you leave the telephone; and remember that if he fails to get it, even after several attempts, he is not of necessity a fool.

In telephony casual conversation is one thing; the passing of vital information is quite another thing. Speech-signalling of this kind is not the simple thing most of us imagine it to be. There should be compulsory courses of instruction in it.

I am, Sir, your obedient servant,

A. LLOYD JAMES

## The Angelus in Alabama

*From Mr Sidney Lanier Gibson*                    *15 July 1940*

Sir,

During the last two years of the last World War the Methodist church bell at Verbena, Alabama, was rung every afternoon at 5 o'clock, and residents of this little town and residents for miles around stopped for a moment and, with uncovered heads, offered a silent prayer for peace. This was kept up until the Armistice came and was published in your London paper.

Yesterday, June 24, Verbena's Angelus bell was started again at 5 o'clock in the afternoon and at the same church; and once more residents of our hamlet and residents living within the sound of the pure tones of the 80-year-old bell are stopping with bared heads to offer a silent prayer to the Great General of the Universe for peace in America, victory for you, and peace to you and all nations.

May you keep very near you the all-wise and all-powerful God, who will lead His armies to victory, while we pray for America and for you.

Yours, &c.,

SIDNEY LANIER GIBSON

## Internment

*From Mr P. F. Wiener*                    *16 July 1940*

[Modern language master, Rugby School]

Sir,

You kindly published a letter of mine in November, 1939, in which I tried to describe the kindness with which we 'enemy aliens' had been treated by all the officials and the Aliens' Tribunal since the outbreak of war. Since then I passed a second tribunal (which again exempted me from all restrictions), and was interned three days later. I am now at my second camp, and as one of the camp leaders I am in daily touch with the military authorities. We are treated with a friendliness and kindness which is of the greatest comfort in our odd situation. We have all come to consider officers and men in charge of us not as pure military authorities and watchdogs but as real friends, who try to help and understand us as much as possible.

There are, of course, many things we complain about. We are since our internment without any news from our families and friends, we lead an open-air camp life, and it is very difficult for old people and great scholars to get used to sleep in crowded tents and wash unsheltered in the open; we all are used to different and more food. But the greatest complaint of most, if not all of us, is the inactivity into which we are forced. Many of us have outstanding technical, scholarly, or industrial qualifications; others are young and healthy as myself, and very fit for military service or agricultural work. It is a most bitter disappointment to us that we have to sit quiet behind barbed wire, and are not allowed to do our bit in any way whatsoever in this fight against our common mortal enemy, for our great common cause.

Yours faithfully,
P. F. Wiener

## Faith in the Führer

*From Mr H. A. Smith*            *6 July 1940*

Sir,

In this Gloucestershire village yesterday, a man remarked, 'Oh, well, if the Germans win, at any rate I have my pension, and they can't touch that.'

Can nothing be done by the Press, the BBC, or the Ministry of Information to bring home to people some of the implications of a German victory?

Yours obediently,
H. A. Smith

[The above letter may have been inspired by the 'Phoney' war response of the Secretary of State for Air, Sir Kingsley Wood, when asked to set fire to German forests: 'Are you aware it is private property?']

## 'Saved'

*From the Reverend P. B. Clayton*       *19 August 1940*

Sir,

They say that recently a naval wife whose husband since September has been dumb received a wire from him. The wire

read: 'Saved.' The wife then wrote her thankfulness as follows:
'My dear Man, I am glad to know you're saved. Was it a bomb
or mine, or was it done by the Salvation Army? In any case, we
shall expect you home. Your loving wife.'

Yours faithfully,<br>P. B. CLAYTON

## How to Combat Rumour

[The word 'jitterbug' was normally used to describe those
who participated in an energetic form of dancing to hot
rhythm music. Lord Haw-Haw was William Joyce whose
broadcasts from Germany were heard by few but discussed
by many]

*From Mr Edward Thompson*                 *13 July 1940*

[Fellow of Oriel College, Oxford]

Sir,

This new energetic drive against 'jitterbugs' and 'chatterbugs'
– the anti-Lord Haw-Haw hammer-hammer-hammer of some
crude broadcasters, the over-elaborate dry asides of others
whose sarcasms miss most of their audience – spreads fear that
things must be worse than we are told, since our rulers are so
afraid of our talking and listening; the dull-minded and literal-
minded will soon be bringing prosecutions for remarks they
simply did not understand and never would understand; and
there may come a time when really vital news, instead of
spreading like wildfire (as it should), will be suppressed close to
its source, because people are afraid it might prove false and
they would get into trouble. Suppose parachutists do descend
somewhere and that wires are cut?

Who listens to this damaging Lord Haw-Haw? Where is all
this widespread defeatism? This country has not the conditions
that made for the French disaster. Our Air Force, our Navy, our
Army are finer than they have ever been, we are in the greatest
adventure since Marathon, after years of self-treachery we are
even able to tell the truth about the Italian dictator. Only one
nightmare troubles the country's self-possession, and that is the
occasional dread lest our rulers might let us down by timidity
towards Italy or Japan or even by the final despair of the
Bordeaux Government. The conviction of the utter faithlessness
of the Nazi régime has gone so deep that the only thing the
present campaign is doing is to make people who long ago gave

up listening to the German broadcasts wonder whether they sometimes contain truth that explains why our rulers are so worried lest we hear them. No doubt there is some unwise talk about – why should it cease merely because there is a war on? But so long as the Government does its job as it has been doing it lately there will be no defeatism worth wasting B.B.C. time on.

Yours, &c.,
EDWARD THOMPSON

['Our Air Force, our Navy, our Army are finer than they have ever been' – as the Army had lost virtually all its guns, tanks and heavy equipment during the evacuation from Dunkirk, the above statement was untrue]


## A Bet at Brooks's

*From Mr Anthony Compton-Thornhill*     *10 February 1941*

Sir,

The Racing Calendar for 1781 has the following entry under 'Newmarket July Meeting, Tuesday, the 10th': –

'L$^{d.}$ Egremont's Spitfire by Eclipse, 8st., beat L$^{d.}$ Clermont's Dictator, 8st. 8lb. R.M. 300gs. 6–4 on Spitfire.'

Yours, &c.,
ANTHONY COMPTON-THORNHILL

## In Place of Tobacco

*From Sir Stephen Tallents*     *1 September 1941*

[an eminent civil servant who was an authority on the collection of thistledown for pillows]

Sir,

Pipe tobacco is none too plentiful nowadays and briars themselves are in short supply. Can I persuade your readers to pool any experience they may have of home-grown substitutes for either?

Coltsfoot, as the old botany books show, is the countryman's traditional substitute for tobacco. The French, I read, are being advised to smoke the leaves of lime, ash, or nut trees. I have lately come across memories of a clergyman who always smoked watercress and of a Scotsman who preferred lavender – whether flowers, stalks, or leaves is not clear. I have experimented with these last two herbs and with a few others primitively dried. My results so far are instructive rather than alluring either to the smoker or those about him; but I have hopes of devising before winter some more tolerable blend.

Of pipes I can write more confidently. I have lately made, out of both pear and medlar wood, pipes which, if they do not as yet colour or polish so handsomely, taste just as well as briar and better than cherry. But here, too, your readers may have wisdom to contribute.

Yours faithfully,<br>STEPHEN TALLENTS

*From Dr J. A. Stewart*                               *3 September 1941*

Sir,

I have been smoking home-made pipes for over a year. Pipes made of *pàdauk* (Pterocarpus macrocarpus, Kurz), holly, and yew all give a satisfying smoke. I have recently tried Burma teak, which promises to be equally good.

Yours faithfully,<br>J. A. STEWART

*From Mr J. M. Symns*                               *3 September 1941*

Sir,

The other day in one of our local almshouses an old man assured me that he always smoked the sun-dried leaves of the chrysanthemum; I tried it, but found it rather over-scented. I have since found that mixed in equal proportions with tobacco it makes a good smoke and reduces one's tobacco bill by 50 per cent.

Yours faithfully,<br>J. M. SYMNS

*From Canon R. G. F. Wyatt*                               *3 September 1941*

Sir,

I wonder if Sir Stephen Tallents has tried a mixture of raspberry leaves with his tobacco. One can get them from the chemist at about 4d per oz., and I have used them in the proportion of one to two of tobacco. They are not bad. My gardener always has a supply of coltsfoot drying off, and mixed with equal quantities of tobacco it smells very good.

Yours faithfully,<br>R. G. F. WYATT

*From Miss Eleanor Adlard*           *3 September 1941*

Sir,

Why not grow our own tobacco on ground already proved suitable? For over 100 years tobacco growing was a flourishing industry in Gloucestershire in spite of fines and high taxes against the growers. Armed forces of the Crown destroyed no less than nine plantations of it near Bristol in 1692, the idea being to encourage the Virginian trade. A reversal of this policy now seems indicated.

Yours truly,
ELEANOR ADLARD

*From Mr G. A. Tomlin*           *5 September 1941*

Sir,

No correspondent has yet, so far as I can perceive, mentioned smoking for medicinal purposes, such as *Datura Stramonium* in asthma cigarettes. Coltsfoot (*Tussilago Farfara*), mentioned by a correspondent, forms the basis of a herbal smoking mixture. I have also seen lavender smoked in a hookah.

Your obedient servant,
G. A. TOMLIN

*From Mr A. G. Philipson*           *5 September 1941*

Sir,

Why not follow the example of Sherlock Holmes and save all the 'dottles' for future smoking?

Yours faithfully,
A. G. PHILIPSON

*From Mr R. E. D. Cunningham*           *6 September 1941*

Sir,

As good a substitute for tobacco as any of those yet suggested, and one which should easily be procurable by many of your correspondents, is the stuffing from an old hassock. Nice smokers will prefer it in a churchwarden's pipe, if the churchwarden has no objection.

Yours faithfully,
R. E. D. CUNNINGHAM

## A Meat-pie Story

[The Personal column had included a request for 1,000 kittens, a leading article dismissing the thought of using them for pies]

Sir,

As I read your delightful article on kittens I wondered whether you knew the subtle story of the twopenny hot meat-pie shop in Lambeth Road much patronized by people going home from work. The proprietor quarrelled with his assistant. A few evenings later this man walked into the shop when it was full of people and swung a dead cat on the counter, saying, 'That makes the dozen.' People looked at each other and began to melt away.

I also wonder whether you are familiar with the limerick which runs: –

> 'A Chicago meat-packer named Young,
> One day when his nerves were unstrung,
> Pushed his wife's Ma – unseen –
> In the chopping-machine –
> Then canned her and labelled her TONGUE.'

I am, &c.,
BEATRICE H. DERRY

# Per Ardua Ad Astra

———◆———

*From the Reverend John T. Watson*     *25 September 1941*

Sir,

For a number of weeks now I have tried, unsuccessfully, to discover the origin of the phrase 'Per ardua ad astra,' the motto of the Royal Air Force. I have gone so far as to ask many members of the R.A.F. themselves, but nobody seems to know. It occurs to me that many besides myself would like to know, for the motto is our daily inspiration, as it must be, too, of the R.A.F.

Yours faithfully,<br>
JOHN T. WATSON

*From Major-General Sir Frederick Sykes, MP*<br>
*27 September 1941*

[Unionist MP for Nottingham, Central]

Sir,

In answer to the Rev. John T. Watson's letter, in 1912, when I was raising and commanding the Royal Flying Corps (Military Wing), one of our difficulties was that the officers and men were all joining in different uniforms or in civilian clothes. I was convinced that for practical utility and *esprit de corps* a distinctive uniform was essential. The War Office accordingly approved the double-breasted khaki uniform and folding cap which will be well remembered by all who knew the Royal Flying Corps. Brigadier-General David Henderson, then Director of Military Training at the War Office, also agreed that a badge for pilots was desirable, and together we sketched upon a War Office blotting pad the 'Wings' which were afterwards sanctioned by the King.

I then asked my officers to put forward ideas for a motto, and 'Per ardua ad astra' was suggested to me by a young officer of the name of J. N. Fletcher, who had joined the Royal Flying Corps from the Royal Engineers. The motto had been suggested to him by another officer of the Royal Engineers, J. S. Yule, who is now a member of the Historical Section of the War Cabinet Secretariat. It seemed to me the best possible motto, and I referred it to the War Office, where I remember incidentally that one of the pundits, I think it was Harold Baker, then Finance Member, expressed the view that it was bad Latin. However, I pressed the point and the motto was accepted.

Early in 1918 an approved light-blue uniform was introduced, and the khaki double-breasted uniform discarded, as a compromise between the Army and Navy when the Royal Flying Corps and Royal Naval Air Service were amalgamated. The 'Wings' (with the letters R.A.F. replacing R.F.C. in the centre) and motto were retained.

I am, Sir, your obedient servant,

FREDERICK H. SYKES

. . Several correspondents have, in addition, written pointing out the similarity of 'Per ardua ad astra' to various Latin quotations, particularly Virgil's 'Sic itur ad astra' (Aeneid, ix, 641) and Seneca's 'Non est ad astra mollis a terra via' (*Hercules Furens*). Other writers draw attention to 'Ad astra per aspera' (the motto of the State of Kansas); 'Ad astra per ardua' (motto of the Drummonds of Midhope Co. Perth); and 'Per ardua ad alta' (motto of Birmingham University and of 'the old Galloway family of Achannay or Ahannay, now known as Hannay or Hanney').

*From Mr A. C. Rayner-Wood*      *29 September 1941*

Sir,

In your issue of September 25 the Rev. J. T. Watson asks for information as to the origin of the motto of the Royal Air Force.

The following facts, though slight, may be of interest. In the course of the last war — I do not remember the exact date — the late F. H. Rawlins, Lower Master of Eton, asked me to come to see him. I found him with various pieces of paper before him and he said, 'I have to choose a motto for the Air Force.' The result was what has become perhaps the most famous motto in the world. I remember that the final choice was between that and Virgil's 'Sic itur ad astra' and there were other suggestions which I have forgotten.

Your obedient servant,

A. C. RAYNER-WOOD

. . There seems to be evidence that the staffs of other schools were also consulted in this matter.

*From Mr J. R. Mulvany*      *30 September 1941*

Sir,

With reference to the correspondence in your columns, will you allow me to say that 'Per Ardua ad Astra' is the motto of the Mulvanys, an old Irish family, and my recollection is that my cousin, the late Sir Archibald Boyd-Carpenter, made some helpful suggestions to the authorities at the time of its adoption?

Yours faithfully,

J. R. MULVANY

## Flugzeugabwehrkanone

*From Dr Victor Grove*                    *20 September 1941*

Sir,

'Flak' is the abbreviation of the German word-monster *Flugzeugabwehrkanone*, which consists of five parts. *Flug* is our word flight or flying. *Zeug* is stuff, implement, craft, and thus the two words together mean aircraft or flying-machine. *Ab* is our preposition off, and *Wehr* defence, a body of armed men, which makes *Abwehr* mean warding off, fighting off. *Kanone*, of course, is our cannon or gun. No wonder even the Germans, who are somewhat fond of 'word sausages,' thought it advisable to reduce their word for an A.A. gun to the monosyllabic *flak*.

Another recently adopted German word, *Panzer* (pronounced puntser), is the medieval German word for a coat of mail and now signifies armour and armoured. Thus a German *Panzerkreuzer*, *e.g.*, is an armoured cruiser and a *Panzerauto* an armoured car.

Yours, &c.,

V. GROVE

## Teutonic Brevity

*From Mrs W. Murdoch*                    *23 September 1941*

Sir,

Last time I was in Bayreuth a friend had a slight accident to her car. The garage to which she took it for repair had painted across the front: Kraftfahrzeugreparaturwerkstatt. To-day's specimen of German (Flugzeugabwehrkanone) at least only takes one line of capitals in your columns. What about mine?

Yours faithfully,

DOROTHEA MURDOCH

# Wimpey Egg?

*From Bomber*                           *2 July 1941*

Sir,

I think your readers may wish to hear of a typical example of that well-known British sang-froid. A few nights ago, while one of our heavy bombers was over the Ruhr, being subjected to a heavy barrage of *flak* fire, the pigeon − which, as you know, is carried in case the crew find themselves in distress − laid an egg.

Business as usual!

Yours, etc.,

BOMBER

[The raid was on either Duisburg or Dusseldorf. Credit for the above letter shall go collectively to the squadron commanders − all of Wing Commander rank: 103 B. E. Lowe, 150 R. A. C. Carter, 214 unknown (Wellingtons, popularly 'Wimpeys'); 51 B. K. Burnett, 102 C. V. Howes (Whitleys); 83 H. V. Slatterly (Hampdens)]

# Man-power

*From Lieutenant-Colonel W. M. Campbell*     *1 February 1941*

Sir,

After 17 months of war the following appeared in your yesterday's (January 29) issue: − 'Second footman or second parlourmaid required at once; four in family, 13 servants, including four in pantry . . .'

Yours faithfully,

W. M. CAMPBELL

[The address was Warfield Hall, Bracknell, Berks]

# Military Genius

[*The Times* had printed the three lectures − The Art of Generalship − which General Sir Archibald Wavell had given at Trinity College, Cambridge, in 1939 on the Lees Knowles Foundation]

Sir,

As the author (in 1938) of the first full and consecutive account of Count Belisarius's campaigns published in English for more than a century, I am pleased to learn that Sir Archibald Wavell ranks him with Marlborough at the top of his list of good generals. Personally, I should have put Scipio Africanus in Marlborough's place, because he commanded less dependable troops with equal skill, fought under greater political disadvantages, and succeeded in consolidating his gains.

Scipio and Belisarius were set the same apparently impossible task (which General Wavell himself faced in 1940): that of defeating with inadequate forces a strong and well-posted enemy in North Africa. Belisarius's campaign, fought in A.D. 532, when he was in his early thirties, is however of more topical interest than Scipio's, because he operated from a distant base against an enemy who held Sicily as well as Africa and was extremely strong at sea, and because this enemy was German, and because later Belisarius had to free the Italians from their German masters, beginning with an invasion of Sicily.

Belisarius was unique among the generals of antiquity in his sensible and humane conduct of war. It was his rule never to terrorize a civil population, always to avoid pitched battles whenever the same advantages could be achieved by forced marches, by the cutting of enemy communications or by digging in, and never to force a defeated enemy to desperation. He was apparently of Slav blood (Beli-Tsar means 'White Prince') and had the Slav talent for what your former Military Correspondent, Captain Liddell Hart (by the way, the only modern biographer of Scipio), has named 'dynamic defence.' One sentence of Belisarius's speech made near Callinikon on the Euphrates on Easter Saturday, 531, in which he tried to restrain his pugnacious army from fighting an unnecessary battle, has often recurred to me during the past three years: 'Steady, soldiers! Providence may be counted upon to rescue men from unavoidable dangers, but not from ones that they bring upon themselves needlessly.' They threatened to mutiny, and he had to give way; he fought with inadequate forces and supplies, and took the only beating of his career.

Belisarius's declared preference for indirect means of victory is the more remarkable because it was apparently he who invented the prototype of the modern tank – the cataphract, or heavily armoured horse-archer, with whom in his classic defence of Rome he did such terrible execution against Wittich's corps of German lancers.

Yours, &c.,<br>
ROBERT GRAVES

*From Mr A. H. Burne*                                    *30 October 1942*

Sir,

I am glad to see that General Wavell does not place Julius Caesar high on his list of great generals. From a careful study of his *De Bello Gallico* it seems clear that the British leader Cassivellaunus (or Cassibelan) soundly defeated him. Unfortunately Cassivellaunus could neither read nor write, so Julius Caesar has had it all his own way with the historians — with the possible exception of Mommsen. Cassivellaunus was undoubtedly our first great national hero.

Yours faithfully,<br>
A. H. BURNE

## The Five-inch Bath

*From Mr William Keay*                                    *3 October 1942*

Sir,

I am reminded by your recent leading article on economy in the use of water that there are certain devices on the market for automatically regulating the quantity of hot water for a bath. The plimsoll-mark on the inside of the bath is a great test of character and the temptation to exceed the ration is great.

One such simple device, installed in a large Midland hospital some years ago, has proved successful in effecting appreciable economy in hot water. It consists of a small cylinder containing a float which turns off the supply when a predetermined quantity of hot water has been delivered. No more hot water is obtainable until the bath is emptied and the operation repeated.

Your obedient servant,<br>
WILLIAM KEAY

## Jet-propelled Aircraft

*From Mr M. J. B. Davy*                                    *14 January 1944*

[writing from the Science Museum, South Kensington]

134

Sir,

The successful development of a jet-propelled aircraft emphasizes how few are the really new ideas and how long it takes to realize some of the old ones.

Hero of Alexandria described about AD 50 a machine demonstrating the principle of propulsion by the reaction of jets (of steam) and the Abbé Miolan attempted in 1784 to apply it to the navigation of a hot-air balloon. The project was dismissed as having 'no aviating merit,' but this did not deter J. W. Butler and E. Edwards from patenting in 1867 (36 years before the Wright brothers flew) a design for an aeroplane which envisaged propulsion by the reaction of jets of compressed air or gas, or by 'the explosion of a mixture of inflammable gas or air' emitted through jets.

Your obedient servant,<br>M. J. B. DAVY

[When Adolf Galland tested the Messerschmitt 262 jet-fighter in 1943, it flew 'as though an angel's pushing.']


## An Old Soldier Remembered

*From Field Marshal Lord Wavell*                    *12 April 1944*

[writing from The Viceroy's House, New Delhi]

Sir,

In reading *The Times* of March 16 I saw an obituary notice of Mr Tom Byrne, VC. I do not know whether it would interest any of your readers to know that one of his last jobs in the Army was as groom to my father in Dublin about 1901–02.

I had just joined the Army then, and remember him well as a dignified old soldier with whom I had many talks in the stables at Dublin Castle. He liked especially to speak of Captain De Montmorency to whom he had been batman and to whom he was entirely devoted. I remember him showing me his Victoria Cross and telling me of his experience in the 21st Lancers' charge at Omdurman. He was typical of the best type of old soldier.

Yours truly,<br>WAVELL

[Captain De Montmorency also won the VC at Omdurman, where Byrne saved the life of a Lieutenant Molyneux. Shot in the right shoulder and wounded in the chest, Byrne nevertheless charged three Dervishes.

Winston Churchill described Byrne's act as the bravest he had ever seen performed]

## Store of Memories

*From Mr Michael Charlesworth*          *30 October 1981*

Sir,

The forthcoming demise of that famous Piccadilly store brings to mind an incident at New Delhi in the War.

Two new swans had arrived to grace one of the Viceregal ornamental ponds. Lord Wavell was asked to name them. Members of his personal staff stood silent as the well-stocked mind of the scholar-statesman was applied to the problem.

Which pair of names would be produced from classical history or legend or indeed from other men's flowers? The Viceroy broke the silence. 'Call them Swan and Edgar', he said.

Yours faithfully,

MICHAEL CHARLESWORTH

[*Other Men's Flowers*, Wavell's anthology of verse, appeared in 1944]

## President Roosevelt

*From Mr Charles J. Seymour*          *14 April 1945*

Sir,

Some Americans may be asking how the man in the street in this country feels about the death of Mr Roosevelt.

The old paper-seller who has a pitch near my home handed me my copy and pointed, mutely, to the headlines. We stood looking at one another for several moments and neither could speak. Then he said: 'The man next door heard it on the wireless, in the midnight news, and came and knocked me up. The missus and I were so upset that we couldn't sleep and were glad when it was time to get up.'

I think that describes, as well as they can be described, the feelings of most British people.

Yours truly,

CHARLES J. SEYMOUR

# Children from the Camps

*From Mr Alfred Edwards, MP*    *7 May 1945*

[Labour Member for Middlesbrough East]

Sir,

The most shocking discovery made after the liberation of the concentration camps is the large number of children found in these 'cities of sorrow.' These, mostly orphans of parents who died fighting Hitlerism, were regarded by the Nazis as hereditary unreliables and potential rebels.

The story of 're-education' in the Third Reich as practised in the *Erziehungslager* (educational camps for children) has yet to be written. If children after having passed through such a place still showed signs of moral or mental integrity, they were outlawed by being pronounced *wehrunwuerdig* (unworthy of serving in the army) and were assigned to penal battalions or thrown into concentration camps for the most trifling offences.

What is to be done with these children? The final answer to this question lies with the future administration of Germany. Allied Military Government cannot be more than a stop-gap. No doubt, here is a task for Unrra and for the Economic and Social Council, the enlargement of whose authority is understood to be among the British suggestions at San Francisco. Rehabilitation for the victims of Hitlerism is not a case for charity. These men, women, and children hold title to help as of right. That principle must be clearly established and observed; but some time must elapse before the necessary machinery can be set up.

In the meanwhile something must be done. I suggest the opening of a national fund for the purpose of removing a group of these children (for instance, the juvenile inmates of Buchenwald) to suitable surroundings to give them a new start in life. They may – for the beginning at least – be more a task for the doctor and psychologist than for the teacher. But the chances are that under normal conditions they will recover quickly and be fit to become the first unit to benefit from what we understand by education. If we succeed the victims of to-day will be the vanguard of the free world to-morrow and could play a proper part in the so much talked of – and so little thought out – re-education of the German people.

    I am, Sir, your obedient servant,
        ALFRED EDWARDS

# The Atomic Bomb

*From the Bishop of Chichester*          *14 August 1945*
  [the Rt. Rev. George Bell]

Sir,

At a pace almost breathless, and by a means without precedent, the war against Japan is being brought to an end. The very fact of cessation of hostilities will mean an immeasurable relief to millions of human beings. The achievement of victory over the first beginner and last survivor in a trinity of aggressors will be hailed with the deepest satisfaction, not only by the indomitable people of China but by all the United Nations, and those who value freedom and the reign of law.

But there must be many who feel that the manner of delivering the final blow casts a cloud on the victory. As Sir Henry Dale said in his important letter of August 8, science, 'an unwilling conscript,' has become the direct agent of indiscriminating devastation at long range. At the beginning of the European war no words were too bad for the bombardment of Warsaw and Rotterdam; and in its closing stages the use of the V-bombs was similarly censured. But the havoc then wrought by German forces cannot be compared with the ruin caused in Hiroshima and Nagasaki by the atomic bomb.

As the President of the Royal Society says, the moral factor cannot be ignored. The discovery of the enormous energy available in nuclear reactions is more revolutionary for good or ill than any other discovery of modern times. But that the motive impelling the discovery should have been destruction, that the scientists making the discovery should have been unwilling conscripts in the cause of death, and that the first use of the new power should be the indiscriminate obliteration of two vast towns, these surely are things which all who care for man's moral equipment are bound to condemn. In the allies' agreement signed on August 8, establishing the War Crimes Tribunal, 'war crimes' include 'wanton destruction of cities, towns, or villages, or devastation not justified by military necessity.' In the same document 'murder, extermination, enslavement, deportation, and other inhumane acts committed against any civilian population, before or during the war' are described as 'crimes against humanity.'

There are certain deeds which science should not do. There are certain actions for which scientists should not be made conscripts by any nation. And surely the extermination of any civilian population by any nation is one of these.

              Yours, &c.,

              GEORGE CICESTR

# The Election of 1710

[The General Election of July 1945 produced 174 fewer Conservative Members than that of 1935, and 227 additional Labour Members]

*From Lord Merriman*                    *14 August 1945*

Sir,

The following description of the general election of 1710 provides an interesting historical parallel: –

'Two hundred and seventy Members lost their seats. In the new Parliament the Whigs were not a third of the House of Commons. . . . Thus was ended . . ., as it now appeared, by the will of the electorate, the ever-famous administration of Marlborough and Godolphin, which for eight years had led the league of European nations to victory against the exorbitant power of France, which had made the British Island one United Kingdom, and had raised Great Britain from despondency and weakness to the summit of world affairs.'

The quotation is from *Marlborough, his Life and Times*, fourth volume, page 329, by Mr Winston Churchill.

Yours, &c.,

MERRIMAN

# Suits for King Zog

*From Major J. H. Churchyard*                *15 February 1946*

Sir,

In your issue of today (February 13) you report on page 4 the departure for Egypt of King Zog from this country, with the remark that 'the King had 30 suits specially made for him in England'.

How did he get his coupons?

I am, Sir, yours, etc.,

J. H. CHURCHYARD, Major (retd.)

[On 18 February Sir Stafford Cripps, President of the Board of Trade, informed the House of Commons that since 1 June 1941 King Zog of Albania had been in receipt of 242 clothing coupons, plus a special supplementary allowance of 100 in 1942, and an extra 80 on leaving for Egypt. Total 422. The coupons needed for 30 suits depended on whether King Zog wore a waistcoat; if he did, then 780 coupons was the number, if not 630.

Members then converted King Zog's Egyptian wardrobe into clothing coupons: one nightshirt 8, one pair of spats 3, etc. The matter was eventually cleared up by one of the King's aides; His Majesty had placed an order for suitings for himself and family to be sent to Egypt as export goods, these requiring no coupons]


## 'This Bastard Product'

*From Lord Winterton, MP*                    *5 April 1946*

[Conservative member for Horsham 1904–51]

Sir,

The Attorney-General is reported in your columns (and in *Hansard*) as having said on the third reading of the Trade Disputes Bill: –

> . . . this bastard product – I am using the language used in this House the other day by Lord Winterton because I felt I could not choose better language – this bastard product of narrow legalism . . .

I have never used any such inelegant language in the House at any time. When supporting a recent Bill to validate the election of three members of Parliament who had broken the electoral law I said: 'We are legitimatizing a piece of Parliamentary bastardy.' That was an actual statement of fact, and bears no sort of resemblance to the Attorney-General's use of an abusive phrase about an Act he dislikes.

I am, Sir, your obedient servant,

WINTERTON

[The Attorney-General was Sir Hartley Shawcross]


## Picasso

*From Mr Justice Asquith*                    *8 January 1946*

[later Lord of Appeal]

Sir,

Having read with interest a number of letters written by apologists of the Picasso and Matisse pictures at present on exhibition, I should, as a conscientious fumbler after aesthetic truth, much value a little first aid from their writers. The letters in question appear to an uninstructed intelligence to be based on a number of non-sequiturs – *e.g.*: –

(1) That because in the past certain works of art which were derided by contemporary critics have been acclaimed by posterity as masterpieces, therefore any work which incurs a sufficient amount of obloquy on its first appearance must be first class. This fallacy seems to involve at least two sub-fallacies: – (*a*) That later opinion is always sounder than earlier. Yet is not a decline in public taste a frequent phenomenon? Would anyone today back nineteenth-century taste in, say, architecture, against that of the eighteenth and seventeenth centuries? (*b*) That works condemned by contemporary opinion are generally or always approved later; whereas much (I should have thought most) of the works which are thought rubbish by contemporary critics continue to be thought rubbish by posterity, if indeed they are thought about at all. Bilge they were, and bilge they remain.

(2) Another non-sequitur seems to me to be involved in the assumption that because 'pretty-pretty' art is not beautiful, ugly-ugly art must necessarily be so. Rather than elaborate this, I would insist that what the common man finds even more difficult to understand is the claim that Picasso's latest phase is enormously 'modern' and portentously 'significant.' Making the questionable assumption that the 'modern' is better than the old, has Picasso done more than, in Johnson's phrase, to be 'dull in a new way'? Has he indeed done so much? Is his method so different from that of the 'abstract' painters of 20 or 30 years ago, who painted half a guitar with a tram ticket under the strings and a human ham in the offing, and commended the result to us as the last word in aesthetic power and profundity? As to the claim that these pictures are 'significant', of what are they significant? What truth, shattering or healing, is revealed, what inscrutable riddle or inenarrable mystery is resolved, by painting a woman with the eyes in the scalp, and one above the other, instead of side by side?

These are fair questions, and I would add another. Why are these pictures given the titles they bear? In railway dining-cars, in the old days, there was offered to the public, under the name of turbot, what has been described as 'a bone, an eye, and a piece of wet black mackintosh.' Something not materially distinguishable from this is offered to the public at the Victoria and Albert Museum, but is described as 'Woman in Armchair.' To me at least the nomenclature seems as arbitrary in the second case as in the first.

I am, Sir, yours, &c.,

CYRIL ASQUITH

# Out of Print

*From Mr Stanley C. Dunn*                    *21 May 1946*

Sir,

Shakespeare is out of print.

Yours truly,<br>
STANLEY C. DUNN

P.S. – The above was the information given me at the fourth well-known bookshop which I visited today in search of the works of William Shakespeare.

[That was the world in Surrey; in Fleet Street a correspondent was offered an alternative]

*From Mr Brian Edsall*                    *23 May 1946*

Sir,

'Shakespeare is out of print'; but the *Board of Trade Journal* is printed on one side of the paper only!

I have the honour to be, Sir, yours faithfully,

BRIAN EDSALL

# Russian Foreign Policy

[The Russians were unilaterally retaining troops in Persia (Iran). On 5 March 1946 Winston Churchill made his 'Iron Curtain' speech at Fulton, Missouri]

*From Lord Dunglass*                    *12 March 1946*

[Parliamentary Private Secretary to the Prime Minister (Neville Chamberlain) 1937–40; later, as Lord Home and then Sir Alec Douglas-Home, Foreign Secretary and Prime Minister; now Lord Home of the Hirsel]

Sir,

Recent manifestations of Russian foreign policy prompt me to recall the summer of 1939 and the failure of Mr Chamberlain's Government to secure an Anglo-Soviet alliance. Towards the end of protracted talks the price of co-operation was raised until it stood at a demand that Great Britain should assent to the forcible absorption of the three independent States of Latvia, Lithuania, and Estonia into the Soviet Union. Mr Chamberlain, although he realized to the full the strategic value of such a deal, felt bound to refuse it on those terms.

Apart from the price, another aspect of the negotiations

caused much concern. Whenever agreement seemed to be in sight the Soviet delegates found some excuse for delay or introduced some irrelevancy with an irritant value, and they carried this technique so far as to throw serious doubts on their sincerity of purpose. In the event, the Russian-German alliance and the smooth occupation of Poland by the Soviet armies proved that these moves must have been prepared while Anglo-Russian talks were proceeding.

During the war Mr Churchill and Mr Eden made many sacrifices in order to secure Russian co-operation, but no sooner had the common enemy been defeated than the treaties and agreements which they signed were broken in rapid succession. With the peace, Mr Bevin and his party came into office with the declared determination to work with Russia. They have found that the price of co-operation is still on the 1939 level — namely, the sacrifice of the sovereignty and political freedom of independent countries. The tactics, too, are unchanged.

Many people in Great Britain censured Mr Chamberlain and the Conservative Party, but it is to be hoped that they now have more understanding and will realize that co-operation and friendship with Russia do not depend upon the personality of the British Prime Minister or Foreign Secretary, or the nature of the party in office. Friendship can only grow from action based upon common moral and ethical principles, and so long as Communists direct Soviet foreign policy these are not there.

Yours sincerely,<br>DUNGLASS

## Under Tarpaulins

*From Miss E. Havinden*                    *14 November 1946*

Sir,

I wonder if I am the last person to be living under tarpaulins. This house was damaged by a bomb in July, 1944. The landlord says that the delay is due to the War Damage Commission at Cambridge. I dread having to catch the rain-water in basins for a third winter.

Yours faithfully,<br>E. HAVINDEN

# The Charge of the Light Brigade

*From Sir Lenthal Cheatle*                    *9 March 1946*

[a consultant surgeon]

Sir,

With your authoritative permission may I be allowed to place on record, before I die, a conversation that was indelibly fixed in my memory five decades ago? Dr Ligertwood was then in medical charge of the Chelsea Pensioners, and after taking me to see an old bed-ridden Balaclava hero who was in hospital after being 'knocked about by his wife' told me the following story. He was on the staff of Lord Raglan and saw the charge of the Light Brigade. He saw Lord Raglan write the despatch and Nolan deliver it. Lord Cardigan after reading spoke to Nolan, who waved his arm in the direction of the Russian lines. He then saw Nolan killed on his return ride, and was present when Lord Cardigan rode up to Lord Raglan after the charge and heard him say, 'Those fellows have been pulling me about.'

Dr Ligertwood then told me the despatch in question stated, 'The Light Brigade will advance,' saying nothing about a charge. When Lord Cardigan had read the despatch he said to Nolan, 'The Light Brigade will advance, but where to?' and Nolan, waving his arm towards the enemy said, 'Well, my Lord, if you don't know where the Russians are, they are over there.' Lord Cardigan may have been piqued by Nolan's behaviour, for they were on unfriendly terms. Dr Ligertwood told me finally it was afterwards learnt from the Russians that the officer on the chestnut horse had his steed to thank for his escape. That officer was Lord Cardigan.

I am, Sir, your obedient servant,

G. LENTHAL CHEATLE

[Sir Lenthal died in 1951 aged 85]


# W. C. Fields as Micawber

*From Mr James Agate*                    *28 December 1946*

[drama critic of *The Sunday Times* 1923–47; author of eight volumes of autobiography, *Ego*; to be remembered with Hazlitt, Lewes, Shaw, Walkley, Beerbohm and Tynan]

Sir,

Your obituarist says of W. C. Fields that he was 'an almost ideal Mr Micawber in the film of *David Copperfield*.' Sir, you

144

will permit me to say that he was not, and demonstrably not, and could not be. Consider Micawber's first appearance in the novel. ' "This," said the stranger, with a certain condescending roll in his voice, and a certain indescribable air of doing something genteel, which impressed me very much, "is Master Copperfield. I hope I see you well, sir?" ' There was nothing remotely genteel about Fields's Micawber, who in the film made his first appearance by a highly ungenteel fall through the roof of his own house.

Consider again. ' "Under the impression that your peregrinations in this metropolis have not as yet been extensive, and that you might have some difficulty in penetrating the arcana of the Modern Babylon in the direction of the City Road — in short, that you might lose yourself — I shall be happy to call this evening, and install you in the knowledge of the nearest way." ' Fields's Micawber would not have used the word 'peregrination,' or known the meaning of 'arcana.'

Mr Micawber's manners which 'peculiarly qualify him for the Banking business'? Not even Mrs Micawber at her most doting could have said that of Fields. Micawber is a gentleman who keeps his fallen day about him, and if he is not played like this he is not played at all. Fields was a glorious buffoon. But being possessed of no more gentility than a pork pie he could do no other with Micawber than turn him into an obese Ally Sloper, with very much the same nose and hat. And that, I submit, is not Dickens's character.

I am, Sir, your obedient servant,

JAMES AGATE

[In his youth a great juggler admired by Edward VII, Fields had three funerals — non-sectarian, Catholic and Spiritualist — the first organized by the ventriloquist Edgar Bergen]


# A Return to Learning

*From the Poet Laureate*                    *24 January 1948*

[John Masefield, OM]

Sir,
Some weeks ago you kindly printed a letter from me about some of the grievous afflictions hindering the revival of learning here. Since I wrote that letter I have read defences of those afflictions. Men who ought to know better have declared that

the nation wisely prefers other things to books and that much paper used for books is wasted on 'trash.' May I protest against these claims, now repeated and repeated?

There is no humanist in Europe who would not deny himself bread so that children might have instruction. The want of school books, of text books, of professional course books is cramping and crippling a generation of youth already shaken by years of horror and misrule.

As to the waste of paper on 'trash,' may I relate my own experience? I go much into book-shops: books are necessary in my profession: and though I can now seldom find the histories I need, I notice the high general level of the modern output, and the marked absence of light work. Paper can be wasted in other ways than in the publication of rubbish. I have in the past years received from one Government Department alone enough useless forms to make from 30 to 40 crown octavo pages. One postcard would have sufficed for the 12 months; yet these forms have reached me, as I do not doubt they have reached from five to ten millions of my fellow countrymen. A hundred and fifty million crown octavo pages have been flung thus, not into the dustbin, where they might be salved, but into that waste of time, life and hope now strangling every effort of man.

'People do not need books.' Even this infamy is circulated. Was there not a scoundrel in an infamous time who said 'The Republic does not need experiments'? Our young people cry aloud for books: the released generation calls for books: the suffering world asks for the glad abundance and free importation of books that we old ones remember from the happy past. Some tell us that there are no ships to bring paper. This is a strange cry, no ships, in a maritime land, when lands not maritime can find ships, almost every week, for the transport of illegal immigrants. It is not a lack of ships that brings this barrenness: it is a lack of will and a lack of light: and by such lacks a great land may be herded into a Dark Age in a very little time.

Yours sincerely,
JOHN MASEFIELD
(courtesy of The Society of Authors)


## The Oxford Gasworks

*From Dr Julian Huxley*                    *12 April 1949*

[Director-General of UNESCO 1946–48, Dr Huxley was knighted in 1958]

Sir,

Last week I revisited Oxford after a considerable period abroad. The first thing that struck me was its incomparable beauty. If Paris be the most beautiful large city in the world, Oxford shares with Venice the distinction of being, each in its own very different way, the world's most beautiful small city.

The second thing that struck me was the marring of that beauty by the gasworks. Instead of making the best of our treasure, we allow it to be defaced in a monstrous and quite unnecessary fashion. The third thing that struck me was the urgent need for planning in Oxford. New traffic routes are the most obvious need, but they must fit in to an overall plan, and one which takes account of the need for preserving and developing Oxford's beauty, and not only of economic considerations and so-called 'practical' matters (as if living and working in beautiful surroundings, and the pilgrimages of visitors from all over the world to Oxford's beauty, were not 'practical').

If the gasworks are allowed to remain, not only does the beauty of Oxford thereby continue to be diminished but there is no hope for an enlightened overall plan for Oxford. And without that the beauty of Oxford runs the risk of being progressively drowned in banality. If the Oxford gasworks are allowed to remain where they are it will be an index of our failure to conserve and develop our unique heritage through proper planning.

Yours, &c.,

JULIAN HUXLEY

# A Volga Boatman

*From Mr Laurence Viney*                    *1 April 1949*

Sir,

Coming to London in the train this morning, a man sitting next to me was reading the *Daily Worker* while all the time softly whistling the Eton Boating Song.

I am, Sir, your obedient servant,

LAURENCE VINEY

# An Actor's Entrance

*From Mr Raglan Hill*                    *25 May 1951*

Sir,

In the theatre, the habit of applauding the stage entrance of every well-known performer is one which, since the war, seems to have become more prevalent. Sensitive playgoers as well as the actors themselves are irritated by the outbursts which greet every star, because the dramatic effect of the entrance is ruined and the tension of the play slackened. Some people, it may be held, are unable to control their emotional reactions and must needs make a noise, but that this is not true was proved at the recent first nights, on consecutive evenings, at the St James's Theatre. On the first occasion, every set and each actor's entrance was greeted with applause. On the following night, *Antony and Cleopatra* was played without such interruptions and, in his curtain speech, Sir Laurence Olivier said: 'Thank you, above all, for your silence.' Cannot managers ask audiences to restrain their clapping until the end of each act for their own benefit and for that of the actors?

I am, Sir, your most obedient servant,

RAGLAN HILL

[The other play, which occasioned applause, was Shaw's *Caesar and Cleopatra*]

# 'Pocket-boroughs'

[The university franchise ended in 1950]

*From Sir Alan Herbert*                    *15 June 1951*

Sir,

Mr Attlee spoke, no doubt, in a heated moment; and I am sure that, after reflection, he would like to apologize for his description of the university constituencies as 'pocket-boroughs.' He is a member (and an Honorary Doctor) of Oxford University. In 1945 he publicly supported the candidature of Mr G. D. H. Cole (standing 'as a member of the Labour Party') for that 'pocket-borough'; and I should be surprised to hear that he did not use his vote. To acquire that vote he had to be of good behaviour for three years and pass an intelligence test, which is not required of the electors of Walthamstow (West).

I myself defeated an official Conservative in 1935 and an official Socialist (Mr Cole) in 1945; and I should be grateful if the Prime Minister would explain whose pocket I was in. Would he also comment on my sad suspicion that if Mr Cole had been elected the 'pocket-boroughs' would have been preserved? By the way, would not the description be more appropriate to members who are chosen and financed by wealthy trade unions, and bound, more or less, to do their will?

I am, Sir, your obedient servant,

A. P. HERBERT

## A Political Paradox

*From Mr J. M. A. Talbot*                    *1 November 1951*

Sir,

From the welter of facts and figures concerning the General Election, I am surprised that it has not emerged that, while the birthplace of the Co-operative movement, Rochdale, is now a Conservative seat, the birthplace of the Conservative party, Tamworth, is a Labour seat.

I remain, Sir, yours faithfully,

J. M. A. TALBOT

## Reading the Meters

*From Lord Braybrooke*                    *22 January 1952*

Sir,

A barber recently asked me why it could not be arranged for one and the same man to read both gas and electricity meters, seeing that both undertakings are nationalized. The more I think about it, the more am I convinced that there can be no real reason for two men to visit each house in question to read meters.

Yours, &c.,

BRAYBROOKE

# Tribute to a Queen

[King George VI had died on 6 February 1952]

*From Mr Isaac Foot*                    *19 February 1952*

   [father of famous sons]

Sir,

   In your issue of February 12 you refer to Mr Walter Elliot's felicitous quotation of 'a verse, penned by an American, of testimony to the Queen Mother's gallant bearing in the air raids.' Our knowledge of that verse we owe to you, Sir, as it was quoted in a letter to *The Times* on December 5, 1940. In 1943, at the request of the Minister of Information, I made a prolonged tour in the United States, and while speaking in New York I quoted the verse (which I had transcribed), and expressed the wish that I might meet the writer. My wish was gratified, and on July 22 at a public luncheon in Chicago I made a presentation to the author and thanked her for her tribute to our beloved Queen.

   I learned that the 'tribute' had been widely published in the United States and throughout Canada. The author was Mrs Mary Winter Adams, of 425, Sheridan Road, Lake Forest, Illinois. I had the honour of sending to the Queen a signed transcription of the poem. The correct version of the lines is as follows:

### TRIBUTE TO A QUEEN

London Bridge is falling down,
   My fair lady.

\*　　\*　　\*

Be it said to your renown,
That you wore your gayest gown,
Your bravest smile, and stayed in Town
When London Bridge was falling down,
   My fair lady.

      I am, Sir, your obedient servant,

ISAAC FOOT

151

[Her Majesty was once asked if her daughters would be evacuated to Canada. 'The children can't go without me. I can't leave the King, and of course the King won't go.']

## Buses in Convoy

*From Sir Pierson Dixon*                    *10 April 1952*

[Permanent Representative of the UK to the UN 1954–60]

Sir,

The late Mr Ernest Bevin was fond of telling the story of the impatient Londoner in the war who, after a long wait for a Number 11 bus, eventually boarded one of a string of three or four. In response to his grumbles the conductor replied: 'Well, Sir, we always travel in convoy and we haven't lost a bus yet.'

I am, Sir, your most obedient servant,

PIERSON DIXON

## Strikers' Votes

*From Mr Andrew Caird*                    *16 March 1953*

Sir,

The strike of Austin motor-car workers is kept alive by the daily votes by a show of hands. Men hesitate to vote against striking while their comrades can see how their hands indicate their decision. I had experience of this matter years ago. It was my duty to ask about a hundred printers in Manchester to work on Saturday to produce a special edition of a newspaper because a railway strike prevented copies coming from London. They asked for a meeting and a vote. It was taken by a show of hands. Two men voted to work; all the others voted to refuse. The two secretaries made new speeches and asked for a vote by secret ballot. Two men voted to refuse work; all the others voted to work. So the newspaper was produced without any bother.

Our rulers might consider whether it would be possible to enact that secret ballots should be the rule for trade unions. I believe it is the fear of criticism by their fellow workers which induces so many men to vote for strike or no work in the show of hands. Let them have the secret ballot as a right.

Yours faithfully,

ANDREW CAIRD

# U.S. Attitude to Britain

[Churchill and Eisenhower respectively occupied
10 Downing Street and the White House]

*From Mr Richard Goold-Adams*                    *9 April 1953*

Sir,

Like your other correspondents, I too have just been in the
United States. I was there for several weeks on a lecture tour
sponsored by the Foreign Office; I spent most of my time in the
western half of the country. I agree strongly that the curve of
Anglo-American friendship has reached an alarmingly low level
– a lower point, in fact, than is generally recognized here in
Britain. When doing my best to present our case on various
aspects of foreign and economic policy, I found myself
constantly thanked with real warmth for what I had said, by no
means necessarily because people agreed with my views but
because they were pleasantly surprised to find that I had such
vigorous ones. Much of the misunderstanding is certainly due to
sheer lack of knowledge about happenings and conditions in
Britain.

It would be wrong, however, to believe that this is the whole
cause. The American people are going through a period of
intense frustration. Having become the strongest Power in the
world, and having leapt into the active leadership of the free
community of nations within a decade, they are beginning to feel
their own muscles. It irks them very deeply, therefore, to feel
that they have always been made to dance to the Communist
tune, that the men in the Kremlin always seem to make the first
moves, to which the free world must then reply. They are
consequently searching, both consciously and, even more,
subconsciously, for a way out of this impasse.

As a result, two constant dangers exist: first, that America will
seek to act alone in an emergency – there have been examples
of this already; secondly, that it will place the main blame on its
biggest ally, Britain, if, as we seem to, we always try to put the
brake on its policy. Professor Brogan recently made the first
point admirably in writing of America's basic tendency no
longer being towards isolationism but to an 'illusion of
omnipotence.' The second point emphasizes the fact that
irritation with Britain has been endemic as a result of the
apparent insolubility of so many present international problems.
And if, as seemed likely until the present *volte-face* in Russian
policy, the new Administration were still to be confronted in a
few months time with most of the same difficulties as it is to-

day, the dashing of many high hopes now placed in it by the American public would risk putting Britain more than ever in the position of a scapegoat.

Perhaps we cannot do much about this except to take much more care than we do to explain the reasons for our point of view as fully as possible on all and every occasion. But we do fall into a trap which we could and should avoid. We are quite mistaken if we imagine, as many British people do, that this country stands on a special pedestal in America. President Eisenhower is trying to get the view generally accepted in Washington that Britain is America's 'most valuable ally.' The fact that he is doing so emphasizes the fact that it needs doing. If that is true in Washington, how infinitely greater is the need in the rest of the country. It is absolutely no use our blandly assuming either that all we do is immediately seen to be right and proper just because we do it; or that Americans necessarily understand and appreciate our motives; or that most of them think of us as special allies apart from the rest of Europe; or that the United States will ever consequently underwrite Britain and British policy just because we are us. Unless we learn to act on these truths I fear that the dangerous decline in Anglo-American friendship will continue. That in the long run spells disaster not only for us but for the whole free world.

I am, Sir, your obedient servant,
RICHARD GOOLD-ADAMS

# Preference for Green

*From Mr Ralph Wade*                    *18 March 1953*

Sir,
Some years ago in order to use up random lengths of rug wool I made a rug in small squares — reds, blues, greens, greys, &c. This rug was for four years in store, and on getting it out I find all the green squares are moth-eaten, but, with rare exceptions, all the other colours have been ignored.

Yours faithfully,
RALPH WADE

# A Building by St Paul's

*From Lord Esher*                                   *29 May 1953*

[President, The London Society]

Sir,

The comments in the Press have shown the strength of feeling which exists against the prevalent tendency to permit great blocks of offices in the heart of London to rise in ever increasing height and bulk. The size of the proposed new building hard by the east end of St Paul's had already increased our fears that worse is in store for us and that the City we love is about to be engulfed in a tidal-wave of brick and stone. If what we now hear is true, these fears have been alarmingly justified, and we shall be faced with a gigantic block of 14 storeys and of a height of no less than 170ft. in the very middle of the City barely 500 yards from the cathedral.

The London Society is second to none in wishing to see the devastated areas of the City rebuilt at the earliest possible date, but its members, and surely all true lovers of London, both here and throughout the world, will be shocked beyond measure if the rebuilding takes the form of a faint imitation of the skyline of New York when we already have our own incomparable skyline dominated by the dome of St Paul's Cathedral and Wren's exquisite spires.

Yours, &c.,

ESHER

# Sordid Reading Matter

*From Mr F. W. Saunders*                           *6 October 1954*

[Chairman, the Royal Merchant Navy School]

Sir,

The Board of Management of the Royal Merchant Navy School is appalled at the amount of crude and sordid printing matter easily procurable for a few pence from many bookstalls and shops, which coming into the hands of children cannot be other than extremely harmful, and contribute to the modern tendency of gangsterism and delinquency.

This is not only causing deep concern to this school but to headmasters generally, as well as to parents throughout the country. We feel that the time has come to put a stop to the publication of this dangerous literature with its attendant effects on the moral character of young persons.

I should, therefore, be glad to hear from any public body or persons who would like to be associated with us in initiating appropriate action to end further publication of this undesirable matter.

I am, Sir, your obedient servant,

F. W. SAUNDERS

[In 1947 Thornton Wilder addressed some American Rhodes scholars at Oxford. 'Yesterday I searched a station bookstall for a work by Miss Austen. I was offered some lewd literature.']

## Memorials in London

*From Mr John Parker, MP*                                    *9 July 1955*

[Labour Member for Dagenham]

Sir,

Just before the last Parliament rose authority was given by the House of Commons for the erection of a statue to commemorate Lloyd George. A decision as to where such a memorial should be sited was left over for discussion by a committee.

I would like to support the suggestion made by the then Prime Minister, Sir Winston Churchill, that it should be placed in the Palace of Westminster, preferably in the Members' lobby near the House of Commons.

It is high time that the number and siting of our memorials to those who have been prominent in public life should be reviewed. We have had three pantheons for our statesmen since just before Victoria's accession, the Palace of Westminster, Parliament Square, and Westminster Abbey. Two of our Prime Ministers (Palmerston and Peel) are commemorated by bust or statue in all three places; four (Canning, Russell, Disraeli, Gladstone) in two of them and three (Derby, Salisbury, and Asquith) in only one.

Of statesmen who were never Prime Minister only one (Joseph Chamberlain) is commemorated in two of these places. Others – all in the Palace of Westminster – include Earl Granville, Stafford Northcote, Vernon Harcourt, and – hidden round a corner – John Bright – and down a corridor Randolph Churchill and W. H. Smith.

Surely one national memorial should suffice however distinguished the Prime Minister? The list of lesser politicians is a curiously assorted one and cannot be reckoned as a considered judgment of posterity. Furthermore, there is no statue commemorating Rosebery, Balfour, Campbell Bannerman, Bonar Law, or any subsequent Prime Minister. One of the principal parties in the country, the Labour Party, has no statue in any of the pantheons.

I therefore suggest that any recommendations as to the siting of Lloyd George's statue should be accompanied by proposals for setting up machinery to review our political statuary. The following principles would, I feel sure, command wide support. First, there should be only one memorial in the three pantheons, however distinguished the statesman, and that the best work of art. Secondly, there should be no increase in the number of statues in Parliament Square, which would be spoilt if allowed to become overcrowded. Thirdly, lesser lights, no longer so highly valued as at their deaths, should be removed and memorials commissoned for those whom time has shown more worthy.

There should be no difficulty in finding a home for all 'displaced persons' in the towns they represented in Parliament or their birthplaces.

Yours sincerely,
JOHN PARKER

## The Nursery Years

*From Mr Charles Partridge*                    *4 January 1955*

Sir,

I should like to put on record that one of the greatest losses to English society since the Second World War is the ever-increasing disappearance of the nanny who used to reign supreme in the nurseries of our childhood.

Her code of manners and morals, of good and bad behaviour, of respect due or parents and visitors − many of these foundations of well-bred society are nearly gone. Also her traditions and folk-lore, and her knowledge of family history and genealogy, for often she came of villagers who in various capacities had for generations served 'the Quality' of her neighbourhood. The cult of the old-fashioned nanny occupies much space in the delightful novels of Mrs Angela Thirkell.

Visiting our friends' houses we realize this loss: we have to see and hear too much of their very young children. They used to be kept under 'Nanny's' control in the nursery, but nowadays they are generally with their parents, and are often a nuisance to everybody, even to people 'fond of children.' One result is that the parents are far less free than they used to be to pay visits and calls and to get away on holiday. Nowadays, too, the mothers, having to act as nanny, and often also as cook and house-parlourmaid, have no leisure for culture, and so families and homes that were formerly the best-cultured are losing more and more that high standard. The communistic 'wireless' is taking its place, and minds are being lowered to the same dull level.

Another result is that 'the Quality' that ought to breed larger families than 'the Quantity' is – 'prudently' – breeding, and will continue to breed, smaller. In short, the disappearance of 'Nanny' is affecting the social life of the nation adversely in several different ways. *Sic transit* . . .

I have the honour to be, Sir,<br>your obedient servant,<br>CHARLES PARTRIDGE

## Rule of the Road

*From Mr R. A. Palmer*                    *27 April 1955*

[writing from St Paul, Minnesota]

Sir,

My grandmother, Eliza Slocum (Slocomb in one Bible), was born at Westbury*, Somerset, England, on December 9, 1824. She often told me about the early years of her life in Somerset and about her school days. Among other things, she told me that all schoolchildren in England, at the time that she went to school, had to commit many things to memory. One of the selections she recited many times was this: –

> 'It is the rule of the land
> That when travellers meet,
> In highway or by-way,
> In alley or street,
> On foot or on horse-back
> By day or by night,
> Each favours the other
> And turns to the right!'

It is that last line that gets me and makes me wonder, and it is because of this that I thought you could enlighten me: Now, when driving an automobile, do you pass on the left (as I understand one does in England)? Has the rule been changed or is what the schoolchildren learnt all wrong in so far as passing on the right is concerned?

Respectfully yours,
R. A. PALMER

[*Presumably Westbury-sub-Mendip, 4 miles north-west of Wells]


*From Lieutenant-Colonel S. G. M. Lynch*          *2 May 1955*

Sir,

In Mr R. A. Palmer's letter I suggest a misquotation has been made in regard 'to the traveller on horseback.'

I have always understood that the mounted man kept to the left, in order that his right hand in which he carried his weapon, sword or lance, should be between him and the approaching stranger. The mounted man who was frequently armed with a lance or spear, which could not be sheathed, carried his weapon while mounted constantly in his right hand, and so kept to the left-hand side of the road when approaching an oncoming person.

When, with improving road conditions, horse-drawn coaches became more general on the roads, the coach drivers followed the custom of keeping to the left of the road. The dismounted man kept to the right of the footpath, in order to keep his sword arm free from the approaching stranger afoot. The origin of the right hand being the weapon hand dates back thousands of years, when it was thought that the heart was contained in the left chest, consequently requiring more protection. The left became the shield hand, the right hand being reserved for the lance or sword.

With the introduction of motor-cars, the driving seat was placed on the right hand or off side, as in the horse-drawn vehicles, which they have so unfortunately, in my opinion, displaced.

Yours faithfully,
S. G. M. LYNCH


## Pins in a Shirt

*From Mr C. Gower Robinson*          *27 April 1955*

Sir,

This morning I put on a new shirt. In addition to the normal complement of buttons it was held together by eight pins; all of

159

these were inserted from somewhere inside, so that it was impossible to find the heads; seven of them were inserted by a left-hander; three of them served no apparent purpose, as I was able to wear the shirt for some little time before they advertised their presence by sticking into me.

Yours, &c.,
C. GOWER ROBINSON


## What Mahler Ordered

*From Sir John Barbirolli*                    *29 November 1955*

Sir,

In his generous notice of the Hallé performance of Mahler's First Symphony which appeared in your issue of November 23 your Music Critic includes the following: 'and it was not really necessary for Sir John Barbirolli to ask his horn players to stand up, like jazz musicians, when playing the triumphant chorale at the end.'

Might I be allowed gently to point out to him that the standing up of the horn players for the triumphant final statement of the chorale at the end of the symphony, far from being an unwarranted act of vulgarity on my part, arose simply from what is by now, I hope, my well-known passion for precise detail, and fidelity to the composer's intentions. If your writer will kindly refer to a full score of the Mahler First, he will find quite elaborate instructions for the precise moment at which the horn players are to stand. My knowledge of German being, to say the least, rather sketchy, I took the precaution of asking an eminent Viennese colleague to translate the pertinent paragraph for me.

Yours, &c.,
JOHN BARBIROLLI

[Bar before cue 56: '*Alle hornisten stehen auf . . .*'

A supreme Mahler interpreter, Sir John was aged 54 when he first conducted a complete symphony by the composer]


## Landings in Egypt

[On 26 July 1956 President Gamal Nasser nationalized the Suez Canal. On 29 October Israel attacked Egypt; seven days later an Anglo-French force intervened.

160

Meanwhile on 4 November the Russians began to suppress an anti-Stalinist rising in Hungary]

*From Lady Violet Bonham Carter*                    *6 November 1956*

[daughter of H. H. Asquith; one of the most formidable public speakers of her time]

Sir,
I am one of millions who watching the martyrdom of Hungary and listening yesterday to the transmissions of her agonized appeals for help (immediately followed by the description of our 'successful bombing' of Egyptian 'targets') have felt a humiliation, shame, and anger which are beyond expression. At a moment when our moral authority and leadership are most direly needed to meet this brutal assault on freedom we find ourselves bereft of both by our own Government's action. For the first time in our history our country has been reduced to moral impotence.

We cannot order Soviet Russia to obey the edict of the United Nations which we ourselves have defied, nor to withdraw her tanks and guns from Hungary while we are bombing and invading Egypt. Today we are standing in the dock with Russia. Like us she claims to be conducting a 'police action.' We have coined a phrase which has already become part of the currency of aggression.

Never in my life-time has our name stood so low in the eyes of the world. Never have we stood so ingloriously alone. Our proud tradition has been tragically tarnished. We can restore it only by repudiating as a nation that which has been done in our name but without our consent – by changing our Government or its leadership.

Yours faithfully,
VIOLET BONHAM CARTER

[Philip Zeigler shows, in his *Mountbatten*, how the Chief of the Defence Staff and the Chiefs of Staff also had misgivings over the landings in Egypt.]


## Behaviour in the Commons


*From Miss G. Middleton*                    *4 November 1958*

Sir,
With millions of others I watched enthralled the opening of Parliament on television. In only one episode was I disappointed.

161

My grandmother once had the privilege of being present in person at the ceremony during the life of Queen Victoria. She often described this to me and I remember most vividly the story of the rising excitement when the Commons were summoned. According to my grandmother her Majesty said 'Summon my faithful Commons.' There is complete silence while the command is obeyed; then in the distance down the long corridor which separates the Chambers was heard a rumbling, a shouting and scurrying, a stamping and shuffling of feet as the faithful Commons rush to the Bar higgledy piggledy all fighting for a place to be near the throne, almost tearing off one another's coats and collars like, as my grandmother used to say with an indulgent smile, 'a lot of unruly school-boys.'

I waited breathless for this enthralling moment. What fun to see this wonderful football scrum in the midst of all the pomp and dignity. But nothing of the sort happened.

The commentator told us the ceremony had remained unchanged for 400 years. Have the Commons become better mannered, are they allotted places by ballot, or is all this something I have imagined?

Yours truly,
GERTRUDE MIDDLETON

## Children at the Opera

*From Mrs J. H. Sharp*          *18 November 1958*

Sir,

Some 35 years ago, when we were living in Naples, we often attended the San Carlo Opera. On these occasions several of the boxes were always occupied by large family parties, including the latest arrival in the charge of the *balin*, or wet nurse, in her picturesque costume, from whom he took nourishment in the course of the performance.

A friend of ours, an Oxford don, witnessing this intimate domestic scene, remarked: 'I wonder how that would go down at Covent Garden.' Incidentally my own son attended his first opera on his first birthday.

Yours, etc.,
ELSIE SHARP.

[One of Sir Thomas Beecham's fashionable audiences of the 30s (see *The Second Cuckoo*, p. 111) would doubtless have concluded that a bassoon was being patted]

162

Sir,

Your correspondent's charming account of 'Children at the Opera' causes me to recall a Sunday evening a couple of years ago at the Royal Festival Hall when my wife found herself (a) dressing her husband, (b) feeding our youngest son, and (c) taking her seat for the concert in time for the overture, all apparently simultaneously. His parents visited the boy between concerto and symphony, to find him peacefully asleep in the conductor's room amidst grease-paint and tights (Mr Dolin was in occupation during the week).

And at about the same time a distinguished cellist, giving a recital accompanied on the piano by his daughter, was compelled to alter the order of his programme so as to open with an unaccompanied Bach suite (with all repeats) to accommodate his grandson's feed-time.

Yours faithfully,
JOHN RUSSELL

*From Sir George Cuffe*                    *1 December 1958*

Sir,

I suggest that one point that your correspondence on 'Children at the Opera' has not touched on is how few 'Grand Operas' have both dramatic and musical distinction and could also be given a 'U' certificate. At the moment *Die Meistersinger* is the only one I can think of as really qualifying. Operas such as *La Tosca* or *Wozzeck* should clearly be banned for young people.

And there is another class of opera where the dramatic action is not objectionable but the music, to those that understand it, is 'Horrific': *Gotterdämmerung*, *Boris Godounov*.

Yours faithfully,
G. E. CUFFE

# Without Asking for More

*From Miss E. M. G. Swann*                    *18 March 1959*

Sir,

While travelling recently on the Southern Region of British Railways the passenger opposite me ordered tea from the dining-car attendant. It arrived on an immaculate tray but was quickly reduced to a dismal lake of milk and tea by the rock 'n' roll of the hurrying train.

When the tray was collected and paid for the lady remarked good-naturedly that she had been able to drink only one mouthful. This seemed to close the incident, but a quarter of an hour later the attendant appeared with a fresh tray and said the going was now smoother and 'you'll be able to enjoy it.'

This was courtesy with a heart-warming something more — and restored my faith in British Railways.

Yours faithfully,<br>E. M. G. SWANN

# Who's Who

*From Earl Russell and Lord Russell of Liverpool*
*28 February 1959*

Sir,

In order to discourage confusions which have been constantly occurring, we beg herewith to state that neither of us is the other.

Yours, &c.,<br>RUSSELL (Bertrand, Earl Russell).<br>RUSSELL OF LIVERPOOL (Lord Russell of Liverpool).

[As one was a philosopher and the other a lawyer, the confusion was perhaps natural]

# Almost Victorian

*From Mr C. E. Vines*　　　　　　　　　　*20 January 1959*

Sir,

In your Law Report, January 14, a Q.C. is reported to have said his client 'was a man of very high, almost of Victorian, principles.' What an admission. The assumption is that people of the highest principles to-day fall below the Victorian level. Is this true? I hope not.

Yours faithfully,<br>C. E. VINES

# Odd One Out

*From Mr T. C. Batty*                    *18 March 1959*

Sir,

Among the 'odd one out' type of questions which my son had to answer for a school entrance examination was: 'Which is the odd one out among cricket, football, billiards, and hockey?'

I said billiards because it is the only one played indoors. A colleague says football because it is the only one in which the ball is not struck by an implement. A neighbour says cricket because in all the other games the object is to put the ball into a net; and my son, with the confidence of nine summers, plumps for hockey 'because it is the only one that is a girl's game.' Could any of your readers put me out of my misery by stating what is the correct answer, and further enlighten me by explaining how questions of this sort prove anything, especially when the scholar has merely to underline the odd one out without given any reason?

Perhaps there is a remarkable subtlety behind it all. Is the question designed to test what a child of nine may or may not know about billiards – proficiency at which may still be regarded as the sign of a mis-spent youth?

Yours faithfully,

T. C. BATTY

*From Professor Hyman Levy*                    *20 March 1959*

[Professor of Mathematics Imperial College of Science and Technology, 1923–54]

Sir,

Mr T. C. Batty has put his finger on what has long been a matter of great amusement to me. Of the four – cricket, football, billiards, hockey – each is unique in a multitude of respects. For example, billiards is the only one in which the colour of the balls matters, the only one played with more than one ball at once, the only one played on a green cloth and not on a field, the only one whose name has more than eight letters in it. Hockey is the only one ending in a vowel. And so on with each of the others.

It seems to me that those who have been responsible for inventing this kind of brain teaser have been ignorant of the elementary philosophical fact that everything is at once unique and a member of a wider class. Mr Batty's son, in his school class, could be underlined as the only member who was Mr Batty's son. Similarly with every member of the class.

Yours faithfully,

HYMAN LEVY

Sir,

Quite clearly 'hockey' is the correct answer to Mr Batty's question. Every child should know that of the four games quoted hockey is the only example of one which, at present, no player is ever paid to play. The examiners are plainly anxious to discover how aware the child is of the problem of choosing a career.

Yours faithfully,
T. P. GODFREY-FAUSSETT

## 'Working Class'

*From Mr E. Marriott*                    *20 October 1959*

Sir,

The view has been expressed in your issue of to-day that one of the reasons by which the Labour Party lost the election is the extinction of the 'working class.'

On the contrary, 'working class' in its literal sense now includes practically everyone under 65. Socially we have become divided into only two classes – the 'striking class' and the larger 'non-striking class', a division made, curiously enough, by those who most loudly aspire to a classless society.

The strike is Labour's nuclear weapon, and one that is being more and more irresponsibly used. Trade unionists are forced into this warfare irrespective of their wish, with the alternative of persecution and unemployment. Meanwhile, the whole country suffers from the repercussions of local squabbles.

The Labour Party, rightly or wrongly, has come to be regarded by many as the striking class's chosen party, and this association has done them untold harm in the eyes of voters who settle their working grievances in more civilized ways.

Your obedient servant,
E. MARRIOTT

## South Africa

*From Mr Laurens van der Post*                    *11 April 1960*

[Knighted 1981]

Sir,

It is with much regret that I am compelled to ask you to dissociate me from the advertisement you published on behalf of

Christian Action on March 25, to which my attention has only just been drawn, and to which my name was added without my consent. I was not consulted and I have not given permission for my name to be used by Christian Action save for two specific ends: to raise money for the Treason Trial Fund and the subsequent Defence Aid Fund.

I, myself, have been an opponent of *apartheid* ever since it was adopted as policy by the Nationalist Government, and also opposed its forerunner, General Hertzog's policy of segregation. In fact, ever since I was a boy I have fought with every positive means at my disposal against colour prejudice and racial discrimination in Africa. But no matter how much I deplore the handling of this tragic situation by the Government of South Africa, no matter how fully I sympathize with the object of the advertised appeal, I cannot identify myself with its mood and wording of unqualified condemnation of 'the whites.'

To-day the situation in Africa in general, and South Africa in particular, is so grave that the need for the utmost precision in our thinking, feeling, and example is imperative. In my opinion in this country the lack of this precision is doing irreparable damage and adding to the confusion in the minds of my countrymen of all races. One example of it, as illustrated by the boycott, is the increasing inability in this country to distinguish between the Government of South Africa and its people. General Smuts, who was born a Boer as I was (unlike Dr Verwoerd, who is a Hollander and studied at a university in early Nazi Germany), once said to me: 'Outsiders will never understand South African politics unless they realize that they are essentially a battle between Afrikaner and Afrikaner over the role the British should play in our country.'

I would amend this to-day by saying that no one can understand our politics unless they realize that they are increasingly a struggle between white and white over the emancipation into full citizenship of our black countrymen.

As an example of the injury done by this lack of precision let me give you the reaction of a Boer on reading the Christian Action advertisement. He has been a gallant opponent of colour prejudice all his life and was involved in the first tragic riot near Vereeniging. 'Last week,' he writes, 'was a bitter week for us Afrikaners. There was not one of us, and very few among the Nationalists, who did not deplore such a tragic loss of life. But there is not one of us who was not shocked also by the denial in the outside world of our right to defend our lives against violence. Imagine, 150 police find 20,000 angry Africans advancing on them. They realize they are outnumbered by 130

167

to one. Only a few weeks before eight of their colleagues had been stoned to death by "unarmed" Africans. The police try to telephone for reinforcements and find the telephone wires cut. Not until three shots have been fired at them by the "unarmed" mob do they open fire. Had they allowed themselves to be overpowered they would have lost their lives. Even worse for the community that it was their duty to protect, their arms would have been snatched from them. I myself have no doubt that a massacre of the whites would have followed. What seems so strange is that, in the world, European blood in South Africa apparently is cheap, and African blood alone is sacred. Apparently Christian Action, judging by its advertisement in *The Times*, condones in the African the violence it deplores in the whites.'

May I myself make one personal appeal to the people of this country? Remember that under the South African system of voting it was possible for Dr Verwoerd's Government to have a majority in Parliament although it polled less votes than the Opposition. Be positively for the good rather than merely against the evil in South Africa, resisting violence without yourselves becoming violent in spirit. Finally, keep open the bridges, whatever they are, between yourselves and the creative forces struggling for expression in all races in my country. Like the Pharisee, it is never enough to pass by on the opposite side of the road.

Yours sincerely,<br>
LAURENS VAN DER POST

## 'Instant Beer'

[An American firm had produced a syrupy concentrate of about one-fourth the volume of beer, water and carbon dioxide removed]

*From Mr Peter Mathias*                 *8 January 1961*

[Fellow of Queens' College, Cambridge; now Professor of Economic History, University of Oxford]

Sir,

Finding historical precedent is a fascinating pursuit. The British Admiralty in the eighteenth century was much exercised to find a beer concentrate. Enough beer could not be stored, or kept good, in warships cruising on distant, often tropical stations. Hence it was a common practice to supply the men with diluted French brandy — a distasteful substitute, their Lordships considered, for a home-produced drink.

In 1774 the Commissioners of Victualling thought they had solved the problem with a beer concentrate, developed under their initiative. Captain Cook had reported enthusiastically on the trial kegs he had taken with him to the South Seas. Only after a general issue had been made to the Fleet in 1779 did the Commissioners acknowledge failure, admitting that 'the said essence . . . will not be accepted on board HM Ships but as a medicine.' Only from this point did the Navy turn to rum as a substitute — and to lime juice as a remedy for scurvy. Their beer concentrate was to have dealt with both problems.

Yours, etc.,

PETER MATHIAS

*From Mr C. L. Shaw*                    *13 January 1961*

Sir,

It is long since the Army, too, first showed an interest in 'instant beer'. In 1854 it carried out tests of its own on beer concentrate. The idea was no doubt to find out whether this could be shipped to the troops then at Varna and later sent to the Crimea. According to the *United Services Gazette* of April 1854, the process of reconstituting the beer from the concentrate was 'most simple and only required a certain quantity of hot water to produce a palatable drink.'

Ten Guards n.c.o.s were 'told off to try its effects' and to report after a week of being 'allowed to drink as much as they pleased but restricted from taking any other beer or spirits.' They duly reported that 'the porter is approved but the ale is not a favourite.' The findings seem to have been thought unenthusiastic, for nothing more was heard of the concentrate.

The project may also have been considered unnecessary. As supplies to the Army in the Crimea improved in 1855 regular consignments of bottled beer began to arrive from British breweries.

Yours faithfully,

C. L. SHAW

# The Purpose of a National Theatre

*From Mr Laurence Irving*                    *28 April 1961*

[designer; biographer and grandson of Sir Henry Irving]

Sir,

The establishment of a National Theatre, if it is at all desirable, calls for clear thinking, particularly by those upon whom the Government must rely for professional advice.

The theatre is the domain of the actor; all other artists are ancillary to his performance. Though at this time his authority and prerogative have been usurped by others, it must be the purpose of a National Theatre to restore to him a stage whereon he can maintain and demonstrate the highest standards of his art, assured of continuity of possession and freed from the speculative hazards of the so-called commercial theatre.

How can this be done? Let a noble theatre be built, with all its services under one roof, fitted for the production of plays on any scale and for the comfortable participation of the audience. Let a young actor-producer be appointed to direct it − one who will commit himself entirely to the living theatre. Let him enlist a company of similarly dedicated players − young enough to mature and to grow to full stature in the new dispensation. Let the salaries of these players be sufficiently generous for them to be able to ignore the distraction of films and television. Let the board of management give the director a mandate to re-create a style of acting and presentation capable of interpreting to perfection the whole range of drama from *Oedipus* to *The Caretaker*. Let it be made clear to him that for five or 10 years he must work to this end, disregarding favourable or adverse criticism and popular success or failure. Let no leading players be asked to give more than three performances of a major role in one week. Let all members of the National Theatre, artists and staff, be assured of pensions commensurate with their service.

Is all this the expression of Utopian folly? For certain the English theatre (including its critics) is in some disarray. Young players visiting European countries, which they have been led to believe are less enlightened than their own, return amazed by their glimpse of exemplary theatres in which all those who serve in them from director to call-boy strive only to aid and reinforce the actor in his task of creating illusion on the stage. Among these young people are many with high professional ideals who are resigning themselves to an acceptance of second-rate standards and to the surrender of their artistic integrity. Never was there so much promise in the English theatre; never was the outlook for theatrical artists so unpromising.

Sir Ralph Richardson wrote recently that a National Theatre is not comparable to a National Gallery in that the exhibits are alive and kicking. Yet it can be compared with a national or municipal orchestra. In both cases, under the hand of an ardent director an association of artists with individual skills can reach a measure of perfection interpreting classic and modern repertory conscious of their corporate being and assured continuity of purpose.

Those who disagree may well ask what I mean by style. Perhaps it is totality of presentation in a well-conducted, well-equipped and disciplined theatre. The Royal Shakespeare Theatre and the Old Vic have whetted our appetites for a National Theatre; neither, owing to its chartered obligations, can qualify as a substitute.

The experiment will be costly and, at first trial, may fail. So it is with rockets.

Yours, &c.,
LAURENCE IRVING

## Indexes

*From Mr Evelyn Waugh*                    *13 October 1961*

Sir,

You say in your leading article today, 'No one has ever suggested that novels should have indexes'.

I possess a translation of Tolstoy's *Resurrection*, published by Messrs Grosset and Dunlap of New York and 'illustrated from the photoplay produced by Inspiration Pictures Inc', which has a particularly felicitous index. The first entry is: 'Adultery, 13, 53, 68, 70'; the last is 'Why do people punish? 358'. Between them occurs such items as: Cannibalism, Dogs, Good breeding, Justification of one's position, Seduction, Smoking, Spies, and Vegetarianism.

I am, Sir, your obedient servant,
EVELYN WAUGH

## Forward from Jeeves

*From Mr Laurence Meynell*                    *20 April 1961*

Sir,

Most of us have become innured to the transatlantic 'mortician', but it was with some surprise (not unmingled with

171

admiration) that I saw two days ago over a Lóndon clothes-renovating shop the legend: –

EXPERT VALETICIAN

Yours, etc.,
LAURENCE MEYNELL

*From Mrs D. M. Kellett Carding*         *27 April 1961*

Sir,

My butcher's bill on Saturday morning bore the printed heading: –

MEAT TECHNOLOGIST

Yours, etc.,
JOAN KELLETT CARDING

## Menace to Clubs

*From Mr Nathaniel Gubbins*         *10 January 1962*

Sir,

As an old clubman (20 years a member of The Savage Club and more than 40 years a member of The Press Club) I was alarmed by your Correspondent's report (January 2) on the growing menace of women invading men's clubs, even to the point of becoming associate members.

We all know they are now allowed to enter club premises on special occasions such as cocktail parties, not because we want them but because men are inclined to show off in front of women and spend more money at the bar – the only institution that keeps most clubs solvent.

But those who contemplate making them members, associate or not, seem to have forgotten that most men join clubs to avoid women. After all, you can meet women anywhere without paying a subscription for the privilege.

Members regard their clubs as male sanctuaries, not because they hate women, but because women are never happy on mixed social occasions unless a man is dancing attendance on them. They are too tired to light their own cigarettes (if they have any), too weak to open doors, and too fragile to stand if there is a man to offer his chair or bar stool.

If women become members of our clubs shall we be expected to leap about like a jack-in-the-box, giving up our seats, opening doors, lighting cigarettes, and, yes, buying all the drinks, if only to stop them fumbling in their handbags?

If this happens most men will resign from their clubs and that will be the end of clubland.

Yours faithfully,
NATHANIEL GUBBINS

# Priorities at the Post Office

[Mr J. R. Bevins was postmaster-general]

*From Mrs Joan Ommanney*                    *15 January 1962*

Sir,

Mr Bevins says he has stopped all parcel post from and to London in order to make possible a clearance at the main sorting offices.

Would it not have been better if instead he had stopped the posting of all football pools and their attendant literature which would not in any way have affected the industrial life of the country?

Yours faithfully,
JOAN OMMANNEY

# Deliveries Banned

*From Mr S. P. Walker*                    *12 October 1963*

Sir,

It is sad to see that the law is stopping the delivery of newspapers by milk lorry in Cheriton Fitzpaine. When I lived in a remote part of Cornwall I could rely on getting cigarettes if the postman had any letters to deliver, and often lovely fresh mackerel came out of the back of the afternoon post van – as the shops only opened for one hour on Thursday afternoons *everyone* helped everyone else. The 'local' grocery, six miles away, called once a fortnight collecting and delivering orders, but if rung up early enough would bring out a few tins of paint or a Calor gas cylinder – and one would wait three months for the library van from 'town' to bring something unobtainable nearer.

What a pity such kindnesses should be 'agin' the law'.

S. P. WALKER

# Much Ado About Nothing

[Franco Zeffirelli's production of Shakespeare's play for the National Theatre — with Maggie Smith as Beatrice, Robert Stephens Benedick, Albert Finney Don Pedro, Ian McKellan Claudio, Derek Jacobi Don John and Frank Finlay Dogberry — had caused *The Times* drama critic to remark that 'one of the most Italianate figures is Dogberry — a wrong-headed reading if ever there was one']

*From Sir Laurence Olivier*                     *18 February 1965*

[Life peer 1970; Order of Merit 1981; Director of the National Theatre 1962–73]

Sir,

First of all, let me say, that the idea that the sound of the production should be Italianate, as well as the look, the feeling, and the atmosphere of it, was one that I most strongly encouraged and I promised the director that I would take full responsibility for it if it was brought into question.

What your critic has to say brings into the open a question which has been vexing me, and I am sure many of us in the theatre business, for some years. How should the peasant class speak in a Shakespeare play? What also vexes us is how these people should sound in English adaptations in foreign plays of all periods. These two questions are not unrelated, and I feel we can take them together to some extent.

We do not know, we cannot guess, how Shakespeare would like his plays to be interpreted in this day and age, any more than we know how Cervantes would like Sancho Panza to speak in an English version. We can only hazard that both would like the interpretation to be made so that the work can be appreciated by the greatest number of people, including intellects both high and low.

In general practice, and in the general way of vaguely localized Shakespearian presentation, our peasant can get away with regional, Mummerset, or a vaguely 'off' accent, or has done so up to now. Nobody has required Bottom the Weaver to have Athenian characteristics, and the Fourth Citizen in *Coriolanus* has not been reproached for coming straight from Salford, but I can't believe that Shakespeare intended an English atmosphere to pervade all his plays, much as I feel some people would wish it to be so.

There are times when his specified choice of place and character-naming brings this very much into question and invites

174

exploration and expedition into further fields. I think that most would agree that *Romeo and Juliet* invites an Italian atmosphere, *Macbeth* a Scottish one, and *Antony and Cleopatra* largely an Egyptian one. The porter in *Macbeth* has been presented with a native accent with impunity on countless occasions.

For some mysterious reason the Cockney accent is very seldom welcome in Shakespeare except in the Eastcheap scenes in the histories.

On the very 'First Night of Twelfth Night' (January 6, 1601, according to Leslie Hotson), the most daring jape lay in the fact that a distinguished member of the audience was a Duke Orsino, Italian Ambassador to the English Court, and popularly supposed to have a béguin for the Queen. Did the first actor playing Orsino speak with an Italian accent by any chance? I'm only asking.

Now every producer has the right to express a point of view on any play, in fact that is one of the main things required of him and if the point of view taken is one that requires strong local characteristics, then this promotes a problem that has yet to be solved somehow or other.

In his production of *Much Ado About Nothing*, Mr Zeffirelli has been inspired by the tradition created by the Teatro San Carlino in Naples. This tradition has ceased to exist in Naples for some years but still survives in Sicily. This influence, being applied to this production, must bring with it a strong atmosphere, redolence and impression of Sicilian character and characteristics in the behaviour of the people concerned, and consistency requires that it sounds as well as it seems.

What would the captious find preferable in these circumstances? Cockney? Mummerset? English regional? I think not.

Proper logic is not by any means always to be applied to the stage which owes far more to the instinctive, the intuitive, the inexpressible, even to clown's logic. (Grock's way of getting down from a high piano stool.)

True logic will dictate to us that if a play is translated into the English language it must therefore be translated into English custom and characteristic, but do we really believe it is more fulfilling to Shakespeare to have Don Pedro behave like a gentleman from the Marlborough Club, than to suggest the kind of blood and ésprit that made Shakespeare choose his name and station.

Is Dogberry worse and less real as a low down carabiniero or a Warwickshire buffoon? The question I say is a vexed one and

175

it cannot be answered by the bigoted or the severe logician. The answer can only lie in the mysterious impulse of stage logic.

Yours faithfully,

LAURENCE OLIVIER

[There is another answer — see Bernard Shaw's *Our Theatres in the Nineties*, vol. III, p. 325. 'Of all Sir Henry Irving's manifold treasons against Shakespeare, the most audacious was his virtually cutting Dogberry out of *Much Ado*.']

# Ad-lib

[Adlai Stevenson, probably the most civilized man to contest the US Presidency (he lost to Eisenhower in 1952 and 1956), had died in London on July 14, 1965]

*From Mr Cyril Clemens*                    *4 August 1965*

[Editor, *Mark Twain Journal*; writing from Missouri]

Sir,

Your readers may be interested in what the late Adlai E. Stevenson wrote me shortly before his sudden passing: —

'My grandfather who was Vice President of the United States from 1893 to 1897, and had the same name as myself, was often asked how his name was pronounced. Many called him "Ad-*lay*", and many "Ad-*lie*". He was a good friend of Mark Twain, and at a banquet Mark Twain said he had resolved once and for all the controversy about the pronunciation. Whereupon he recited the following, he had just composed on the back of a menu: —

> "Lexicographers roar
>     And philologists bray.
> And the best they can do
> Is to call him Ad-*lay*.
> But at Longshoremen's picnics
>     When accents are high.
> And fair Harvard's not present
>     They call him Ad-*lie*." '

CYRIL CLEMENS

# Travel by Rail

*From the Bishop of Llandaff*           *19 January 1966*

[the Rt Rev Glyn Simon]

Sir,

What can be done about British Railways? I had occasion to go to Paddington last Friday. The heating of the train on the way up was barely adequate; on the way down it hardly existed. The ticket-collector told us 'the boiler had gone', but that 'the engine would be changed at Swindon'.

Either it wasn't, or that boiler had 'gone' too, for the carriage was, if possible, colder from then on. This is the third long winter journey in two years on which I have had this experience.

Of course the train was late, in both directions, though less than the hour or more late that I experienced not so long ago on three journeys out of four. No one can now rely on the help of British Railways in keeping important engagements.

Of course, too, we came into a longish and unexplained stop, in the middle of a remote and snow-bound countryside. Cannot British Railways in some way broadcast information on such occasions? Or do they think, like the more old-fashioned doctors, that the less the sufferer knows the better?

Yours faithfully,

†GLYN LANDAV

*From Mr Timothy West*           *10 August 1978*

Sir,

I think I have good news for my fellow railway enthusiasts who feel that the nationalization of 1948 destroyed the peculiar individual flavour of the four main lines — the spirit of devolution is abroad.

I planned to make a journey this week from Taunton to Bournemouth — not far as the crow flies, but necessitating a change at Castle Cary and allowing nine minutes to get by foot from Dorchester West Station to Dorchester South.

No one at the Paddington enquiry office could tell me whether these two stations were sufficiently adjacent for me to achieve this, because Dorchester South is a Southern Region station, and so neither geographically nor spiritually within their province. Waterloo enquiries felt the same way about Dorchester West. I decided to risk it, and in the end the point proved academic.

The train from Castle Cary was late, and as the guard pointed out with some asperity, 'a Southern train won't wait for a connexion from a Western'.

In reply to my inquiry about a possible later train from Dorchester South to Bournemouth, he explained that as a Western guard he was not expected to carry a Southern timetable. He was very sorry. 'A few old Weymouth guards', he went on, 'still carry the times in their heads. But not me.'

The ticket collector at Bournemouth refused to believe I'd come from Taunton at all. I do see his point.

Yours faithfully,
TIMOTHY WEST

## Page or Pop?

*From Mr R. Hume-Rothery*                    *11 April 1967*

Sir,

I wonder if someone could explain why small boys can be dressed in the exact replica of an Army uniform as pages at a wedding, whereas an adolescent whose dress vaguely resembles that of one of the Services must be forever in fear of prosecution by the police should he appear in public dressed in such a way?

Yours faithfully,
R. HUME-ROTHERY

*From Captain S. A. J. Howieson*                    *13 April 1967*

Sir,

I can answer the question which Mr Hume-Rothery poses. Small boys who attend as pages at society weddings are never more than, at most, six or seven years old. They wear a replica of the uniform of the bridegroom's regiment – and they never use them again, and certainly not in public.

The youths who obtain service uniforms – some authentic and most of them not – parade them in the public street. There is a load of difference.

Yours faithfully,
S. A. J. HOWIESON

## Nottingham Forest 3 Chelsea 0

*From Lady Brunner*                    *26 September 1967*

Sir,

Yesterday afternoon, boarding the Clyde-Thames Express at Leicester, one had to struggle through corridors choked with a milling crowd of Chelsea Football Club supporters in the 13–16

178

age range, who had got on at Nottingham. Shouting and singing, they made a considerable hullabulloo.

While the train was still in the station there were sounds of intensified pandemonium and a crash of glass in the next coach, which contained the Buffet Car. The Chelsea supporters then tried to leave the train and surged onto the platform but were circumvented by two policemen. The situation seemed extremely confused but the supporters were got back on the train and the journey was continued. An elderly ticket collector reported that the Buffet Car had been wrecked, and that cans and bottles of drink had been looted. This was evident as the boys paraded up and down the corridors quaffing their ill-gotten gains.

The resulting inconvenience to passengers with the Buffet Car out of action for the rest of the journey, and the continuous shouting and pushing in the corridors can be imagined. But, worst of all, a tribe of young hooligans, some of them mere children, had got away with it. They sat where they liked, leaving trails of litter, and they never sat anywhere for longer than five minutes.

Arrived at St Pancras the police picked up one of them who was seen to have some sort of primitive weapon. The others surged off in various directions. For lack of evidence of identification nothing could be done. In the turmoil of the Buffet break-up the attendants had difficulty in identifying any particular culprits, set upon as they were by what they later described as 'young animals'. At St Pancras I went back to look at the Buffet out of curiosity and spoke to the attendants. One's feeling of sympathy for them standing there in an absolute shambles was very great.

If the refusal of British Rail to run special trains for football supporters because of the damage done results in them boarding, as these young people did, an important long distance train and smashing that up, then British Rail must think again.

Sitting in the train and afterwards, brooding over the whole nasty incident, it seemed both frightening and shaming. One felt shame that decent railway attendants should have been treated as they had been, that foreigners may have viewed the sorry exhibition. And it was frightening to realize that those boys in their formative years, with one exception, had been free to flout authority and to indulge in such behaviour. What sort of adults were responsible for them, what parents, what schoolteachers? What environment had produced them?

Yours faithfully,
ELIZABETH BRUNNER

[After the Second World War, sociologists attributed juvenile delinquency to the absence of fathers in the

Armed Forces, 1939–45. However, Lady Brunner's 13–16 year olds would appear to have been born 1951–54]

# A Silent Scene

*From Mr P. W. Rowley*                              *29 April 1968*

Sir,

A silent scene witnessed on a busy inner-London bus route.

A bus driven by a young white man with long hair.

A surly looking bleach-blonde white conductress.

At the bus-stop an old brown-skinned man wearing dark glasses and carrying a white stick.

The blonde conductress leaves her platform and gives her arm to the old man.

The bus remains stationary until he is seated.

He holds out his cupped hand with his fare.

He is ignored and all other fares except the old coloured man's are collected.

Silent notice and appreciation by other passengers.

Yours faithfully,

P. W. ROWLEY

# Footing the Wedding Bill

*From Mr Terence Allan*                    *31 March 1976*

Sir,

In the days when a girl didn't go out to work, and stayed at home until an acceptable suitor could be found, her marriage was a financial as well as a social achievement for her parents – and it was the measure of a father's relief that he stumped up for the wedding.

But nowadays, when equal pay and opportunity give a girl financial independence, and changing social patterns mean that parents have little or no influence on her choice of husband, it is surely something of an anachronism that the bride's parents should still foot the bill.

As the father of three daughters of marriageable age, I admit to bias – and I do not doubt that my counterpart, with sons, would defend the practice to the pop of the last champagne cork!

Yours faithfully,
TERENCE ALLAN

*From Mr Alastair Morrison*                    *3 April 1976*

Sir,

I am accustomed to looking at the bottom right-hand corner of your correspondence page for an insight into some of the most pressing problems of the world today. As the father of four daughters I am sure that Mr Allan's letter on the cost of paying for weddings falls into this category.

I believe that it is the practice in many countries for such costs to be shared between the two families. In default of this I can only look forward to the prospects of financial ruin, unless it is possible to arrange such expedients as enforced elopements or a multiple wedding.

There is much to be said for a system of bride price which seems to be a custom in societies with a more realistic view than ours.

Yours faithfully,
ALASTAIR C. MORRISON

Sir,

I am the father of three daughters who are not yet of marriageable age but have no prospect of being able to afford grey topper and champagne occasions when the time comes. Mr Allan could obtain some relief by insisting on a double wedding of any two from three. This would save the cost of one outing for his side of the family.

My solution is to provide a stout ladder suitable for elopement. At the moment the girls think I am joking – over the years they will become conditioned to the fact that I mean it!

Yours faithfully,<br>W. E. G. MANNING

*From Miss Caroline Allan*        *7 April 1976*

Sir,

My father, who put the cat among the pigeons with his letter about wedding expenses, is quite obviously in cahoots with Mr Morrison who suggests that brides might be sold.

So be it, but if I am to be auctioned, I make the following stipulations:

1. That the price I fetch should be paid to me personally – out of which a small proportion would be set aside for wedding expenses.
2. That the balance should be nonrefundable.
3. That under no circumstances should my father get a cut. 'Lot No 1 – Caroline Allan. . . .' May the bidding be brisk!

Yours faithfully,<br>CAROLINE ALLAN

*From Dr Peter J. Simons*        *9 April 1976*

Sir,

As it is now clear that Miss Caroline Allan is about to be sold by auction, may I inquire where and when this is to take place and whether there is a reserve price? Generally speaking of course, period pieces fetch better prices than those of rather more recent date though one hopes that this will not be the case with Miss Allan. But, most important of all, where can the article be viewed?

I am, Sir, yours speculatively,<br>PETER J. SIMONS

Sir,

Adverting to Miss Allan's letter, wherein she makes the stipulation that after deduction of wedding expenses from the auction price for herself as a bride, 'the balance should be non-refundable.'

I am reminded that the Supply of Goods (Implied Terms) Act 1973 states that goods must be substantially suitable for the purpose for which they are supplied.

May I suggest that Miss Allan or her estimable father arranges for a prospectus to be issued so that would-be bidders can make suitable assessment of the 'goods' offered. *Caveat emptor.*

Yours faithfully,

P. DONNELLY

Sir,

As an Inspector of Taxes I am taking a proper interest in the arrangements being made for Miss Allan's future. I am considering whether her case falls to be considered as a disposal of a chattel having a value in excess of £1000; in that event she will be subject to capital gains tax in her father's hands and the Inland Revenue will want to know her value on Budget Day 1965.

There is another possibility. It cannot be denied that value has been added to her in recent years and there may thus be a liability to VAT, at the luxury rate of 12½ per cent I should say.

If on the other hand Miss Allan were unchivalrously judged not to be a 'capital asset', the Inland Revenue would assess her father on any sums paid to him; they would fall to be treated as income or proceeds from a random or spare-time activity.

I hope that no one will suggest any sort of bartering arrangements. There is a precedent, it is true, but the Revenue would certainly regard such an expedient as tax evasion.

Yours truly,

STEPHEN HIGHLOCK

[Mr Terence Allan was contacted early in 1985 for further intelligence. His eldest daughter, Caroline, was married on August 21, 1982; his youngest, Elizabeth, would be the occasion of another bill in June 1985]

# The Dustman's Life

*From Mr J. S. Chaloner*                    *21 February 1969*

Sir,

Having been a dustman for just one day I would offer a small amount of authority to support the view that the Lambeth dispute and its probable extension are unnecessary.

On the occasion last year when I worked as a dustman I was a London Borough Councillor and reported to the refuse collection depot at 5.30 a.m. to find out, by personal experience, just what the job involved. Between starting time and finish at 3.30 in the afternoon, with the other three members of the crew, I emptied 800 dustbins, and saw the refuse disposed of to the wharf. As one of my other occupations I am a farmer, and therefore not unfamiliar with heavy manual work, out of doors and in all weathers. Sir, the work of a refuse collector is still one of the toughest, dirtiest, and most thankless tasks performed for the community, whatever the pay rate.

The public frequently complains of mess left behind by collectors. Little is heard of bins that are filled too full to carry, of lids left off bins so that rain-soaked contents make them too heavy for even strong men to lift, or of broken glass that falls out of the top of bins and can cut a man's neck. In this country, too, we still expect our dustmen to carry from back doors, basements, and driveways, in comparison with most other countries where householders are obliged to place their loaded bins ready at the kerbside.

Totting — the sorting out and reselling of rag, metal, cardboard and anything else found in refuse collection — is the only faintly intriguing thing that can maintain men's interest in what is otherwise a brutish and sad occupation. What is against householders', ratepayers' or the community's interest in this traditional practice? I fear it is only the tidy mind of local government officialdom that instinctively dislikes the irregular 'flea market' aspect of this operation within a civic function.

The fact is that totting is carried out under well-controlled conditions; the remuneration it provides is the subject of continuous statistics, and tax assessments. By forcing its cessation nobody's interests are better served. Continuing it means no more than acceptance of a human foible which is surely understandable to anyone who has ever contemplated doing the dustmen's job themselves.

Yours faithfully,

J. S. Chaloner

# Income Tax Delays

*From Mr Geoffrey de C. Parmiter*          *3 October 1969*

Sir,

For many years I have suffered, with such patience as I can muster, the bizarre methods by which the Inland Revenue conducts its business, but a recent letter from an inspector of taxes has finally brought me to such a state of exasperation that I feel impelled to write to you.

The present conduct of the income tax department of the Inland Revenue can very easily lead, in some cases, to a grave denial of justice, and in many others it must cause serious prejudice to a great many people. In an attempt to persuade you, Sir, to use your great influence to bring about some improvement in this deplorable state of affairs, I will tell you my story.

In September, 1964, my solicitor began correspondence with an inspector of taxes in Red Lion Street, W.C.1, concerning my liability, if any, to income tax on premiums taken on the leases of two flats. The matter was not a simple one, and the correspondence went on for some 12 months, when the inspector suddenly started to write to me instead of my solicitor. When I suggested that he continue to deal with my solicitor, he wrote on November 22, 1965, asking whether he had my permission to correspond direct with my solicitor!

On my assuring him that he had my permission, the correspondence with my solicitor was resumed and it continued until the middle of June, 1966, when the inspector, in a letter dated June 9, 1966, and beginning 'I regret the delay in replying to your letter of January 19', abruptly stated that he proposed to make an assessment, despite the fact that the discussion on my liability to tax was far from completed. An assessment was made, an appeal was lodged, and the correspondence between the inspector and my solicitor got under way again, but after a letter from my solicitor dated October 27, 1967, no more was heard from the inspector.

He began to show signs of life again nearly a year later when he wrote a letter on September 19, 1968, beginning 'I regret the long interval which has elapsed since you last wrote to me . . .' In this letter he conceded most of what my solicitor had been arguing since September, 1964. It had taken four years and much unnecessary expense to reach this point, and at long last the assessment was recognized as nothing more than a wildly inaccurate guess.

The correspondence has since continued on matters of detail, and the last letter from the inspector that I have seen was dated August 11, 1969, and began, as usual, 'The delay in dealing with your letter of June 23 is regretted.'

Thus, owing to the extraordinary delays of the Inland Revenue, my income tax liability for the year 1964–65 is still unsettled. This, however, is not the end of the story. I have five claims for repayment of income tax still outstanding. The claims were made on July 9, 1965, May 17, 1966, August 5, 1967, August 4, 1968, and June 16, 1969, and although the first of them was made over four years ago, no attempt has yet been made to deal with any of them.

The burden of writing so many letters regretting delay seems to have lain heavily upon the inspector of taxes, for he had, apparently, no time to send me the forms for my tax returns for the three years 1967–68, to 1969–70; at any rate, I did not receive them. However, as the result of a most uncharacteristic burst of energy, there was sent to me, on August 18, 1969, a bulky package containing all the forms for those three years.

I was on holiday at the time and I did not receive this package until I returned home; nevertheless, only a little over a week after I got back I received a letter from another inspector (this time, rather unexpectedly, in Salford) demanding that I send him the three returns 'as soon as possible'.

Following the dreary history of the past five years this letter was the last straw which has induced me to write to you. I have told the inspector that I will send him the returns at a time entirely convenient to myself. To hell with the inspector of taxes!

I am, Sir, your obedient servant,

GEOFFREY de C. PARMITER

[Elite tax inspectors are now being lured into the private sector where they may double their salaries. – *The Times*, February 5, 1985]

# Chinese Style

*From Mrs Evelyn Gibson*                    *4 February 1969*

Sir,

My favourite quotation from the New China News Agency has always been:

'The peasants are enthusiastically paying their taxes.'

Yours faithfully,

EVELYN GIBSON

# A Headmaster for Roedean

*From Miss Elizabeth Manners*                    *20 June 1970*

[Headmistress, Felixstowe College]

Sir,

Many women, especially those in my own profession, must have smiled somewhat wryly at Marc's cartoon (June 18) of the beauty queen whose ambition is to be the first headmistress of Eton. Far too many coeducational schools are actually schools run by men for boys with some girls attached, the Headship, Deputy Headship and most departmental Headships being filled by men.

When women protest about this highly undesirable state of affairs, they are always told that the reason why women are not appointed to these responsible positions is that they do not apply. Yet many of us know this to be untrue and could cite numerous instances of excellent women candidates who have been rejected time and again, simply because they were women. The vacant Headship of a coeducational school is nearly always advertised as 'Headmaster' and women teachers, however well qualified and experienced, know that it is a waste of time to apply, even when the wording (Head) indicates that their applications could, in theory, be considered.

Every reorganization plan brings in its wake more coeducational schools with fewer Headships available for women. It is therefore with considerable dismay that I note the appointment of a man to the Headship of one of the fast dwindling number of all-girls' schools, Roedean. Had there been no women applicants at all, I could have understood this, even though I should still have deplored it. Such an appointment with seven women on the short list is incomprehensible.

One wonders how many of Roedean's governors are men and by what hurtful reasoning they decided that a married man was preferable to an unmarried woman. The head of a school should not need to use the talents of his or her marriage partner in order to do the job. Many women in coeducational schools have suffered from the Headmaster's wife who has been, though totally unqualified, the unofficial Headmistress. It is a great pity if the same situation is now to be found in girls' schools.

A Wykhamist friend of mine hailed the Roedean appointment as a splendid idea. His look of stupefaction, almost of horror, when I asked him if he would then welcome a Headmistress, be she married or single, at Winchester, told its own story.

On the whole, women have sufficient sense of fitness not to

covet the Headships of boys' schools. It is a great pity that their male colleagues, not content with these schools and the coeducation schools, are now greedily grabbing the only Headships open to women, those of the girls' schools.

Yours faithfully,<br>ELIZABETH MANNERS

## The Causes of Industrial Unrest

*From Professor Elliott Jaques*          *1 September 1970*

[Head of School of Social Sciences, Brunel University]

Sir,

Through absence I have only today seen your leader of August 27 'Why are we all so bloody-minded?' You are right to display such intense concern. You are far too sanguine, however, in your conclusions. We are faced by an unremitting problem that will continue to mount in fury during the 1970s if not tackled at source.

The short answer to your question is that the power-bargaining procedures by which we determine payment depend upon bloody-mindedness and always have. It is a testimony to the good sense of the nation that, despite these back-handed procedures, things are no worse than they are.

You ask why the outbreak of trouble now? Because we are now completing the process of becoming a fully industrialized country in which nearly everyone must gain his livelihood by earning a wage or salary. But we have failed to accept that we have used no just or honourable principle in deciding what the differential pattern of those wages and salaries should be. We leave it to power.

During the 1960s it was noticeable that everyone had come to compare their pay levels with everyone else's – Civil Service, industrial workers, office staff, teachers, dustmen, managers, nurses, firemen. Everything was set fair for the present disturbances, but the productivity-bargaining incomes policy staved off the trouble for the past four years. But that policy, despite your praise in a leading article a year ago, far from ameliorating the situation, has proved an added disaster. It callously rewarded those who had restrictive practices to sell or who threatened to introduce restriction.

It was a disingenuous policy amounting to social dishonesty in its effect. Management, trade unions and government all played their part. It has left a national legacy of despair, suspicion and resentment. Now the only apparent way to get a real improvement in standard of living is to get an increase big enough to lap the rest of the field and hope that the advantage will not be overrun too quickly by inflation.

The question of how differential payment is decided inevitably becomes an explosive question in every industrialized society. Everyone wants to know the basis on which society is to distribute its rewards among them. The C.B.I. and management and the T.U.C. are frozen in their power stance and have proven incapable of recognizing the problem; and Mr Carr, any more than Mrs Castle, shows no sign of being aware of it.

Nothing short of the survival of our democratic way depends on our resolution of the need for a just answer to the question of differentials, in a form that is explicit, understandable, and implementable. How long before that lesson sinks in; and how much disruption are we to suffer meanwhile?

Yours faithfully,
ELLIOTT JAQUES

## Promenader

[Mr Edward Heath was Prime Minister in 1971]

*From Dr Malcolm Arnold*  *12 March 1971*

Sir,

As the Government proceeds with its plan to hive off the profitable parts in the public sector and sell them to private enterprise, when it comes to the turn of the BBC to be so used, may I put it on record that I have made first bid for the Henry Wood Promenade Concerts?

Yours faithfully,
MALCOLM ARNOLD

## The Brighton Belle

*From Mr T. L. J. Burfield*  *22 March 1971*

Sir,

The passing of the 'Brighton Belle' into history is indeed a sad event, not only to commuters, but to the many hundreds of thousands of people who travel between the South Coast and London. The 'Belle' seems to have become associated with the theatrical profession, but whilst many theatricals use this train so also do businessmen, residents and holidaymakers. To those who commute, the luxury of travelling by the 'Brighton Belle', either in the early evening, or late after theatres and dinners, has been appreciated by millions.

It may well be said that the train is not economic and British Rail cannot afford a replacement, but with the vast expenditure of British Rail, incurring quite frequently major losses, surely the 'Brighton Belle' should be retained or replaced by a new train which has character at perhaps even only a fraction of cost in relation to British Rail's overall expenditure.

If everything in this country is reduced to the lowest common denominator and we admit that nothing can be done that is not wholly economic, surely the outlook for Britain is a sad one. I would like pressure to be brought upon British Rail to reconsider their decision and retain the 'Belle' until a suitable alternative, other than a plebeian canteen — otherwise called a buffet car — can be provided as a replacement for our much-beloved 'Brighton Belle'.

Yours faithfully,
TREVOR L. J. BURFIELD

[When Lord Olivier made his maiden speech in the House of Lords (20 July 1971), part of his peroration ran: 'I believe in the Common Market, in the Concorde, in Foulness and the Brighton Belle.']


## Interrogation Methods Used on Detainees in Ulster

*From Dr Garret FitzGerald*                    *20 November 1971*

[Fine Gael Member of the Dáil Eireann for Dublin South East; Prime Minister of the Irish Republic June 1981– March 1982, and since December 1982]

Sir,

I write as a member of the Parliament of the Republic of Ireland utterly — and vocally — opposed to the IRA, North and South. I oppose them because I oppose intimidation, ill-treatment, brutality and murder, and because their actions have tragically, and I believe knowingly, deepened the divisions between the two communities in Northern Ireland.

I suspect that some at least of the strength of my reaction against them reflects the impact on my country of the British democratic and liberal tradition and of British ideas of justice. These ideas have taken deep root in Ireland, and it is by these standards that we judge each other in this country, and frequently find each other wanting. By these standards also we must judge others.

And by these standards the combination of the 'hood' treatment, electronic noise, up to 43 hours leaning against a wall by one's fingers tips with legs apart (just try it for 10 minutes), deprivation of food other than bread, and of sleep, during interrogation constitutes an offence against humanity and must be stigmatized as psychological torture. To say − as Compton incredibly does − that it is not brutality unless there is evidence that those concerned were indifferent to, or took pleasure in it, is to degrade language, as the treatment itself degraded those imposing it and those receiving it.

If any reader doubts this, let him exercise his imagination on the reactions of British opinion, the British Press, and British politicians if a *foreign* government were conclusively shown to have imposed such treatment on British citizens neither charged with nor convicted of an offence, some of whom were later released as innocent. Would we then see a jubilant, self-congratulatory chorus of politicians rejecting the word 'brutality', or would we see screaming headlines about brutality and torture, and demands for action in defence of the rights of British citizens?

The behaviour of some British politicians in relation to this matter in the past 24 hours has displayed some very unlikable characteristics. The senior minister who twice described as 'murderers' men who have not even been charged with an offence and some of whom have since been adjudged innocent and released by security forces themselves, for which he is responsible, showed a lamentable disregard for what we in Ireland have learnt to regard as British standards of justice.

And others who have complacently justified what even the Compton report describes as ill-treatment on the grounds that the end of securing information justifies these means, have put themselves in a moral position distressingly close to that of the Nazis − any difference being one of degree rather than of principle.

The terms in which the Compton report purported to evaluate the facts it had established through the admissions of the security forces themselves, and the reactions of many British public figures to it, will have done Britain immense damage in the eyes of her friends everywhere − one need not bother with the predictable reactions of her enemies. And, by adding strength to so much of the IRA propaganda about Britain, terrible damage has been done to the cause of peace in Ireland. This can yet be retrieved if a cry of anger is seen to erupt in Britain against all those who have betrayed Britain's traditional standards in the past 24 hours.

I write in sorrow, restraining anger.

Yours, &c.,
GARRET FITZGERALD

# A Union for Pupils

*From Mr A. S. Neill*                    *26 November 1971*

[founder of Summerhill School]

Sir,

For 50 years Summerhill has had self-government, living by majority rule. True it has limitations; I don't ask the children to decide whether Smith or Brown should teach maths; on the other hand if Brown is a bad teacher they won't go to his lessons and he has to leave. If this principle could be applied to state schools there would be lots of teachers on the dole.

The school meeting makes wise decisions about things like bedtimes, social behaviour, bathing – no pupil can bathe unless a life-saver is present. Naturally some rules are often broken, especially the bedtime ones, and at the moment we are having trouble with the non-smoking rule. Luckily drugs have not reached the school.

It is not easy to judge the results of self-government unless in a negative way. In 50 years no child has appeared at a juvenile court; I cannot think of any old pupil who would go to see a porn film or play. As far as I know only three ex-pupils have sought psychotherapy later . . . and in our time we have had more than our share of problem children.

We are as real a democracy as possible. I cannot invite a visitor because of the latest law made by children who have been a zoo to often 100 visitors a week for years . . . the law: no more visitors. And there is no leadership in our assemblies. I am glad to say that half my proposals are outvoted.

Granted that we are a small community of 64 children and 12 staff, and our self-government could not apply to a large day school, but a beginning could be made by abolishing the gulf between staff and pupils. I am sure that if a child in a large state school could address his headmaster as Charlie school discipline would benefit enormously. Children have the power of governing themselves but only in an atmosphere in which there

192

is no fear, no staff dignity, no childish rules about length of hair or colour of jacket.

Child freedom works and the late Sir Herbert Read wrote that Summerhill has proved it.

A. S. NEILL

## In Fortune Green

*From Miss Elizabeth Chillingworth*       *2 February 1972*

Sir,

> My heart leaps up for I have seen
> A sign saying 'Bangladesh cuisine'
> In Fortune Green.

Yours faithfully,<br>ELIZABETH CHILLINGWORTH

## Horror in Haberdashery

*From Mrs Richard Manley*       *21 February 1973*

Sir,

May I please protest about the constant process of Americanization?

On a recent visit to England I went to Marks and Spencer to buy some underwear. I fought my way to where, above the heads of the crowd, a banner proclaimed I should find pants, only to discover to my horror a counter full of trousers. Pants, I was informed, are known as 'briefs'.

What is it that makes perfectly respectable English institutions adopt these alien usages? I simply didn't dare go in search of vests or suspenders.

Yours faithfully,<br>JANE MANLEY

*From Mrs H. P. A. Kempthorne*       *24 February 1973*

Sir,

Re Mrs Richard Manley's alleged Americanization of underwear, is it not rather a case of *autre temps, autre moeurs*? She found that a chain store banner proclaiming pants led her to trousers and was told her need was briefs.

My grandmother wore drawers; my mother knickers (Directoire for winter and French for summer); at school I had bloomers (parking a catapult up one leg), later cami-knickers*

193

and now enjoy the exiguity of pants or briefs when I don't choose tights like my niece.

Upper-deck it was long-boned stays for my grandmother and a flexible foundation for my mother. Now I have a bra, plus a suspender belt when not wearing tights, and my niece opts for a body stocking.

Pants and briefs have become unisex terms so possibly Mrs Manley was shopping for a male relative and not herself, though in that case I am puzzled over her fear about suspenders — surely she is not using an Americanization for braces?

Incidentally my grandfather wore long drawers (colloquially long johns) in winter and short drawers in summer; my father pants (long) or trunks. My husband who has briefs recalls part of his kit when going as subaltern to Africa was a spine pad, but I don't suppose one could find that under any name at all in a chain store.

Yours faithfully,<br>BETTY KEMPTHORNE

[*Ladies who shop at Eulalie Soeurs in Bond Street may have observed the Countess of Sidcup (formerly Madeline Bassett) buying cami-knickers from which she heaves sighs at moments of emotional stress]


## Living in the Computer Age

*From Mr J. D. Pertwee*                    *21 August 1973*

Sir,

For many months I have been pestered with computerized letters from a firm of television maintenance service engineers, insisting quite wrongly that I owed them £2.74. I made unsuccessful efforts to get them off my back by appealing to the branch I used to deal with, to the head office in London, and their central accounts office but the letters, increasingly threatening in content, kept coming.

Finally I recalled some advice given in the correspondence columns of your Business News, and addressed my last missive in a foreign language (Swedish). The response was dramatic. Within seven days I had a letter of apology (in English) and an assurance that the necessary steps had been taken to see that I would be troubled no more.

I had prepared further letters in Swahili and Serbo-Croat, but one was apparently enough for the monster.

Yours faithfully,<br>JOHN D. PERTWEE

[Mr Pertwee's presumed ability to translate Swedish into Swahili must make him unique among English readers of *The Times*]

## Correct English

*From Mr J. R. Colville*                    *27 June 1973*

[Sir John Colville served successive prime ministers – Chamberlain, Churchill and Attlee – as assistant private secretary; later private Secretary to Princess Elizabeth; author of *Man of Valour*, a biography of Lord Gort]

Sir,

I hope you will lead a crusade, before it is too late, to stop what Professor Henry Higgins calls 'the cold blooded murder of the English tongue.'

It is not merely a question of pronunciation, which is to some extent regional and which changes with every generation, painful though it be to hear BBC speakers describe things as formīdable, compārable, lamēntable, or even, the other day, memōrable. Contrōversy and primārily are particularly vile. However, the Professor's and my main objection is to the mushroom growth of transatlantic grammatical errors and, in particular, to the misuse of transitive verbs.

It would be a pleasure to meet you and, no doubt, profitable to consult you on a number of matters. On the other hand to meet with you, or to consult with you, would be distasteful to us. The newspapers, including *The Times*, are increasingly guilty of these enormities, and on June 12 a formal motion in the House of Commons about Maplin descended to the depth of demanding that there should be a 'duty to consult *with* certain statutory bodies'.

Professor Higgins and I also deprecate the infiltration of German constructions into our language. This is doubtless due to too literal translation of German into English by the early inhabitants of Illinois. 'Hopefully it is going to be a fine day', translates back well into German; but it is lamentable English.

Amongst the other adverbial aberrations threatening us, the Professor and I, who were brought up to believe that short words of Anglo-Saxon origin are (except when obscene) preferable to long words of Latin origin, strongly object

195

to the substitution of 'presently' (which used to mean 'soon') for 'now'.

All this, Sir, is but the tip of a large German-American iceberg which, we fear, will presently become uncontrollable.

I am, Sir, your obedient servant,

J. R. COLVILLE

[On 4 January 1985, a *Times* leading article, dealing with Cabinet papers in 1954, could write: 'Churchill in 1954 was old and tired − but not beyond the prose memoranda of a cogency to put modern ministers to shame.']

## Craftsmen and Scholars

*From Mr Peter Watts*                    *12 December 1973*

Sir,

The scholar is not higher than the craftsman, he *is* a craftsman − *of words*. My father was a classical scholar and a life-long teacher of the classics who could never knock a nail into a piece of wood without damaging his thumb and the wood. For more than 30 years I have been a sculptor in wood and stone, and I could never construct the simplest Latin sentence without committing at least three major howlers. Yet both of us were sufficiently adroit in our own spheres to realize that our paths were exactly parallel, and that the semblance of perfection which he loved and pursued all his life was the same beacon as mine.

The greatest happiness that life can afford is to be found in the pursuit of these paths, and their number is almost without count but the goal is one. The chief aim of our educators should be to direct our young people into one path *or another* and not to insist on the priority of academic learning.

Yours faithfully,

PETER WATTS

## By Horse and Rail

*From Mr R. J. Ogle*                    *4 March 1975*

Sir,

There seems to be considerable public concern about the railways' attitude to carrying bicycles. Those of us to whom a horse is a preferred alternative to the motor car are in far worse case than the bicyclist. The railways will not carry horses by passenger train at any price, while hitching-posts in shopping precincts are few and far between.

Yours faithfully,<br>R. J. OGLE

[British Rail (Western Region) guarantee to carry Mr Ogle's horse if the beast occupies one seat and reads *The Times*]

## 'Dear Reverend'

*From the Reverend E. H. W. Crusha*                    *12 March 1976*

Sir,

May I enlist your support in restraining the use of 'Dear Reverend' and 'Dear Reverend So-and-so' in letters to clergymen? It appears to be increasing among people of standing and education who might be expected to be readers of *The Times*.

Yours faithfully,<br>EDWIN CRUSHA

*From Mr Arthur Bond*                    *16 March 1976*

Sir,

As a boy in a solicitor's office I was taught that a clergyman one knew and liked was addressed as 'Dear Vicar' or 'Dear Rector'. If one disliked him or did not know him well enough to form a view one said 'Reverend Sir' unless his help was needed, in which case one said 'Dear *and* Reverend Sir'. It seemed to work very well.

At home at the manse callers who asked 'Is the Reverend in?' were usually gentlemen who had already been to the Presbytery but decided that, on this one occasion, and strictly off the record, they would like a second opinion.

Yours faithfully,<br>ARTHUR BOND

*From Mr Peter du Sautoy*                    *16 March 1976*

[Chairman, Faber and Faber Ltd]

Sir,

I learnt from T. S. Eliot, the politest of men, that letters to clergymen one does not know personally should begin 'Reverend Sir'.

Yours faithfully,<br>PETER DU SAUTOY

*From The Reverend R. W. D. Dewing*     *18 March 1976*

Sir,

A certain firm which had my name on its mailing list as 'The Rev Dewing', sent me a 'personalized' circular letter which commenced 'Dear The Dewing' and continued in the same fashion: 'You see The Dewing . . .', and, 'The advantages to you The Dewing are . . .'

When I wrote and expressed my surprise and amusement at this strange form of address, I was told that the fault lay with the computer, which was unable to distinguish between clerical and other gentlemen. Programmed to omit initials, had I been entered on the mailing list as Mr R. W. D. Dewing, my letter would have commenced 'Dear Mr Dewing', but, concluding that Rev must be initials, it obeyed its instructions and produced 'The Dewing'.

> I remain, yours faithfully,
> R. W. D. DEWING

*From the Reverend F. P. Coleman*     *19 March 1976*

[Rector, St Andrew-by-the-Wardrobe, with St Ann]

Sir,

Reverence to whom reverence is due. The morning's post recently included a letter addressed to 'The Reverend St Andrew-by-the-Wardrobe'.

> Yours truly,
> F. P. COLEMAN

*From Mr Peter Faulks*     *20 March 1976*

Sir,

I remember being told by a clergyman that when in India a parishioner wrote to him as 'Reverend and Bombastic Sir.'

> Yours faithfully,
> PETER FAULKS

*From Canon Allan Shaw*     *23 March 1976*

Sir,

There are degrees of reverence. When I was a Dean and very reverend I once received a letter addressed to 'The Very Shaw'. I thought that took some beating.

However, it was bettered by the present Bishop of Lincoln. He once told me that he had received a letter directed to 'The Right Phipps'.

> Yours obediently,
> ALLAN SHAW

# 'Dear Rabbit'

*From Rabbi David J. Goldberg*                    *24 March 1976*

Sir,

While Christian clergymen ponder their correct form of address, they might also spare a thought for the difficulty experienced by their Jewish colleagues. On several occasions (and usually from the Inland Revenue) I have received letters which address me as 'Dear Rabbit'.

Yours sincerely,

DAVID J. GOLDBERG

# A Major Problem

*From Mr Adrian R. D. Norman*                    *25 March 1976*

Sir,

Your surprised and amused correspondent, the Revd R. W. D. Dewing, reminds us that though to err is human, to mess things up consistently requires a computer. On behalf of my colleagues and fellow acolytes at the shrines of the computer, may I beg his forgiveness for those sins of commission, our programmes, and invite through you, Sir, the help of your readers?

Those who have finished the crossword 20 minutes short of the terminus today might bend their minds to devising an algorithm for deducing accurately and infallibly the correct form of address from the name line of a properly addressed envelope containing up to 36 capital letters and punctuation marks. It may be that the problem is insoluble because, as with the crossword, logic alone cannot decide whether the clue conceals an anagram or a classical allusion. The computing profession will be greatly in the debt of the solver of this now classic problem and the usees (alias: victims of the computer's users) will have one less cause for complaint.

For those who take up the challenge, the test data base contains records with the following name line fields: Danie Van Der Merwe, The Master of Ballantrae, The Mistress of Girton, C. M. Gomez de Costa e Silva, Mrs Mark Phillips, Earl Mountbatten, Count Basie, Sir Archie McIan of that Ilk, Adm. Hon Sir R. A. R. Plunkett-E-E-Drax, J. Smith Esq, Sister Mary-Paul, A. d'Ungrois, the Revd Dewing.

Of course, any abbreviation needed to fit into 36 characters must be accepted. Confident of the continuing superiority of

199

that product of unskilled labour, the human mind, over its most marvellous artifact,

I remain, yours faithfully,

ADRIAN R. D. NORMAN

# Back Gradually to Reverends

*From His Honour Judge Irvine*        *25 March 1976*

Sir,

The clergy may have their tribulations in the modes of their computerized address, but the law is not without its trials in that respect. At least the Lord Bishop of Lincoln remained 'Right', but judging from the nature of the particular envelope's contents I fear as 'Honour Irvine' I may have changed my sex.

I have the honour to be, Sir,

your obedient servant,

J. E. M. IRVINE

*From the Bishop of Repton*        *26 March 1976*

Sir,

His Honour Judge Irvine is not alone in having his sex changed by letter. The Gas Board have just stopped addressing me as Archbishop and simply begin 'Dear Grace'.

I have the honour to be, Sir,

your obedient servant,

† WARREN REPTON

*From the Reverend D. F. C. Hawkins*        *27 March 1976*

Sir,

A young member of my congregation in Nigeria once addressed me in a letter as 'My dear interminable Canon'. I try to believe he intended it kindly.

Yours obediently,

D. F. C. HAWKINS

*From the Reverend S. H. Chase*

Sir,

Surely few can rival my claim to temporary reverend fame.

When serving in Holland in 1944, as Chaplain to the 7th Bn The Duke of Wellington's Regt, a parcel of games and other comforts arrived from a well-wisher at home.

The parcel was addressed to 'The Rev The Duke of Wellington', and without a moment's hesitation was handed to me.

Yours faithfully,
STEPHEN CHASE

*From Mr Christopher Child*                    *27 March 1976*

Sir,

It is not only the style of an opening address that can be reverent. As a young District Officer Cadet, I received an application for employment as a junior clerk in the District Office. After setting out his qualifications, the writer finished his letter by saying that 'nightly, I pray to the Almighty, to whom Your Worship closely resembles, that my application may be successful.'

I have the honour to be, Sir,
your obedient servant,
CHRISTOPHER CHILD

*From the Reverend Adrian Benjamin*              *29 March 1976*

Sir,

Further to the Revd R. W. D. Dewing's letter on his being persecuted by a computer, may I as a fellow clergyman suggest that this is by no means a lone martyrdom? Tired of replying to the National TV Licence Records Office's constant enquiries as to why we did not possess a TV Licence, with the statement that it was because we did not possess a TV, my wife and I gave way, bought one, and wrote and told them of our surrender. A month later there came yet another letter with the question reiterated.

I had snatched up my biro ready and angry to reply — when suddenly I noticed the address to which the letter had come. This time, All Saints' Vicarage having had a TV safely installed, the letter had come to 'The Present Occupier, All Saints' Church . . .'

Should I tell them that we have more interesting things to do there? That the Almighty manages without? Or simply give way and install one in the pulpit, so we can watch ours at home?

Yours faithfully,
ADRIAN V. BENJAMIN

Sir,

The clergy are not the only body of men to attract unorthodox forms of address. Since my appointment as a magistrate I have kept a list of what people have called me. Top of my chart, on one occasion only, is 'Your worshipful Holiness', a distinction to which I venture to believe comparatively few parsons can lay claim, 'Your Majesty' twice, and lastly 'Me old cock'.

Yours truly,
ST JOHN HARMSWORTH


## The Labour Succession

[On March 4, 1976, the Prime Minister, Mr Harold Wilson, announced his retirement as leader of the Labour Party.]

*From Mr John Thirkell*                    *20 March 1976*

Sir,

A Prime Minister should be an intellectual with common sense. This is a rare combination of qualities. James Callaghan has common sense but is short on intellect, Wedgwood Benn is an intellectual who lacks common sense.

This narrows the choice down to Healey, Roy Jenkins and Crosland, all of whom are approximately equal in brains and judgment. My own choice, on balance, would be Crosland, because he has the added quality of style.

Yours truly,
JOHN THIRKELL

[The succession went thus: Callaghan 1976–80, Foot 1980–83, Kinnock 1983– . Crosland had died in 1977.]


## Long Distance Walking

[The following received the supreme accolade of being discussed in a *Letter from America*]

*From Mr Mark Godding*                    *8 July 1977*

Sir,

Regarding the current enthusiasm for walking to extend one's life, may I point out that if one walked 10 miles a day, then having lived to the ripe old age of eighty, one would have walked for approximately nine years? It would also have cost a considerable amount in shoe leather. Is it worth it?

Yours faithfully,
MARK GODDING

['I put this letter,' said Alistair Cooke, 'in a file of human wisdom that contains such gems as Aristotle's "A play has a beginning, a middle and an end", Dr Johnson's "Much may be made of a Scotsman if he is caught young", Mark Twain's "The human being is the only animal that blushes, or needs to", and H. L. Mencken's definition of self-respect: "The secure feeling that no one, as yet, is suspicious".'

An appreciative Godding then wrote asking for Cooke's autograph, adding 'I am aged 15']

## Laughing Bishops

*From the Reverend Dr William Strawson*     *16 April 1977*

Sir,
Whenever newly consecrated bishops are photographed with the Archbishop the whole party appears to be convulsed with laughter. What is the joke? Is it an episcopal pun known only to our fathers in God? Or a demonstration of the church hilarious? Or do rochets tickle when first put on?

Yours faithfully,
WILLIAM STRAWSON

## Metternich's Journey

[A politician's downfall had been described as the most undignified since Metternich left Vienna in a laundry basket]

*From Dr C. A. Macartney, FBA*     *16 April 1977*

[sometime Fellow of All Souls College, Oxford]

Sir,
Your second leader of April 12. Metternich did not leave Vienna in a laundry basket. From his office in the Ballhausplatz he walked across on the morning of March 14 to the nearby palace of Count Ludwig Taaffe. Prince Karl Liechtenstein then provided him with a carriage, in which he was driven to the

203

Prince's castle of Feldsberg. The later journey to England (for which Baron Rothschild paid) was uncomfortable, but not humiliating. Metternich travelled by train, under a false passport.

> I have the honour to remain, etc,
> C. A. MACARTNEY

## Field Sports

[Prior to the 1983 General Election Mr Michael Foot pledged himself to abolish hunting. A group of Leicestershire miners disagreed; so, too, did . . .]

*From Lieutenant-Colonel Sir George Kennard, Bt.*

2 June 1983

Sir,
  To abolish Field Sports would cost several hundred jobs. To prohibit cheerful efforts to place hooks in fishes' mouths would cost several million votes. Is Mr Foot's dog too wet to chase a mouse?

> Tally Ho,
> G. KENNARD

## A Voice from the Past

[Mr Ronald Brittain, MBE, had died on January 9, 1981, aged 81]

*From Lieutenant-Colonel O. R. Nicholas*    16 January 1981

Sir,
  I would like to add a footnote to the obituary on RSM Brittain. I am not sure that his voice was the loudest in the British Army, but it was undoubtedly the most penetrating.
  He was, indeed, fair. When one officer cadet dropped his rifle on parade, a mortal military sin, several Warrant Officers and NCOs converged at the double upon the miscreant, brandishing note books in which to 'take his name'. They were obliged to slink away when the RSM, lowering his voice to a muted bawl, announced: 'Let him alone – he was trying'.
  He was a great gentleman, not only in size.

> I have the honour to be, Sir,
> your obedient servant,
> O. R. NICHOLAS

# On the Track of Hannibal

*From the Reverend D. L. Graham*       *27 August 1981*

Sir,

Two weeks ago, on August 8, your third leading article concerned itself with the crossing of the Alps in 218 BC by Hannibal and his army with its 37 elephants; this was occasioned by the photograph two days before on your back page of Mina, an elephant, waiting at Dover before crossing the Channel to make her own crossing of the Alps; after taking 33 hours to get through the pass known as the Col du Clapier, she and her entourage reached Sousa in Italy on Tuesday 11th.

'Proof for Hannibal' is the sub-title of the news paragraph (August 12), but does anyone require proof that Hannibal brought his elephants across the Alps? Has anyone doubted it since 218 BC? Yet we are told that Mina's reconnaissance journey is 'the culmination of eight years of research by two groups', and that 'a definitive expedition will be mounted next year with six mountainy elephants from Nepal'.

The historical questions about Hannibal's journey are: by what route did he go from the river Rhône to the Alps, and through which Alpine pass did he march. Sir Gavin de Beer in his book *Alps and Elephants*, published in 1955, though he had proved scientifically and irrefutably that Hannibal used the Col de la Traversette, and the French authorities thereupon called it the 'Route d'Hannibal'. Since 1955, however, opinion among historians has swung back to one of the Mont Cenis group of passes further north, which indeed Napoleon had thought the most likely. Mina's Col du Clapier is perhaps the most favoured of these.

If for Hannibalic reasons elephants are to be led across the Alps, then they might at least be the correct sort of elephant. Every schoolboy knows that African elephants (*Loxodonta africana*), the ones with the huge ears, are bigger than Indian elephants (*Elephas maximus*), but Greek and Roman writers all say the opposite. This is because the African elephant of antiquity was not our big-eared animal, the elephant of the African bush which may indeed never have been seen in the

Mediterranean area; the African war elephant of antiquity was a different animal, the forest elephant (*Loxodonta africana cyclotis*), a sub-species which derives its scientific name, *cyclotis*, from its comparatively small round ears and its name 'forest' from the fact that nowadays it is found chiefly in the forests of the River Congo.

In classical times these elephants were widespread over north Africa from Eritrea, through the Ethiopian mountains, across the Sahara and into the north African coastal regions and the Atlas mountains. The Ptolemies of Egypt got most, if not all, of their war elephants from Eritrea; the Carthaginians got theirs from the Atlas area and the lands along the north African coast. In 1947 it was estimated that there were about 100 of these animals still living in the mountains of Mauretania. A good stuffed specimen of *cyclotis* is in the Kensington Natural History Museum, but the Regent's Park Zoo has no specimen and, it seems, never has had. In 1970 the National Zoo in Washington DC had a specimen, a most attractive beast with its distinctively rounded ears. It was considerably hairier than either its larger Indian and much larger African cousins with whom it was housed. The African forest elephant seldom exceeds 7ft at the shoulder, the Indian elephant stands up to 10ft and more, while the African bush elephant, old Big Ears, grows up to 12ft and more, the huge specimen in the Smithsonian Institute in Washington measuring just under 14ft at the shoulder.

I am not sure that next year's expedition with the six Napalese elephants deserves to be called 'the Kon Tiki approach to an historical question'. I hope they and their human companions will enjoy their trip, but the contemporary question to put to them is: 'Is your journey really necessary?'

Yours faithfully,<br>
DOUGLAS GRAHAM

*From Mrs C. Z. Purcell*                    *4 September 1981*

Sir,

This summer's experiment of taking an elephant on Hannibal's supposed route across the Alps, discussed in your third leading article on August 8 and in the Reverend D. L. Graham's letter to you (August 27), is not the first recent one.

About twenty years ago a party of young graduates took an elephant for the same purpose via the Col du Clapier pass. One of them, John Hoyte, wrote a book about it, *Trunk Road for Hannibal*, published in 1960 by Geoffrey Bles Ltd.

Yours faithfully,<br>
C. Z. PURCELL

Sir,

Could I make a small negative contribution to the 'Hannibal-and-his-elephants' discussion (leading article, August 8)? It is, I suggest, interesting since it reflects on Sir Gavin de Beer's theories.

As your correspondent on Wednesday (August 27) wrote, Sir Gavin's first choice was the Col de la Traversette. But in his second book on the subject he added another possibility, the Col de Mary. I walked over this pass in the autumn of 1975 (with donkeys, not elephants) and became convinced that Sir Gavin had never done the same. If he had he would certainly have eliminated it, for it largely fails to comply with the rules for success as he himself describes them.

These, as all who have played the game will know, are to discover in the chosen pass a number of specific features which match Polybius's (and if possible Livy's) account of the crossing. Certainly there was a rock formation at the entrance to the Col de Mary where Hannibal could have rallied his advance-guard during the Second Battle of the Alps, but no place for him to assemble them beyond the summit and encourage them with an extensive view of the plain of Piedmont below, no rocks on the descent which would have needed splitting with fire and vinegar, and above all virtually none of last year's impacted snow, on which the Carthaginians and their baggage animals, falling through the new snow, could have lost their footing and slithered into gorges below.

On the climate of 217 BC Sir Gavin was original and persuasive, but in other ways I suggest unreliable.

Yours,

THOMAS HINDE

Sir,

In 1911 my late father, Professor of Military History at All Souls College, Oxford, published a detailed essay on his decision that Hannibal crossed the Alps over the Col du Clapier (*Hannibal's March*: Oxford, Clarendon Press). He came to that view after testing the many other possibilities put forward over the years and studying the accounts of Polybius and Livy on the sites.

All this was to the great advantage of his children, who spent happy school holidays in the French Alps, walking and climbing, unwittingly assimilating both history and geography at first hand.

Yours faithfully,

VICTORIA SPENSER WILKINSON

*From Mr W. F. Zeuner*                    *3 October 1981*

[Expedition Leader, Hannibal Expedition]

Sir,

Further to your article by Frances Gibb on our expedition (August 28) and your correspondents to *The Times* on September 4 and 5, I should like to supply you with further information to clarify the record.

Mr Thomas Hinde, whose most interesting book, *The Great Donkey Walk*, includes his crossing of the Alps with donkeys, mentions that Sir Gavin de Beer's first choice was Col de la Traversette. Of the two passes favoured by Sir Gavin I would agree with Mr Hinde that Col de Mary is most unlikely. There are other cols in the area, for example, Col de Malaure, which our expedition have investigated over the years and which fit with Polybius's description fairly well, but these have changed in many ways since Hannibal's time.

At least three, including la Traversette, have been considerably damaged by being blown up for political reasons on more than one occasion during the last 250 years. This makes a serious investigation of the Italian descent and also the views from the top rather difficult, particularly as part of the top has disappeared.

Our researches, started eight years ago, led to our taking an elephant across five passes last month: Col de Clapier, Col de Petit Mont Cenis, Col de Grand Mont Cenis, Col de Mont Genevre and the French side only of Col de la Traversette. We consider that one of these passes must have been used by Hannibal, but we have very large quantities of information on other sections of the route which influence which pass is possible as a crossing point. These have still to be analysed fully before we make our final decision as to which route Hannibal really took. The exercise this summer was mainly a feasibility study and to field test our radio-telemetry equipment.

Your second correspondent, of September 5, refers to John Hoyte's book, *Trunk Road for Hannibal*. We are well aware of this book, in which John Hoyte categorically states that he failed to cross Col de Clapier with an elephant and went over the Mont Cenis down to Italy to Suza, where he had an enormous party and was made most welcome. Nevertheless, stonemasons carved an elephant on the Italian side of Col de Clapier even though Hoyte's elephant never reached that point. It is therefore considerably to the credit of our team, despite previous attempts by others, that we did succeed in crossing Col de Clapier from the French side and down the Italian side in 9¾ hours, absolutely according to plan and without incident.

I hope this clarifies the facts that your correspondents queried.

Yours faithfully,

W. F. ZEUNER

## Greater Love

*From Mr Michael Mabbs*                    *11 December 1981*

Sir,

Page five today (December 10) said: 'That means that an estimated 330,000 women under the age of 50 are living with a man to whom they are not married.' Does he need any help?

Yours in awe,

MICHAEL MABBS

## End of the Line for a Tradition?

*From Mr W. S. Becket*                    *22 April 1982*

[Chairman, The Railway Performance Society]

Sir,

May I through your columns draw to the attention of your readers the impending end that is planned for a 120-year-old British institution?

Apart from a short period in 1917, at 10 o'clock on each weekday morning since June, 1862, the Flying Scotsman has pulled out of King's Cross for Scotland. It is not overstating matters to claim that this is one of the most hallowed of all remaining historical traditions in the field of British transport.

From next June it is proposed to run the 10.00 train from King's Cross to Aberdeen with the title The Aberdonian; the Flying Scotsman leaving at the historically obscure time of 10.35 and running to Edinburgh.

On the face of it, it may appear wholly logical to confer the name Aberdonian on an Aberdeen train. However the Flying Scotsman is, by tradition, a service that terminated in the granite city and is the train that has always left King's Cross at 10 o'clock. To run it at any other time is unthinkable − indeed a suitable analogy would be a proposal to rename Big Ben as the national time-centre.

We are by nature a conservative people. We have the good fortune to be steeped in the most colourful history imaginable.

The rescheduling of the Flying Scotsman is a subtle but significant erosion of our heritage.

The Flying Scotsman has always left King's Cross at 10.00. Let it be so for the future.

Yours faithfully,<br>W. S. BECKET

# Grace Kelly Legacy

*From the General Secretary of the Names Society*
*17 September 1982*

Sir,

The British people would seem to have paid their own warm tribute to the late Princess Grace of Monaco over the last 20 years or so in a way that may not be immediately obvious.

While she was still Grace Kelly she appeared as Tracy Samantha Lord in the film *High Society*, released in 1956. Until that film appeared Tracy was almost unknown as a first name in Britain, but it immediately began to be used in great numbers. Samantha was not such an immediate success, but it came into general use at the beginning of the 1960s and has also been intensively used since.

Meanwhile, Kelly appeared as a first name in 1958 and quickly multiplified. The latest available figures, based on first name usage by the Smiths in England and Wales, show that Kelly is currently the fourth most popular name for girls. Tracy and Samantha, though they have clearly passed their peak, are still in the top 30.

There have been such films as *Gone with the Wind* which have had a major influence on first name habits, and individuals such as Shirley Temple and Gary Cooper who have caused their own names to become highly fashionable. But Gracy Kelly's impact in her last film seems to have been truly remarkable.

Yours faithfully,<br>LESLIE DUNKLING

[Film buffs will recall that the musical *High Society* was the second movie version of Philip Barry's play *The Philadelphia Story*. The first boasted the incomparable Hepburn]

# Line of Potential

*From Dr P. B. C. Fenwick*               *27 October 1982*

[writing from The Maudsley Hospital]

Sir,

As a race we are very poor at making the best of our national
heritage. It is a puzzle to me why the 0 parallel of longitude
is not acknowledged in a way that would attract the tourists
from overseas. When travelling in Africa and passing the 0
parallel of latitude there are Equator hotels, there are
ceremonies which are carried out when crossing the equator
for the first time, but in England, although the 0 parallel
of longitude runs through Greenwich, it is almost impossible
to find it marked.

Why is there no Meridian Hotel, why no ceremony as one
passes from East to West? None of the roads have meridian
bumps in them. Would it not be possible for the local councils
throughout the country to set up large notices marking the
position of the meridian in order to further the tourist trade?

Yours faithfully,

P. B. C. FENWICK

*From Mr R. A. Copeland*               *29 October 1982*

Sir,

Parallels of longitude (Dr Fenwick, October 27)? Are there
people at the Maudsley who believe the Earth is cylindrical?

Surely the idea of a hospital where the psychiatrists have such
strange ideas would make a much better tourist attraction than
a mere bump in the road at Greenwich.

Yours faithfully,

R. A. COPELAND

*From Mr E. J. Wingfield*               *30 October 1982*

Sir,

Zero latitude is fixed by the angle of the earth's axis to the
plane of its orbit. This is one of those brute facts which man can
only respectfully observe, not alter. Longitude, by contrast, is
arbitrarily fixed by man for his own convenience.

Great Britain's former maritime pre-eminence procured
international acceptance of the line joining the poles through the
Royal Observatory at Greenwich as zero longitude for
navigational purposes, but the French, in particular (isn't

211

chauvinism named after a Frenchman?) for road maps of their own country, prefer the line through Paris.

Yours, etc,

E. J. WINGFIELD

*From Mr A. H. Piggott*                               *1 November 1982*

Sir,

Referring to the letter in today's *Times* from Dr P. B. C. Fenwick: if Dr Fenwick could visit our beautiful town of Louth in Lincolnshire and walk along Eastgate, he would see the Meridian Café.

On the wall of this building there is a plaque marking the position of the 0 line of longitude and a metal strip has been placed in the pavement.

In my walks on most days I pass from the eastern to the western hemisphere and back again.

Yours faithfully,

A. H. PIGGOTT

*From Dr E. H. Kronheimer*                          *1 November 1982*

[Department of Mathematics, Birkbeck College]

Sir,

No doubt one reason why the zero of latitude is held in greater awe than the zero of longitude is that, whereas the placing of the equator may be ascribed to God, the decision to run the international prime meridian through Greenwich, Waltham Forest and East Grinstead was taken, in 1884, by a committee.

Yours faithfully,

ERWIN KRONHEIMER

*From Mr J. P. W. Roper*                             *4 November 1982*

Sir,

Perhaps the Greenwich Meridian is not celebrated because of the precedents: first Peacehaven, an unlovely ribbon development of the early twenties on the cliffs a few miles east of Brighton, where the meridian crosses the South Coast. The name was chosen by national competition and the second part at least was never appropriate. A monument was erected at the cliff edge, some 200 feet above the sea, and by the early forties erosion had already reached the enclosure and the southern post stood suspended where the cliff had been.

Indignant residents may tell us what has since become of the monument itself.

212

Finally, the Royal Observatory has itself removed from Greenwich to Herstmonceux, a minute or two off the line.

Yours faithfully,

J. P. W. ROPER

*From Mr John Gates*                                    *4 November 1982*

Sir,

What difficulties latitude and longitude present to some of your readers! Just when we had got the lines of longitude sorted out and meeting at the poles, Mr Wingfield's letter confuses the equator with the ecliptic.

Zero latitude, i.e. the equator, is the line equidistant from the poles, and has nothing to do with the earth's orbit. It is fixed only by the direction of the earth's daily revolution in relation to the surface of the earth.

Yours faithfully,

JOHN GATES

*From Mr Paul Moxey*                                    *5 November 1982*

Sir,

Dr Fenwick is right about the relative obscurity of the Greenwich meridian, though it does have one bizarre monument. Here in Epping Forest, on the summit of Pole Hill, there is an impressive granite obelisk erected by the Astronomer Royal in 1824 to mark the line due north from Greenwich. Unfortunately, an international agreement of 1884 adopted a new position for the meridian, which now passes 19 feet to the east of the pillar.

However, potential viewers of this misplaced curiosity should be warned that the once impressive view southwards across the Thames is now hidden by a dense growth of hawthorn and oak.

Yours faithfully,

PAUL A. MOXEY

*From Mr Bernard Kaukas*                                    *6 November 1982*

[British Railways Board]

Sir,

The suggestion that those imaginary lines delineating interesting angular distances on the earth's surface should be visibly marked for the benefit of casual passers-by can present minor problems.

For the diversion of discerning summer travellers, Bengt Furustam, the Chief Engineer of the Swedish State Railways, has caused a line of white stones to be laid on either side of the track just north of Murjek to indicate that parallel of latitude bounding the region of the earth surrounding the north terrestrial pole — otherwise known as the Arctic Circle.

The only trouble is, he tells me, that whenever his engineers carry out normal maintenance in the area the stones are moved, and he can never be sure they are replaced on the right line. So it wavers somewhat, rather like a movable feast.

The line reverts, of course, to its normal invisibility in winter.

Yours sincerely,

BERNARD KAUKAS

*From Mr T. Limna*                    *9 November 1982*

[Chief Executive, Lee Valley Regional Park Authority]

Sir,

Dr P. B. C. Fenwick should pay a visit to the Lee Valley Regional Park where he would see the '0' line of longitude marked for over half a mile.

The regional park follows the route of the Lee Valley from London's East End to Ware in Hertfordshire. Just north of the town of Waltham Abbey there is a most delightful country park of some 70 acres of woodland and water meadows containing several thousand young trees of more than fifty varieties. Visitors can enjoy a walk part of which is on the line of the Greenwich meridian, marked at each end of its length with a 4-ton stone from Rennie's London Bridge.

It is a very popular feature with visiting school parties who can be seen regularly lined up on the path with one foot in the east and one foot in the west showing that east and west do meet!

Yours faithfully,

T. LIMNA

# Literary Lapses

*From Mr Julian Gloag*                    *2 November 1982*

Sir,

Your literary editor, in his recent animadversions on the Booker Prize, rightly pointed out that what is celebrated today is all too likely to be forgotten tomorrow. What then remains? I am, Sir, in a position to tell you.

Yesterday I took my children to Madame Tussaud's, where English Literature is represented by just seven figures, three of them members of the same family – the Brontë sisters. The others are Shakespeare, Dickens, Sir Walter Scott and, proving indeed how ludicrously misleading all these twentieth-century prizes are, Barbara Cartland.

Yours truly,
JULIAN GLOAG

## Mark of Disfavour

*From Professor Roy Gregory*        *6 December 1982*

[Faculty of Letters and Social Sciences, University of Reading]

Sir,
The significance of the apostrophe should not be decried. Readers may recall the railway carriage skirmish, in pre-nationalisation days, between Sir Thomas Beecham and the lady who reprimanded him for smoking.

Sir Thomas's reaction being somewhat disrespectful, she thought to overawe him with the information that he was talking to 'one of the directors' wives.' To which he is reported to have replied that he would have been no more impressed had she been the director's only wife.

Yours faithfully,
ROY GREGORY

## Dangers in British Neo-Imperial Mood

*From Mr Correlli Barnett*        *29 June 1982*

[of the History Faculty, University of Cambridge]

Sir,
Your leading article on defence policy today (June 21) brilliantly expresses the neo-imperial mood evoked in many British people by the courage, professionalism and ultimate success of our Falklands task force, but it would have done better to have deflated this mood instead. For the Falklands operation has altered nothing in terms of Britain's present and likely future place in the world or her real defence dilemmas.

It does not alter the fact that our GNP is only four times that of Switzerland or about half that of Western Germany. It does not alter the fact that the likely rate of increase in GNP over the next decade will be significantly less than the increase in the real

215

cost of weaponry; and that therefore we face the prospect of repeated defence reviews, each cutting the Armed Forces in one way or another, and each demanding that choices have to be made as to priorities between the three Services.

The lesson of the Falklands crisis is not that we need a bluewater surface fleet in case similar residual bits of pink on the map come under attack, but that we should bring our foreign policy into congruence with our defence policy and shed such unprofitable bits of pink in good time.

The real guilty men of the crisis are the MPs of both parties who, in the past, blocked possible deals with the Argentine with emotional cries of 'sell-out' without apparently reckoning the possible cost of defending the Falklands against the value of the islands to the United Kingdom.

Can it now be really argued that a capability to do another Falklands somewhere in the wide oceans is more important to our security of this country than the preservation of Western Europe, our own outer rampart and our greatest market? Are we really to return to the beguiling fallacies of Basil Liddell Hart and Neville Chamberlain in the 1930s to the effect that the defence of Western Europe was a matter primarily for Europeans, with only a 'limited liability' land-war contribution from us? Have you, Sir, pondered the impact on less resolute members of Nato of a withdrawal of a major portion of BAOR back to the United Kingdom and the follow-on consequences for the cohesion and effectiveness of the whole Alliance?

In conclusion, I would argue more broadly that our besetting national failing since 1945 has been world-role nostalgia and reluctance to confront the realities of our decline. It seemed in recent years that the penny was at last beginning to drop. I now fear that, thanks to the Falklands victory, it may finish Britannia-side uppermost, with disastrous consequences for our national sense of realism.

Yours faithfully,
CORRELLI BARNETT


## 'For the Use of'

*From Mr R. G. Robinson*     *15 October 1982*

Sir,

PHS's mention (October 5) of today's married quarters being equipped with garden fork but no rake, ironing board but no iron, and so on reminds me of 1940, when as a newly-commissioned officer, I was intrigued to find that in our makeshift accommodation my colleagues and I would be credited 'Field Allowance' of 2s. daily by the Paymaster *if* the Quartermaster was unable to supply us with the officially prescribed essentials of furnishing, viz,

One coalscuttle (officer's),
One poker (soldier's),
One chair (Windsor or Fold-flat),
One inventory board.

As we were accommodated outdoors in bell tents, the likely usefulness of the first two items was as baffling as the apparent class distinction between them. Fortunately for us, however, they were in short supply and so we got our 2s. daily to compensate. However, the Quartermaster was able to provide the chair — thus saving himself the ignominy of issuing an inventory board with nothing listed upon it except itself.

Yours faithfully,
R. G. ROBINSON

*From Dr Anthony Rickards*          *21 October 1982*

Sir,

In 1943, when I took over the inventory of the RAF Hospital in Reykjavik, I had to sign for one item entitled: 'Bedpans, rubber, lunatics for the use of'.

Yours faithfully,
ANTHONY RICKARDS

*From Major-General J. P. Crowdy*     *2 November 1982*

Sir,

Mr Robinson's reflections on the vagaries of the Quartermaster's syntax and vocabulary for his stores nomenclature made me think further about the purpose underlying the rigid rank stratification which differentiates 'poker officers steel' from the more mundane 'poker soldier'.

An even more striking example of the class structure, midway between officer and soldier, and with the implicit suggestion that in some way the description fitted the user, is provided by the time-honoured, but now obsolete, piece of military furniture known as 'stool, wooden-headed, sergeant'.

Yours faithfully,
J. P. CROWDY

*From Mr H. K. Matthews*                    *8 November 1982*

Sir,

I wonder whether Major-General Crowdy knows the full extent of the privileges which rigid stratification confers upon his rank?

In 1957 Middle East Headquarters were good enough to house some of the political staff attached to them. We were 'marched in' to quarters in Episkopi. All went well until my wife enquired about the lack of certain fittings.

'Lids?', came the startled reply. 'Only major-generals have lids to their loos.'

Yours faithfully,

H. K. MATTHEWS

*From Mr J. P. Carswell*                    *10 November 1982*

[Secretary, The British Academy]

Sir,

VOS (from which 'pokers, soldiers' – letter, November 3 – comes) is the tongue enshrined in the Vocabulary of Ordnance Stores and certain other military and naval epics. It is unique in containing no singular forms. All its nouns are plural in form, though not necessarily in meaning.

It is a spoken as well as a written language. I once observed two highly articulate VOS speakers (both elderly quartermasters), one of whom was taking over the contents of a cookhouse from the other. As each item was read out by the incoming sergeant cook the outgoing one produced it.

'Skims cooks one', said the first sergeant, and the other held up an implement.

'Come off it, Sergeant Cook', said the incoming quartermaster, 'I wasn't born yesterday. You know bloody well that isn't a skims cooks; it's a slices fish.'

Yours etc,

JOHN CARSWELL

*From Lieutenant-Colonel A. G. B. Walker*    *12 November 1982*

Sir,

Perhaps one of the simplest yet at the same time most incongruous items in military inventories used always to be found (and I dare say still is) amongst glasses – Port, glasses – wine, etc, was glasses – looking, Officers, for the use of.

I have the honour to be, Sir,

Your obedient servant,

A. G. B. WALKER

*From Mr A. R. Isserlis*            *18 November 1982*

Sir,

Under the Raj, VOS (Vocabulary of Ordnance Stores), like Shakespeare, had its devotees amongst the Gurkhas and Indians as well as amongst the British. One of its characteristics which they most readily grasped was its almost invariable reversal of the normal order of words.

Thus, when I was a company commander, I could never dissuade my havildar-clerk, when presenting for signature a stores indent including a demand for razor blades of the kind then normally supplied for troops under the brand name Seven O' Clock, from listing the item as 'blades, razor, Clock, O', Seven'. The demand was always honoured without query.

Yours faithfully,

A. R. ISSERLIS

## Slow Way with Snails

*From the Principal of Romsey House*       *5 March 1983*

Sir,

Having singularly failed to impress you over the years with my letters on profound theological issues, may I try and make my mark with an alternative matter of erudition − gasteropod gastronomy!

*Pace* your Agricultural Correspondent (March 2) it is just not true to say that the process of preparing garden snails for the pot is 'beyond the means of most housewives.' On the contrary, it is just as simple and takes just about as long as growing the lettuces they feed on.

All you have to do is catch your snails, put them in a closed container (with airholes) in a cool place and feed them on clean lettuce leaves for about five days. You then keep them without any further food for about a month, soak them overnight in a salted solution of equal parts water and vinegar, rinse them in about 10 lots of clean, cold water and boil them for about two hours.

Can I just slip in an ecclesiastical commercial? Acts 10:9–16 shows that 'escargot-lovers' like me even have the encouragement of Holy Writ!

Yours faithfully,

DAVID GREGG

['And Peter saw heaven opened, and a certain vessel descending unto him, as it had been a great sheet knit at the four corners, and let down to the earth:

Wherein were all manner of fourfooted beasts of the earth, and wild beasts, and creeping things, and fowls of the air']

## Hallowed Ground

*From Mr Stephen Green*                    *20 June 1983*

[Curator, Marylebone Cricket Club]

Sir,
I do not know whether Cardinal Hume's election to membership of MCC has any bearing in the matter but I have just had a letter from Trinidad which refers to Lourdes Cricket Ground.

Yours faithfully,
STEPHEN GREEN

## Not Content

*From Mr C. L. Fox*                    *30 July 1983*

Sir,
I have read *The Times* for 52 years. I have read it when it invited Hitler to take over the Sudetenland. I have read it when it was known as the London edition of *Pravda*. But I had never thought to read it when it devoted a whole page to a character called Mick Jagger (July 25) and failed to print the Stock Exchange prices – and this when the *Financial Times* was out of action.

Sincerely,
C. L. FOX

## The Lady

*From Mr Ron Martin*                    *19 January 1983*

Sir,
Congratulations to Julian Haviland (report, January 14) on his delightful phrase, 'The Prime Minister was . . . unimpressed with the behaviour in her absence of the foreign exchange

markets . . .' Worthy, surely, to stand beside Queen Victoria's apocryphal lack of amusement?

Yours faithfully,
RON MARTIN

*From the Reverend Canon J. G. Grimwade    28 December 1983*

Sir,

I find it surprising that you give only four lines to the statement in today's *Times* (December 21) that if there were a chance to be anyone else, Mrs Thatcher would choose to be Mother Teresa.

If this is how the Prime Minister feels it implies an immense change in the Government's health and social policies in the coming year.

Yours faithfully,
JOHN GRIMWADE


## Taking 'The Times'

*From Mr Stephen West                           28 March 1983*

Sir,

Travelling first class from Norwich to London yesterday, a copy of *The Times* was stolen from my briefcase.

Is the recession now so severe that top people can no longer afford to buy their own?

Yours faithfully,
STEPHEN WEST

*From Mr Robert O. Plowright                    30 March 1983*

Sir,

Things are even blacker than Mr Stephen West's experience on British Rail might indicate. Last month, my copy of *The Times* was nicked in seconds from the bar of Leander Club whilst I was busy getting some drinks.

Yours faithfully,
ROBERT O. PLOWRIGHT

*From Mr J. N. Machin                           31 March 1983*

Sir,

I recently left my copy of *The Times* in a London saleroom. Due to the thievish propensities of some who frequent there, I did not imagine there would be much point in going back to look for it.

221

However, I was quite mistaken; although well thumbed through and bearing all the marks of extra usage the paper was left folded on the top of the lot, where I'd presumably left it.

Yours faithfully,
J. N. MACHIN

*From Mr Derek Cannon*                    *31 March 1983*

Sir,

Your correspondent, Mr Stephen West, writes: 'Travelling first class from Norwich to London yesterday, a copy of *The Times* was stolen from my briefcase.'

Perhaps it floated away with his participle.

Yours faithfully,
DEREK CANNON

*From Mr James O'Donald Mays*                    *4 April 1983*

Sir,

Perhaps Stephen West, whose copy of *The Times* was stolen, can take comfort from knowledge that the top paper has long been a commodity with a potential second readership within the same day.

Nathaniel Hawthorne, American Consul to Liverpool during 1853–4, was a witness to this truth. Returning by ferryboat to his residence on the Cheshire side of the Mersey after a day's work, he found a beggar peddling a copy of *The Times* 'with an aspect of doubtless newness.'

When Hawthorne, who already took the paper, refused to buy the beggar's copy, the man turned on him saying, 'Well, upon my word, Sir, I'm in want of a bit of bread.' From subsequent observation, Hawthorne concluded the man to be a humbug who knew the value of *The Times* picked up aboard public transport.

Yours faithfully,
JAMES O'DONALD MAYS

*From Mr John Stockton*                    *4 April 1983*

Sir,

One could argue that Mr Plowright deserved to have his copy of *The Times* nicked from the bar of the Leander Club – shouldn't he have been reading the 'Pink 'un'?

Yours faithfully,
JOHN STOCKTON

*From the Reverend Robin J. Ray*          *6 April 1983*

Sir,

The top people will always be able to afford the cost of the best newspaper but not all are able to complete *The Times* crossword.

Could it be that Mr West and Mr Plowright had completed theirs? In which case anyone unscrupulous enough to steal another man's newspaper can just as easily boast that the finished crossword is all his own work.

Yours etc,
ROBIN J. RAY

*From Colonel Anthony Crockett*          *11 April 1983*

Sir,

Those of your readers unfortunate enough to lose their copies of *The Times* to more predatory fellows might look back with nostalgia to the 1870s, when Mr Hutchings, Stationer, Printer, Bookseller, Bookbinder and Dealer in Fancy Goods, of Teignmouth, Devon, respectfully invited 'the attention of Visitors to his large and well selected stock of Hand Books, Books of Views, Note-Paper Views, etc, Children's Seaside Picture Books, Albums, Postage Stamp Albums and Fancy Stationery, New Music at Half-Price and THE LONDON *TIMES* LENT BY THE HOUR'!

Yours faithfully,
ANTHONY CROCKETT

*From Mr Michael Fiorini*          *13 April 1983*

Sir,

I can sympathize with Mr Stephen West. Some years ago, at Victoria Station, there was a poster advertising the fact that '75 per cent of top people took The Times'. Under this dubious statement was added: 'The other 25 per cent pay for it', by an earlier sufferer.

Yours faithfully,
MICHAEL FIORINI

[If Mr West lived in the Bristol area and travelled first class to London, he would find himself surrounded by tabloids. Readers of *The Times* travel second class]

# The Miners

—◆—

## Nationalize the Mines

*From Mr John L. Low*     *29 November 1916*

Sir,

A Government which wished to govern, and not to argue with a nation, would, as a first step, take over the control of the coal mines. If 6 per cent of the profits went to the owners they could have no cause for complaint; already the Government has practically commandeered our American securities, and no one has been so unpatriotic as to protest. From the point of view of the men, their excuse for striking or wishing more wages would be taken away; for they would know that no excess profits were made, and that their fellow-workers and their brothers in the Navy and Army were getting the benefit of the reduced prices.

Thousands of men of military age are exempt from service in the Forces because they are serving the country in this vital industry at home: why should these men refuse to work under the Government at reasonable pay in the same way that their fellow-citizens are working in the Army Service Corps? The nationalization of the coalfields would not only remove many difficulties which might at any moment be surprised upon the country, but it would, by an adjustment of wages, reduce the price of coal for the poor, and place the nation beyond the fear of any panic which might follow the quarrels of private capital and labour.

Yours, &c.,<br>JOHN L. LOW

# Miners' Wages

*From Sir William Davison, MP*                    *2 March 1925*

[Conservative Member for Kensington]

Sir,

It is to be hoped that the Miners' Federation will give attention to the statement made by the Minister of Mines in the House of Commons on Tuesday last in reply to a question which I addressed to him. He then stated that the average wages cost per ton of coal raised in 1913 was 6s 10½d, while the corresponding figure for the last quarter of 1924 was 13s 1d. He also stated that the average output per man shift in June 1914 was 20.32 cwt, as compared with an average output for the last quarter of 1924 of only 17.74 cwt. The public would be glad to know the opinion of the miners' representatives on the above figures, and as to how far they may be considered as accountable for the existing deplorable unemployment in the mining industry.

I am, Sir, your obedient servant,

WILLIAM H. DAVISON

# Miners' Rations

*From Professor Brinley Thomas*                    *22 February 1946*

[Professor of Economics, University College of South Wales and Monmouthshire]

Sir,

The case for increasing the coal miners' rations urged by Colonel W. R. Gordon in your columns on February 13 deserves urgent consideration. With the latest cut in the fat ration and the disappearance of dried egg, there is a danger of a further fall in output a man. I should like to counter the objection that to give the miners extra would introduce an unfair element of discrimination into the distribution of food.

Our rationing system is based on the flat-rate principle which makes no allowance for differences in the physical effort required in various occupations. It assumes that these differences are adequately met by providing works canteens; but experience proves that canteen feeding is not as feasible in coal mining as it is in other heavy industries. Taking a hot meal straight after reaching the surface means breaking deep-rooted habits formed by working underground and it cuts across the established routine of the miner's home. Moreover, owing to transport difficulties, the men may find that they are very late getting home if they stay for a meal at the pit-head. In South Wales there are over 160 colliery canteens, built at a cost of £250,000. On inquiring recently, I found that, for reasons such as the above, the use made of them has been disappointing. There are no canteens for small pits employing fewer than 50 men.

An investigation would probably show that miners are in fact receiving less energy-yielding foods than many sedentary workers. As a contrast we may recall that during the war the German miner, classed as a very heavy worker, obtained a weekly ration of 30oz. (850 grammes) of meat and 20½oz. (582 grammes) of fats.

Food is only one factor in the coal crisis; but it is one on which immediate action can be taken with a fair prospect that it will bring some result. Mr Shinwell has called the nation's attention to a 'very grave' situation. There is surely no section of the community which would have a right to complain if the miners were immediately granted an extra allowance of meat and fats, perhaps on condition that some of it were consumed in the pithead canteens.

Yours faithfully,
BRINLEY THOMAS

[Mr Emmanuel Shinwell had the misfortune to be Minister of Fuel at this time. One correspondent pointed out that during the German occupation of Holland miners were encouraged to achieve the impossible by weekly gifts of cigarettes and gin. If these failed, the Gestapo moved in]

## Not Enough Power

*From Mr Ronald Beale*                    *25 January 1963*

Sir,

The Trade Disputes Act, 1927, was the sequel to the general strike of 1926 and two of its objects were protection of Parliamentary Government and the Constitution against coercion by spreading industrial disputes and of the choice of the individual in his political views. Its partisan repeal by the Socialists in 1946 left no safeguard and by restoring the 1913 Act substituted for the trade unionist the procedure of 'contracting out' instead of personal choice.

Protection against intimidation was also lost and the way thus opened for 'unofficial leaders' to gain sufficient support to hold the whole nation up to ransom, legally and in defiance of their unions. The availability of Public Assistance for the families of unofficial strikers also assists the procedure still further.

Herein lies the weakness of the position now and in spite of promises of consultation with the unions no real effort has been made by subsequent Governments to introduce new legislation to check the subversive elements which are not concerned with working conditions but are dedicated to the complete disruption of the capitalist system. It is all to be found in the *Communist Manifesto*, reissued by the Socialist Party in 1947!

The unions fear the strength of this subversive undercurrent and are reluctant to accept legislation which will enable them to enforce their responsibilities but until both Government and unions jointly accept the fact that where the 'affluent society' has failed only strong legislation can crush organized subversion, which is utterly foreign to our British system, there will be no change.

The simple alternatives are legislate or sink − in or out of the Common Market.

Yours faithfully,
RONALD BEALE

## Miners' Pay

*From Mr P. G. Evans*                    *16 December 1981*

Sir,

Whilst sympathizing with Mr Arthur Scargill's intention to negotiate the best possible pay and conditions for the miners, as is his duty, I submit that government has an equally clear duty to prevent British industry being crippled by overpriced energy.

The miners should be paid what the market will stand, but surely this must include supplies of coal from other sources overseas, including that produced by the miners of South Africa.

Yours faithfully,
PETER G. EVANS

# Slow Motion Dockers

*From Mr M. M. Clark*　　　　　　　　　*10 April 1984*

[University of Surrey]

Sir,

Dockers in Scotland black coal (headline, April 5).

Another Government employment scheme – and who supplies the polish?

Yours faithfully,

M. M. CLARK

[A train awaiting the newly married Duke and Duchess of Gloucester at St Pancras station on 6 November 1935 had a tender apparently full of huge silver nuggets. The LMS Railway directors had decreed that each lump of coal be whitewashed]

# Pointless Picketing

*From Mr A. R. Mayer*　　　　　　　　　*11 April 1984*

Sir,

I was an active trade unionist for nearly 50 years, during which time I was involved in three fairly big disputes, none of which lasted less than six weeks. I know what it is like to be 'out on the cobbles' and trying to exist on strike pay. My sympathies, therefore, are naturally with any body of men or women who are concerned about their jobs and livelihood.

However, as a believer in a democratic society, I find myself repelled by those leaders of trade unions, like Mr Scargill, Mr Buckton, and now, regrettably, Mr Len Murray (for whom I have always had a great deal of respect), who defend mass picketing which, by definition, is intimidatory and which, if it is not intended to be so, is completely pointless.

It does not require much imagination to know that for anyone who, rightly or wrongly, decides to continue working during an industrial dispute and has to run the gauntlet of hundreds of workmates shouting and jeering (and in some cases attempting to use violent methods of coercion), it must be a very frightening experience.

To excuse bully-boy tactics while simultaneously condemning the police for doing their duty to maintain law and order and protect the individual is to indulge in a dangerous form of cynicism; it is, also, to do trade unionists in particular, and the

Labour movement in general, a great disservice. And worse, and more sinister than that, it is to encourage the antisocial elements in our midst to take us down the road to anarchy.

Yours sincerely,

A. R. MAYER


## Loss of Face

*From Miss Barbara M. Elgar*                    *11 July 1984*

Sir,

The influence of the miners' strike is certainly widespread. Asked in her end-of-term exam to name 'a man who digs underground for coal', one of my eight-year-old class wrote, 'a picket.'

Yours faithfully,

BARBARA M. ELGAR


## Unspoken Tariff

*From Sir Charles Fletcher-Cooke, QC*            *17 July 1984*

Sir,

Recently an official of the Kentish miners' union denied that there had been any intimidation by miners' pickets throughout this long strike since there was no record of a single conviction, anywhere in Great Britain, of a picket by a court of law.

There have, of course, been many charges, remands, undertakings, remands in custody. But, it seems, no concluded trials.

I think this official may have got his facts right. If there had been trials with acquittals or convictions the media would have given great prominence to the sentences. Everyone wants to know the tariff for (a) resisting the police; (b) assaulting the police; (c) breaking a policeman's jaw; (d) firing or damaging police property. These figures have not yet been vouchsafed, even to the strikers.

Why this damaging delay? Is it because courts do not wish to appear to accelerate these charges in priority over their normal lists? Or is it due to an understandable but misplaced desire not to 'escalate' the dispute? Or is it just judicial inertia?

I am, your obedient servant,

CHARLES FLETCHER-COOKE

# Summer of Discontent

*From Professor Frank Musgrove*                    *17 July 1984*

[formerly Professor of Education in the University of Manchester]

Sir,

Your timely leading article (July 12) tackles fundamentals. It errs only in underestimating Scargill and the power of unreason.

Scargill is in fact far more dangerous, amoral and powerful than Mosley ever was. Mosley did not effectively control a key sector of the economy. Nor did he lead men of such elemental passions and limited education and understanding.

The NCB has shown quite astonishing naiveté. Letters to miners and big advertisements addressed to them in the press assume not only that miners read but that they understand such words as 'economic' and 'environment'. They do not. Their conceptual range does not extend much beyond 'scab'.

The present strike is a terrible indictment of our educational system, which leaves very simple and unlettered men at the mercy of unscrupulous manipulators. Formerly all the boys in a mining village went down the pit, including some of great intellectual gifts; for the past thirty years only C and D-stream pupils have gone that way. D-stream 'sec mods' make excellent cannon fodder in politico-industrial wars of attrition.

No man should work down a pit. We must hasten the day when there are virtually no miners left and mining is, as far as is humanly possible, automated. It is precisely modernization towards this (genuinely humane) end that Scargill resists.

And now all the claptrap about 'communities': nobody who has actually lived in an isolated mining village could wish to preserve it in all its narrowness and intolerance.

I am, Sir, yours faithfully,

FRANK MUSGROVE

# Under Arrest

*From the Reverend D. C. Darley*                    *10 August 1984*

Sir,

The press, including *The Times*, continues to publish a biased view of the miners' strike. Picketing miners are harassed, maligned as bully boys, intimidated and, in some cases, brutally treated. Arrested pickets have been taunted, ridiculed and have

231

had false charges brought against them. Police snatch squads seize their victims indiscriminatingly.

My son was arrested in such an operation and was one of five miners held in Leicester Prison from July 27. He was remanded by Chesterfield magistrates. It is improbable that the offences with which they were, in my opinion wrongly, charged would carry a prison sentence, even if proven.

The five were being held with convicted prisoners, locked up for 22 hours a day and neither saw nor heard any news. On six days of the week they were allowed a 15-minute visit, but for my family that was a return journey of 160 miles and for three people £25.00 return fare on the railway. I was surprised that prison officers were willing to be gaolers for such men.

On the evening of August 6 my son was released on bail on the orders of a High Court Judge in London. His conditions of bail state that he has not to go to any place involved in the strike including his own colliery.

My son is 24 years old, has worked as a miner since leaving school and has paid his taxes, been in no trouble with the law but is denied any benefit during this strike. Five years ago he sustained serious injuries in an underground accident and still awaits compensation. He uses pain killers daily but received none in prison.

I have two daughters who are nurses. One had her bag snatched in London; the other was assaulted in Harrogate. Months have elapsed but there have been no arrests for these crimes.

The massive police operation in this industrial dispute must be detracting from the task of detecting and apprehending the real enemies of society.

Yours faithfully,<br>DERRICK DARLEY

*From Mrs A. B. Kay*            *15 August 1984*

Sir,

Naturally one must have sympathy with the Reverend D. C. Darley's upset about the arrest of his miner son and also with his daughters who were the victims of crime against their individual persons. But I grew up in Germany. As a child I personally witnessed street violence and later saw the result to my country of organized crowds of bully boys.

There is method in rousing a crowd to the violence we have all seen on our TV screen. The potential danger to the future of a democratic society is far greater than that of an individual act of crime.

The latter should, of course, be punished, but the former is by far the greater evil.

Yours faithfully,

A. BRIGITTE KAY

## Picketing that Goes Beyond the Law

*From Mr Francis Bennion*                    *22 August 1984*

Sir,

In his letter of August 17 Mr Michael Gordon rightly says that for the authorities to allow the law to be flouted is in the long term 'costly and corrosive'. He mentions the failure to prosecute the organizers of the intimidatory picketing at Saltley coke works, which brought down Mr Heath's government. Since the prosecuting authorities continue to be inactive, may I spell out just what they ought to be doing?

The strike operates by preventing miners who wish to work from doing so. This is achieved by planning and carrying out innumerable acts of mass intimidation by thousands of violent men, using the method known as picketing out. You today (August 18) report a National Coal Board spokesman as describing this activity as 'a kind of terrorism'.

In themselves, these intimidatory acts are undoubtedly criminal. Section 7 of the Conspiracy and Protection of Property Act 1875 makes them so.

Despite frequent changes in trade union law over the past century no government, whether Labour or Conservative, has asked Parliament to repeal section 7. It remains good law and renders it an indictable offence, punishable with fine or imprisonment, for pickets to intimidate would-be workers with a view to preventing them from working.

However what makes the intimidatory picketing effective is the *planning* that goes into it. Each day, thousands of men receive orders from union officials telling them when and where they are to picket out on that day. Secrecy is maintained, so that the police can be caught unawares. The union pays the pickets, and arranges food and transport.

Such organizing is made criminal by another Act of Parliament, passed recently under a Labour Government. Part I of the Criminal Law Act 1977 renders it an indictable offence, again punishable with fine or imprisonment, for trade union officials to plan intimidatory mass picketing.

These two provisions, one outlawing intimidatory picketing

233

and the other outlawing the organizing of such picketing, are each undoubted law. Unlike some laws, they are supported by the vast majority of our citizens. Why then have they not achieved their intended purpose, and brought this mischief to an end?

The answer is that they are ignored by the prosecuting authorities. It is not difficult to obtain the evidence needed to bring such prosecutions under them. If the authorities are doing their job, such evidence in overflowing abundance must already be in their possession. So why are Mr Scargill and his fellow organizers not indicted?

It can only be because the prosecuting authorities have decided as a matter of policy that such prosecutions are undesirable. Although Parliament has not itself made the distinction, *they* are distinguishing between the punishing of ordinary crime and the punishing of trade union offences. Unless partaking of the nature of ordinary crime (as with the burning of buses or assaulting of police officers), offences by trade unionists are to go unpunished.

This distinction is foreign to our legal system. By making it, the authorities give a licence to intimidatory picketing that Parliament itself has never conferred, and never would confer. What right have they to do this? If they insist on doing it, is not the nation entitled to an explanation?

Mr Scargill is accused of being undemocratic. It could be said that prosecuting authorities who take it upon themselves to ignore clear and widespread breaches of the criminal law are themselves behaving in an undemocratic manner. With them it is less excusable, for they are no more than officials well paid by the state to enforce the laws laid down by Parliament. While continuing to draw their salaries, they neglect their duty without explanation or account.

If the organizers of Saltley had been prosecuted in 1972 we would not have had Orgreave and the rest in 1984. What future troubles is this 'costly and corrosive' prosecution policy storing up for us?

Yours faithfully,
FRANCIS BENNION

# Pit Strike Implications for Britain

*From the Reverend Eric James*                    *3 September 1984*

[Director of Christian Action]

Sir,

On your front page today (September 1), alongside the headline 'Jobless up 15,000 in steady trend' − to 3,115,888 − is the other: 'MacGregor puts case to the TUC'. Much of the page concerns, of course, the miners' strike.

The issues of the strike are complex, but is there any doubt that it is overwhelmingly by people who *fear* they are the next in line for the 'steady trend'? Those who are already unemployed will understand the strikers only too well. Those in full-time work and whose jobs are not threatened will find understanding more difficult.

A deep-seated fear cannot be cast out by reason alone, especially if that fear is not groundless, e.g., if the 'steady trend' has advanced to your door.

That, surely, is why the situation calls for a new imaginative quality of reconciling initiative.

Yours sincerely,

ERIC JAMES

# Lend-lease

*From Mr Ivor Berger*                              *1 September 1984*

Sir,

Reference your article, 'Saudis find coal in the desert' (August 29), could we not send Mr Arthur Scargill to organize the unions over there on our behalf?

Yours faithfully,

IVOR BERGER

# Reaping the Whirlwind with Mr Scargill

*From Mr Ronald Dore*                              *4 September 1984*

Sir,

Your correspondents' denunciations of the miners' irresponsibility make good blood-warming Saturday-morning reading. They are right of course. The NUM's refusal to discuss

235

economic viability shows a lack of any sense of responsibility for the health of the national economy.

But why should they show a sense of responsibility? Is not limited liability what a market economy is all about? Is every seller of plate glass obliged to worry about the health of his customers' businesses and adjust his prices accordingly? Why should those who sell labour to the Coal Board have any greater concern for the viability of the board's operations?

We know why, but we have deliberately been trying to forget. From Disraeli to the end of the 1970s we were slowly building in this country a society which modified the crudity of contractual market principles.

We were establishing the convention that those who had muscle — financial muscle, intellectual muscle, or picket-power muscle — should use it, with some consideration for the essential interests of those they bargained with, *and* with some awareness of the collective interest which all parties shared in common.

That is what incomes policies were all about, and investment planning and social contracts — about reducing the role that coercion plays in our society and increasing the role of reponsibility and reasoned consent.

We made a botch of it, trying to embody these principles in institutional forms. The Thatcher backlash has thrown the baby of good principle out with the bathwater of bad institutions. 'Marketism', and the go-getting individualism that goes with it, not monetarism, are the central themes of her economic policy.

The talk is now all of how to make labour *markets* more efficient — i.e., of how employers can learn again to treat employees according to the laws of supply and demand, not as partners in a give-and-take relationship in a cooperative enterprise.

Now that we are reaping the whirlwind of Scargillian irresponsibility, should anyone be surprised?

Yours faithfully,

RONALD DORE

## Strange Equation

*From Mr G. E. Thirlwall*                4 September 1984

Sir,

Mr Arthur Scargill (August 31) tells us that 'Decades of mismanagement and a criminal lack of proper investment are the factors which have kept the Coal Board from showing strong, steady profits', but that Britain's coal industry is nevertheless 'the safest and most technically advanced in the world, producing the cheapest deep-mined coal'.

He strains our credulity.

Yours faithfully,<br>
G. E. THIRLWALL

## Enter the Bishop of Durham

*From Lord Hailsham of St Marylebone, CH, FRS*
*25 September 1984*

Sir,

The Bishop of Durham is reported as saying that the Chairman of the National Coal Board should be denied employment inter alia because he was alleged to be an 'imported American'.

Discrimination in such matters on grounds of national or racial origin and incitement to racial hatred are supposed to be against the law of this country.

I have an interest in this matter. My mother, like the late Sir Winston Churchill's and the mother of the present Earl of Stockton, was also an 'imported American' and I am proud of this fact.

I do not know how the Bishop of Durham would defend his language were he brought before the race relations authorities or the courts, or whether he would have used similar expressions had he believed that Mr MacGregor (who is in fact a native Scot returning to his native land) had been 'imported', with a dark skin from Asia or Africa.

But it is possible to hazard a guess as to what the founder of the Christian religion, who did not approve of double standards on the part of ecclesiastical authorities, would have said about the Bishop of Durham.

Yours etc,<br>
HAILSHAM

*From the Reverend J. L. Marshall*          *27 September 1984*

Sir,

I am astonished by the letter from Lord Hailsham.

That the most senior member of the judiciary should consider

237

that the Bishop of Durham's *obiter dictum* is capable of such a
construction makes me tremble for the future of justice.

Yours faithfully,

J. L. MARSHALL

## Bons Mots

*From Mr R. E. Davies*                    *25 September 1984*

Sir,

God bless the Church of England. At last a successor to
Hewlett Johnson in the tradition of the great Anglican eccentric.
With a bishop like this one looks forward to years of happy
entertainment. Even better, I think he may have cost the NUM
the strike.

Yours faithfully,

R. E. DAVIES

*From Mr Michael Foot, MP*                    *27 September 1984*

[Labour Member for Blaenau Gwent]

Sir,

Not odd, said God, I'd have you know
It may seem quite easy down below
To keep the Bishops all in tow
Just propping up the Thatcher show;
Up here, you see, there's hell to pay —
*She* wants to tell ME what to say.

Yours faithfully,

MICHAEL FOOT

## Sacred Cows?

*From Mr A. O. H. Quick*                    *26 September 1984*

[Headmaster, Bradfield College]

Sir,

I have considerable sympathy for the general point that the
Bishop of Durham was making — the lack of hope in the North-
east — but I cannot believe that any Bishop of Durham in my
lifetime would have preached such a muddled sermon.

The mining dispute is largely a red herring, as the mining
industry is a small part of the problem and the miners have been
offered good terms. But the unemployment and dereliction are

very real. I drove through Consett recently; the great works have been levelled to the ground and there is nothing but desolation.

A serious attack on unemployment in the North and Midlands would almost certainly mean attacking two of the present pillars of our policies – the privileges of unions and our membership of the EEC, which so far has had a disastrous effect on manufacturing employment. It is, I think, a pity that the bishop did not challenge these two sacred cows.

Any solution to the unemployment problem is going to require more radical thought than the bishop or anyone else has been able to give.

Yours faithfully,
ANTHONY QUICK

## Contradictions in Miners' Message

*From Professor Emeritus Thomas Wilson, FBA*

2 October 1984

[formerly Adam Smith Professor of Political Economy in the University of Glasgow]

Sir,

Mr Arthur Scargill's mastery of Newspeak is so impressive as to make him the outstanding Orwellian personality of 1984. When he asserts that the NUM is a democratic union, this means 'democratic' in the East European sense. When he claims to be defending the coal industry, this means he is defending its inefficiency to the mutual hurt of the captive British users of coal and of the industry itself.

When he says he is ready to negotiate, this means he is ready to accept the unconditional surrender of the other side. When he complains that Britain is a police state, this means the police should acquiesce in violent intimidation. When he poses as the defender of trade union rights, this means he is pursuing a strategy that would ultimately result in their being made totally subservient to communist-type authority.

His condemnation of Solidarity is an illustration of this attitude. The behaviour of his 'red guards' affords a preliminary indication of the methods to be followed.

There is another aspect of militant Marxist policy that deserves particular attention. This is the perpetuation of conditions in which it would be impossible to cure the mass unemployment of which they complain. Sympathy for the striking miners has naturally been strengthened by the malaise caused by the general lack of jobs, although there will not, in fact, be involuntary redundancies in the coal industry. Moreover the Government, for its part, has given the unhelpful impression of being content with an Asquithian policy of 'wait and see'.

Employment could, in fact, be greatly increased notwithstanding the much discussed problems of 'post-industrial society' — as has been demonstrated so strikingly in recent years in the USA. For this to be achieved, however, it would be essential to have structural change in industry of the kind being so fiercely resisted by Mr Scargill.

It would also be essential to ensure that increases in monetary expenditure did not continue to be so dissipated in rising costs and prices that the rise in output was too small to have much effect on the demand for labour. For a high level of employment can be regained only if, by whatever means, increases in pay are restrained. This is an old warning often given. It is one that, even today, is sometimes conveyed by the dying voices of the Labour right. But the left will have none of it. There must be no restraint — whatever the party in power.

It is not to be inferred that the militants, of whom Mr Scargill is now by far the most prominent, are too stupid to perceive that their various demands are contradictory. It is rather that, with basic aims quite different from those of the democratic reformers, these contradictions are part of the strategy. To be fair, they have never claimed to be revisionists. They seek to subvert, not to remedy, the present social order.

If capitalism fails to generate the fatal contradictions predicted by Marxist theory, it must be provided with them. A 'Catch 22' situation must be deliberately created. Unemployment must be denounced as a social evil but perpetuated as a cause of social unrest. The New Keynesianism must be blocked and defeated just as much as monetarism.

It is of some importance, in the present situation, that the essential features of Mr Scargill's strategy should be widely understood. Natural concern about unemployment should provide an impetus for constructive action but must not be exploited for the benefit of a totalitarian cause.

Yours faithfully,

THOMAS WILSON

# Police Standpoint

*From Police Sergeant R. B. Davies*        *4 October 1984*

Sir,

I am a serving police officer with 26 years' service, nearing the end of my enjoyable and (to me) rewarding career.

Like many other citizens I am saddened and rather fearful of the dreadful violence of recent events, when it is becoming apparent that the police force is being battered unmercifully. I wonder how many more assaults, actual and figurative, they can take.

One of the opposition political parties has now decided that the violence seen in the miners' dispute is the fault of the police, who were acting unlawfully.

No mention has been made of the fact that the police are charged with the duty of upholding law and order and safeguarding the rights of the individual.

It seems to me that the violent person and the bully boy is taking over and anarchy must surely be only around the corner.

I realize that I hold a biased viewpoint, but it is evident that without support the police force will collapse and a state of affairs will exist that does not bear contemplation.

Yours faithfully,

R. B. DAVIES

# Talks as Bar to Return to Pits

*From Mrs Irene McGibbon*        *24 October 1984*

[National Organizer, Miners' Wives Back to Work Campaign]

Sir,

Now that the latest efforts to achieve a settlement of the mining dispute have broken down, it is time to examine the whole process of negotiations between the NCB and the NUM.

From the outset, in a ploy typical of his Marxist mentors, Mr Scargill issued an impossible demand: that no pit be closed, however uneconomic to mine, until total exhaustion of its resources. The object of this ploy is to make his opponents appear intransigent; since the NCB has not conceded Mr Scargill's demands (because it cannot) it is the NCB which is accused of behaving unreasonably.

241

Yet there is a further aspect to the NUM's negotiating stance. Miners contemplating returning to work will not be prepared to beard the pickets if they believe that a settlement is just around the corner. This is the hope held out whilst talks are in progress.

By a succession of negotiating initiatives (in none of which has Mr Scargill moved seriously from his initial position) the NUM successfully deters its disaffected members from returning to their jobs. Making a decision to cross a militant picket line is difficult enough for the miner and his family, without the added disincentive of the false hopes of these formal, but sham, negotiations.

Given that the NCB does not intend to meet Mr Scargill's demands, can there be any purpose, apart from cosmetic public relations, to be gained from further talks? It would be of substantial benefit to the back-to-work movement if the NCB declared that its bottom line offer had been made, and that no further negotiations would take place until the NUM had moved to meet that position.

Not the usual tactics for a trade dispute, of course, but the 1984 miners' strike is not such a dispute, it is a political manoeuvre to challenge the democratic process.

Yours faithfully,
IRENE MCGIBBON

## Mot Unjuste

*From Group Captain Leonard Cheshire, VC, OM*
*13 November 1984*

[The Leonard Cheshire Foundation International]

Sir,

Mr Peter Heathfield is reported as saying (November 9) that when the strike is over the working miners will be treated as lepers. For a man in his position to suggest publicly that people suffering from leprosy should be shunned and badly treated is to render humanity a great disservice.

I appreciate that he may not have come face to face with absolute poverty nor know how urgently the world's 15 million leprosy sufferers require our help and moral support. However, the overwhelming need of our present time is to see more clearly that the poverty of the developing world is also our poverty and that the real key to our economic recovery lies in improving their own economy and standard of living.

If Mr Heathfield could repudiate his statement and indicate

that the poorest members of our human family are also the
object of his compassion this cause would be greatly assisted.

Yours faithfully,
LEONARD CHESHIRE


## Just So

*From Mrs Elspeth Huxley*                    *14 December 1984*

Sir,
   Could we have a moratorium on the use of the phrase 'they
behaved like animals' to describe any especially nasty form of
human brutality? Carnivores certainly kill when they need their
dinners but do so as quickly as they can. Herbivores just eat
vegetation and do not interfere with others.
   Do we hear of dolphins torturing other dolphins, gorillas
cutting, or biting, bits off other gorillas, elephants inflicting
prolonged periods of terror on other elephants, or indeed on any
other animal?
   Rather should dolphins left to die in nets, gorillas killed in
order that their dried heads should be sold to tourists, elephants
dying in agony from poisons for the sake of their tusks, exclaim,
in condemnation of acts of savagery (should these ever occur)
committed by members of their own species: 'They behaved like
humans'.

Yours faithfully,
ELSPETH HUXLEY


## What is a Scab?

*From Mr Alan Wykes*                    *14 January 1985*

Sir,
   When there are more miners working than there are on strike,
thus indicating the views (previously unsought) of the majority,
will the working miners call the striking miners scabs?

Yours &c,
ALAN WYKES

   [The National Coal Board claimed a majority of miners
   back at work on February 27, 1985]

# Unlimited Liability

*From Mr Ian McKittrick*                    *20 November 1984*

Sir,

The Government should not underestimate the strength of the bond between the bishops and the striking miners. Both groups have much in common, not least in the loss of morale each has suffered as a result of the decline in public demand for the product of its labours, religion and coal respectively.

This alliance could provide the solution to the problems of the coal industry if only the Government were willing to back it. The coalfields should immediately be handed over to the bishops, Durham to Durham, South Yorkshire to Sheffield, Kent to Canterbury and so on; thus, at a stroke, placating the miners, providing work for underemployed members of the episcopate, providing financial support for the Church of England, and, perhaps, ensuring for the rest of us a little respite from rhetoric.

I am, yours faithfully,

IAN MCKITTRICK


# Cri de Coeur from the Shipyards

*From Mr Henry Thelwell*                    *8 November 1984*

Sir,

I am 49, have had asbestosis diagnosed, but am trying to keep my job at the Cammell Laird shipyard in Birkenhead for at least the useful life left in me. Each day I go through picket lines to very much abuse with the jeer that there is no way any of us has a chance of saving our jobs.

None of us wants to be identified with the pickets who have given Merseyside a bad reputation, but there is a deep feeling of resentment building up against the possibility of total closure. If this happens, then I and many of my colleagues will be embittered to the extent that, however irrational it may be, we will probably swing over to the views of those who have helped destroy our jobs by their disruptive actions.

My time on earth may be limited but my fervent wish is to have the dignity of working whilst I can to support my wife and family. My work colleagues and I ask the Government to give this very skilled workforce a last chance with a good shipbuilding order.

Surely we have now proved that the majority of us are not militant and only wish to restore our previous enviable reputation as one of the finest yards in the world.

244

The gamble could be well worth the risk in achieving the retention of a skilled workforce and at the same time creating some confidence that determined endeavour to retain one's job can be done without industrial action.

Yours faithfully,

H. THELWELL

## Accusative Ending

*From Miss Lynne Craig*                    *29 January 1985*

Sir,

If I may jump on your linguistic see-saw. . . . Your editorial of January 22 makes reference to 'Scargillite MPs'. Is it by design or whimsy that Scargill spawns 'Scargillite' — thus joining ranks with 'Bennite', 'cordite' and other explosive substances — whereas Churchill is accorded the veneration enjoyed by 'Virgilian', 'Oxonian', 'Georgian' et al?

I think we should be told.

Yours faithfully,

LYNNE CRAIG

## Tomorrow's Question

*From Mr N. J. Daykin*                    *3 December 1984*

Sir,

Is Mr Arthur Scargill to be the first trade union leader to bring down an Opposition?

Yours faithfully,

N. J. DAYKIN

[Mr Arthur Scargill yesterday told Russians that the miners' strike had politicized thousands of young British men and women 'to a degree that seemed unbelievable only two or three years ago'. The struggle itself had been the 12-month strike's most important achievement, 'a brilliant victory', the National Union of Mineworkers' leader said in *Trud*, the Soviet trade union daily . . . Seventy per cent of the strike's aims had been achieved. Mr Scargill made no mention of miners who had opposed the strike. — *The Times*, 29 March 1985]

# Perverted Trade Unionism

[The general council of the TUC called off the General
Strike on 12 May 1926. A. J. Cook was secretary of the
Miners' Federation of Great Britain, Stanley Baldwin the
prime minister]

*From the Bishop of Durham*                                    *22 June 1926*

[the Rt Rev Herbert Hensley Henson]

Sir,

The dramatic defeat of the 'General Strike' has very naturally
given the greatest satisfaction to all good citizens, but I cannot
help thinking that the full measure of the nation's risk has not
been generally realized, and that there is a disposition in many
quarters to assume that the tyranny is overpast, and that we need
not fear in the future any renewal of the challenge to the State,
which the trade unions so recklessly adventured. It is not
sufficiently remembered that the circumstances in which the issue
was joined were in an extraordinary degree favourable to the
country; that the Government had been given ample time, though
at a vast cost, for preparation: that in the Prime Minister the
nation had a leader who united a stiff back with a magnanimous
heart: that the time of year was propitious: and that the trade
unions themselves were divided in mind. Such a combination of
favouring circumstances cannot be counted upon in the future,
and I am persuaded that the country will be indulging itself in a
fool's paradise if it rests on its victory, and takes no steps to render
a renewal of the rebellion difficult if not impossible.

In this view I am confirmed by the attitude of the vanquished
trade unionists. Even the moderate leaders who disapproved the
General Strike (which none the less they sanctioned) are careful
to dwell on its inexpediency rather than on its essential
wickedness, while their more violent colleagues, who forced
their hands, exalt the marvellous solidarity of 'Labour' which
the strike disclosed, and prophesy an early renewal of the
conflict under conditions which will ensure its success. The
generosity of the Nation, which seeks to minimize the
humiliation of defeat by heaping compliments (not in all cases
merited) on the self-sacrifice of the strikers, their unity, and
their abstinence from disorder, assists to obscure the lesson of
the crisis in the eyes of those who most need to learn it.
Meanwhile the prolongation of the 'stoppage' in the mining
industry promises to serve the sinister purpose with which the
General Strike was engineered.

Why is it that this conflict, so plainly destructive of the industry in the prosperity of which the miners are primarily concerned, and so ruinous to the country as a whole, still continues? I am assured on all hands that individual miners freely affirm in private their desire to get back to work, and their readiness to accept, as a temporary arrangement, the eight-hour day. None the less, in public an unyielding attitude is maintained. Mr Cook, an avowed advocate of revolution on the Russian model, is allowed to pose as the mouthpiece of the miners. The truth is that we are beginning to see the result of persistent Communist propaganda in this country. A recent issue of the *Yorkshire Post* contained an illuminating account of the situation in Chopwell, the mining parish near Gateshead which, during the last few years, has gained an evil notoriety for the lawlessness and violence of a section (it is only a section, and, I am informed, a comparatively small one) of its inhabitants. In answer to the question why this place should be thus distinguished, the reply was returned by 'an official of the local miners' lodge': –

If you want to fix the blame you can put your finger on the Central Labour College, followed by intensive propaganda on the part of men who have been there. In season and out of season we have preached Left Wing politics. We have held classes and study circles and meetings, and we have met with extraordinary success.

This evil seed has fallen on prepared soil, for the trade unions now include in their ranks a great number of young men whose boyhood was spent during the war, when every kind of discipline was weakened, and who have been largely, even continuously, unemployed, since they left school. These lawless youths are well-fitted to become the janissaries of Communist Revolution. The older and steadier trade unionists are terrified into acquiescence in the policies which they abhor. It is profoundly humiliating to observe that even Christianity is powerless against this terrorism. 'You are a Churchman,' said a clergyman to a parishioner who had 'come out' in the general strike, 'how can you reconcile your conscience to breaking the contract under which you are employed, and joining in action which you know to be illegal, and believe to be calamitous?' 'You see this house,' replied the man, 'it is my own, and represents the savings of years. If I were to stand out of the strike it would be wrecked, and I myself might be knocked about.' The fact is that the trade unions have got off the lines of their true purpose, and have grown into a formidable menace both to individual freedom and

247

to public order. They have come to be the mocking caricature of anything that can be justly described as democratic – and, indeed, their constitution seems now to have been deliberately manipulated with the object of making the rank and file the hopeless tools of the ruling clique. Unless this tyranny can be broken, an irreparable injury will be inflicted on English character. The mischief has gone perilously far. It is high time to seek a remedy.

And this is the object of my letter. I desire to press on the Government not to let slip the opportunity, which the defeat of the general strike has provided, of so revising Trade Union Law, that 'Peaceful picketing' – a sordid and hypocritical form of organized bullying – may become impossible; that decisions affecting the vital interests of the nation may only be made by trade unions under conditions which shall guarantee their quality as genuine expressions of the mind of their members; and that direct financial dependence on the foreign enemies of Great Britain may in future industrial conflicts be rendered impossible.

I am, Sir, your obedient servant,

HERBERT DUNELM

# Points Made, Missed and Taken

[a brief selection from the bottom right-hand corner]

*From Mr David H. R. Yorke*          *9 August 1983*

Sir,

As part of the Government's spending cuts have secret restrictions been placed on the supplies of paint for punctuation marks by signwriters?

A journey last week yielded three signs whose meaning would have been made clearer (or indeed reversed) by some punctuation after the initial warning or exhortation.

Near the entrance to Ragley Hall is the delightful 'Lambs drive slowly'. By the towpath of the South Oxford canal lurks the more sinister 'Sheep dogs will be shot'. In my neighbouring village of Lindfield a traffic sign proclaims 'Give way markings erased' — should I stop or not?

Yours in confusion (comma),

DAVID YORKE

*From Mr Christopher Martin*      *13 September 1983*

[Head Master, Bristol Cathedral School]

Sir,

I used to think the people of Newmarket knew something about the Turf that the rest of us did not. Approaching it some years ago, however, I was corrected by the road sign: 'Slow race horses.'

Yours faithfully,

CHRISTOPHER MARTIN

*From Mr Antony Atkins*         *12 September 1983*

Sir,

What ominous indication of our future military preparedness is contained in the notice to motorists 'Dead slow young soldiers crossing' at Shorncliffe Barracks, Folkestone? Its position, at the top of Hospital Hill, may be of significance.

Yours faithfully,

A. W. ATKINS

*From Mr Michael Rubinstein*                   *6 September 1983*

Sir,
   At the Hayward Gallery where part of the Sculpture Show is
currently exhibited, I was not surprised to see a notice reading:
'Way out Toilets'.

                          Yours faithfully,
                            MICHAEL RUBINSTEIN

*From Mr E. R. Pinson*                     *29 September 1983*

Sir,
   A notice outside a Scarborough café reads: 'Children reduced.'
                          Yours faithfully,
                                E. R. PINSON

*From Professor H. H. Huxley*              *11 November 1983*

Sir,
   'The American marine base . . . came under sustained fire last
night from 60 millimetre mortals' (*The Times*, page 1, November
8). An economical breakthrough in genetic engineering?
                          Yours sincerely,
                              H. H. HUXLEY

*From Mrs Mary Godden*                      *16 September 1983*

Sir,
   I vividly recall driving three remarkably quiet children
through the Sussex countryside some years ago. They had been
shocked into silence by a notice at the side of the road which
read: 'Oven-ready chickens and Shetland ponies'.
                          Yours faithfully,
                             MARY GODDEN

*From Miss Ruth Golding*                     *8 October 1983*

Sir,
   In a supermarket window I saw this notice: 'OAP's wanted
for shelf filling'.
                          Yours faithfully,
                              RUTH GOLDING

*From Mr T. L. Jones*                       *17 October 1983*

   [Assistant Registrar, University of Bristol]

Sir,
   Ruth Golding's supermarket wanted OAPs for shelf-filling.
In this university registrars do not die but simply fade away and

so we have a shelf (empty) in our filing room labelled: 'Space reserved for Registrar.'

Yours faithfully,

T. LOCKWOOD JONES

*From Mr Gerald Priestland*             *2 November 1983*

Sir,

There is a terrible notice in the basement of the Royal Free Hospital, Hampstead, which says, 'Whole body counting' and another in a service area on the M3 saying, 'Babies may be changed here'.

Yours fearfully,

GERALD PRIESTLAND

*From Dr A. C. Scott*             *27 October 1983*

[Ninewells Hospital and Medical School, Dundee]

Sir,

A door in this hospital bears the legend, 'Neonatal secretary'.

Yours truly,

A. C. SCOTT

*From Dr P. W. M. Copeman*             *1 November 1983*

[Department of Dermatology, Westminster Hospital]

Sir,

Dundee's 'neonatal secretary' sounds to be a more healthy hazard than our hospital's 'pathological laboratory'.

P. W. M. COPEMAN

*From Dr N. D. Groves*             *1 November 1983*

[Nuffield Department of Anaesthetics, The Radcliffe Infirmary]

Sir,

A signpost near the Casualty Department of my previous hospital directed patients to the 'Traumatic Department'!

Yours faithfully,

N. D. GROVES

*From Mr J. Haworth*             *25 October 1983*

Sir,

The choir library register of Holy Trinity, Sloane Street, had an entry: 'God is gone up' − top shelf, right.

Yours truly,

J. HAWORTH

Sir,

Some time ago displayed outside St Paul's Church, Sumner Place, London, SW7, was a large poster announcing 'Christ is coming', and on the railings a notice saying: 'Please do not obstruct these gates'.

Yours faithfully,
ROBERT BUHLER

*From Mr O. J. Makower*            *30 September 1983*

Sir,

Some years ago, on the road to Clontarf, outside Dublin, a car-hire firm displayed the sign, 'Funerals. Self-drive'.

The point was not missed.

Yours sincerely,
O. J. MAKOWER

*From the Reverend Eric James*            *18 October 1983*

[Director of Christian Action]

Sir,

When I was Vicar of St George's, Camberwell, the local 'Co-op' in St George's Way, SE15, proclaimed to passers-by: Co-operative Wholesale Society, Ltd: Butchery: Self-service.

Yours sincerely,
ERIC JAMES

*From Mr J. C. Taylor*            *26 September 1983*

Sir,

On the subject of ambiguous instructions, I was very disappointed, on reaching Canterbury Cathedral last Sunday, to find a sign saying 'Only guide dogs for the blind allowed entry'.

Yours faithfully,
J. C. TAYLOR

*From Mr G. W. Thomas*            *12 October 1983*

Sir,

Sometime ago a notice outside an Edinburgh park which said, 'downputting of uplifted children,' led me to assume an enlightened Scottish attitude to the problems of youth. My view was modified by a longer acquaintance with the vernacular, but now that I am approaching an age which engenders contemplation of the hereafter I am encouraged to find an unequivocal statement of policy on a notice in the cemetery of

Rosslyn Chapel (Borders region) which says: 'No children allowed into this burial ground unless accompanied by parents or guardians'.

Yours faithfully,<br>
G. W. THOMAS

# Unfair Daffodils

*From Dr M. D. Croft*                    *23 April 1984*

Sir,

The daffodils in our front garden are all pointing towards the street and away from our house. I bought them so that I could look at them out of the window, but they seem to reserve their beauty not for me but for passers-by, who did not fork out last autumn for the bulbs, as I did.

My wife tells me they are looking towards the sun, but that does not explain the behaviour of the daffodils in the back garden, which are also facing the other way. Is there something fundamentally wrong about the way we planted them, or are we doing something of which they disapprove?

Short of wringing their necks, or cutting off the flowers and placing them in a vase on the dining-room table, or changing our highly provocative lifestyle, can anything be done? We need an answer fast, as their attitude is already beginning to infect the primroses.

Yours faithfully,<br>
MICHAEL CROFT

*From Mr R. Norton Ellen*                    *26 April 1984*

Sir,

Re the letter of April 23, there are no such complaints from the Lake District.

Perhaps Dr Croft should try gazing at his daffodils from afar, or 'at a glance', instead of so critically staring at them from the window of his house, back and front. Or, perhaps, join them in sprightly dance, or, at any rate, do something to show them that he is 'gay in such a jocund company'.

This should meet with their approval, and may cause Dr Croft to think what wealth the show to him had brought.

Yours faithfully,<br>
R. NORTON ELLEN

Sir,

Mr Croft's daffodils are obviously reluctant to turn their faces to the walls of his house. Perhaps if he lined the said walls with some reflective material his flowers might reconsider. After all, they are narcissi!

Yours faithfully,<br>OLGA E. LOCKLEY

Sir,

The uncooperative daffodils in Dr Croft's garden are simply turning towards the best source of light. Planted near the house they will turn away from it to where the sky is more visible. If Dr Croft has a front garden wall or hedge, daffodils planted near it will look towards the house.

I have north-facing daffodils against a fence on my southern boundary, and south-facing ones on the opposite side of the garden.

It's only natural, if you come to think of it. You would not sit on your patio staring at the house would you?

Yours faithfully,<br>GEOFFREY YORKE

Sir,

With regard to Dr Croft's daffodils, I am surprised that he does not know the old Celtic legend in which the defenders of the marches, being attacked from the rear while facing the enemy, stood back to back and fought to the last man; their bereaved womenfolk planted daffodils on the site, and, ever since, daffodils planted in rows have grown back to back.

There is a reference to this in the *Green Book of Llantrisant (Cenhinen Rhyfelwr)*. The only thing to do is to confuse the daffodils by planting them in odd-shaped flowerbeds or at random all over the lawn.

Yours,<br>ELAINE MURRAY

Sir,

I am delighted to learn from Dr Croft that I am not the only person being ostracized by daffodils.

Mine insist on facing the street when they bloom and are

consequently at right angles to the house. I agree that sun direction has nothing to do with it and have come to the conclusion that they disapprove of my life-style but wish to keep track of me with an occasional sideways glance.

Yours faithfully,

PATRICIA A. TYRRELL

*From Mrs Barbara Milne*                    *30 April 1984*

Sir,

Dr Croft should really not complain about a flower with such highly placed poetic connections, and his wife, as he observes, is quite wrong to tell him that they are looking at the sun. What they are looking at, being aesthetic by nature, is the view.

We have many daffodils in our woodland, which faces north-east, but they too turn their backs on the sun to admire the magnificent view over Porlock Vale and the sea towards Wales, their homeland!

Dr Croft should realize that flowers with such sensitivity cannot be dragooned; rather, he must learn from them and seek solace and peace in these things of beauty, thereby acquiring 'joy forever'!

Yours faithfully,

BARBARA MILNE

*From Mr T. Larsson*                    *1 May 1984*

Sir,

In the spring of 1946, being in need of a complete change, I decided to spend three months in Sweden's Lappland, just north of the Arctic Circle.

I took with me from Stockholm, some two dozen daffodil bulbs in pots which had started to sprout, and planted them out early in May.

At that time of the year, the sun does not set but only dips towards the horizon at midnight and then goes around in a circle rising comparatively high at midday.

The daffodils grew rapidly and within three weeks were in full bloom. Then tragedy. They insisted on following the sun for its full circle and within one week had strangled themselves. All of them.

Yours faithfully,

THEO LARSSON

*From Mr H. C. Robbins Landon*                    *3 May 1984*

Sir,

My daffodils, being particularly sophisticated, are facing neither the sun, nor the extraordinary view of Chepstow Castle (which my garden adjoins) but the house itself.

The reason for this is certainly because most of the time they are listening to the large quantities of eighteenth-century music which pours out of the house in the daffodils' direction; I think they are particularly fond of Mozart.

Yours faithfully,

H. C. ROBBINS LANDON

## Flower Power

*From Mr H. C. Seigal*                    *5 May 1984*

Sir,

Mr T. Larsson (May 1), whose daffodils strangled themselves trying to follow the sun round in the Arctic Circle, should not have attempted to fly in the face of nature. He would have done better to stick to the local flora. The flowers of *Dryas octopetala*, for example, are designed to follow the sun indefinitely as it circles the horizon.

Yours faithfully,

H. C. SEIGAL

## Olympic Spirit

*From Miss Bridget Boland*                    *12 May 1984*

Sir,

My father, J. P. Boland, won two events in the 1896 Olympic Games. He was in Greece because his tutor at Oxford had given him an introduction to the archaeologist, Schliemann, and in Athens he chanced to meet an Austrian fellow undergraduate who was entered for the tennis in the games and who persuaded him to take the place of his doubles partner, who had fallen ill.

When they won and an official was putting up the Austrian flag and the Union Jack, my father said to him with a grin: 'Actually, I'm Irish.'

The apologetic official looked anxiously at his array of flags and my father said: 'It's a gold harp on a green ground, we hope, but that one will do to be going on with.'

When he went on to win the singles the official was even more apologetic, but he soothed him, saying: 'It's a difficult flag to make in a hurry and I'm afraid I'm now entering for putting the weight as well, so why not make one just saying J.P.B.?'

Unfortunately he lost, or he might have started a trend more in keeping with the intentions of the originator of the modern games.

Yours truly,
BRIDGET BOLAND

## Never-never Land

[While sundry bishops drank deeply of Mr Scargill's own potent brew of Buck-U-Uppo, a less militant cleric reacted to a review (June 21) of *The World of Wodehouse Clergy*]

*From the Reverend Canon D. L. Howells*      *30 June 1984*

Sir,

The epic choirboys' race and great sermon handicaps chronicled by P. G. Wodehouse could not possibly have taken place in Twing. There is no such place; the true text must refer to Tring — an error that has doubtless been made by an early scribe.

Since those heroic and early days Tring, of course, has grown much less rural. No longer does the congregation allow the incumbent to preach for 50 minutes — 'he removeth away the speech of the trusty . . .' (Job XII. 20).

Yours faithfully,
DONALD HOWELLS

*From Mr Roger Washbourn*      *17 July 1984*

Sir,

Few modern exegetes would accept your correspondent's identification of Twing as Tring, Hertfordshire.

According to the folio in my possession (third printing) the parish of Twing is beyond peradventure in Gloucestershire. This is attested in two independent sources; a letter from Eustace to his cousin Bertram Wooster inviting his participation in the Great Sermon Handicap and one from the incumbent of Twing, the Reverend F. Heppenstall, scratching his entry and transferring the stable's first colours to his nephew, the Reverend James Bates, of Gandle-by-the-Hill. Both are headed 'The Vicarage, Twing, Glos.'

While it is possible that someone whom Jeeves described as

257

'very high-spirited' may have been uncertain whether he was in Gloucestershire or Hertfordshire, the same could hardly be urged of a senior clergyman, who could not unreasonably be assumed to have known in which county his benefice lay.

Sad it is to reflect that a revival of that splendid event is now unlikely since all those historic parishes, Little Clickton-in-the-Wold, the Bousteads Parva and Magna, Fale-by-the-Water *et al*, must now have been united under a team ministry, presumably based on Twing.

Yours faithfully,
ROGER WASHBOURN

[*Crockford* 1906 has these parishes in the Diocese of Gloucester: Sutton under Brail, Newington Bagpath, Ozleworth, Shipton Moyne and Shipton Oliffe. P. G. Wodehouse's favourite Aunt Louisa – sometimes regarded as the inspiration for Bertie Wooster's Aunt Dahlia – died on 13 December 1906 at Hartley Bourton-on-the-Water]

## The President's Joke

['My fellow Americans, I am pleased to tell you we have signed legislation that would outlaw Russia forever. We begin bombing in five minutes.' – President Reagan, joking in a microphone test during the presidential re-election campaign, August 14, 1984]

*From Mr P. R. Kitson*                    *23 August 1984*

[Department of English, Language and Literature, University of Birmingham]

Sir,

May a philologist remark that technically Mr Reagan's joke was rather a good one? He extrapolated to a preposterous but logical conclusion from two assumptions both of which are actually false but both of which some people might possibly believe to be true, viz., the standard propaganda parody of himself, which he was parodying, and the competence of one country's legislature to abolish another.

He assumed his hearers would be bright enough to spot these for falsehoods, and so share the joke.

The only people who come with discredit out of the episode are those humourless souls, whether in the Kremlin or in your columns, who treat parody as on a par with serious discourse, and those who confuse nastiness with sacredness, which is about what it amounts to to say nuclear war should not be joked about.

Yours faithfully,
P. R. KITSON

## Food of Love

[Towards the end of the 1984 Proms Claudio Abbado conducted the Vienna Philharmonic Orchestra in four symphonies: Mozart's 'Prague' and Bruckner 7; Beethoven 4 and Schubert's 'Great' C major]

*From the President of the Vienna Philharmonic Orchestra*
*24 September 1984*

Sir,
Concert reviews only rarely mention the audience, without whom the artist would yet be as a fish without water. Therefore, we would like to use this way, via your great London newspaper, to express to the friends of the Proms our thanks from the concert podium: to play for you was a truly special experience for us. The tension created by this mutual attraction cannot be expressed in millions of volts.

As an audience, you are a phenomenon; you have overpowered us with your contagious joy and your enthusiasm, your love and attention for the music and your discipline (can it be that among so many thousands of people nobody coughs?) and your affection.

It was sheer pleasure to play for you and we hope to meet you again. You applauded us — we fell in love with you.

Yours sincerely,
ALFRED ALTENBURGER

[The shade of Sir Henry Wood bows acknowledgements]

## Gas and Gaiters

*From Sir Kenneth Hutchison, FRS*          *13 October 1984*

Sir,
An interesting tercentenary is in danger of passing by unnoticed. In 1684, at latest, the Rev John Clayton, MA (Oxon), 1682, later Dean of Kildare, in Dublin, discovered gas-lighting. Inspired by a visit to a ditch near Wigan, where flames

burning fiercely like brandy had been seen for many years, he procured some coal from a pit near by, took it home and heated it in a retort over an open fire.

He observed that the products were three in number, a liquor, a tar, and a spirit which he could in no wise condense. He called it the 'Spirit of Coals' and collected it in bladders and was wont to entertain visitors by pricking a bladder with a needle and lighting the escaping gas, which burned with a clear, white light.

He died in 1725 and when his son Robert, Bishop of Cork, was going through his late father's papers he came across accounts of this and other experiments. Through the Earl of Egmont, a fellow, he communicated them to the Royal Society and they were read at a meeting and published in the Philosophical Transactions in 1739.

The bishop had hoped publication would inspire others to put his father's discovery to some good use. It was not to be and over 50 years passed before William Murdoch, unaware of what had gone before, used coal gas made in his back garden to light the living room of his small house in Redruth.

Yours faithfully,<br>
KENNETH HUTCHISON

## Off the Handle

*From Professor Harold G. Marcus*          26 July 1984

[writing from Michigan]

Sir,

I have frequently noticed that many front doors in Britain are not equipped with handles, especially in London, where one often sees individuals grasping the inside of letter slots or using keys or door-knockers to pull doors shut.

I know that British people equip the doors inside their homes with handles or knobs, so that ignorance of these conveniences does not explain their extraordinary absence on so many entry portals.

Perhaps some of your learned readers might be able to explain this curious lapse.

HAROLD G. MARCUS

*From Mr P. d'A. Willis*                    *28 July 1984*

[writing from The Oriental Club]

Sir,

Is your American correspondent unaware that a Gentleman has no need of handles with which to shut his own front door, a wife or servant usually performing this function?

Yours faithfully,

P. d'A. WILLIS


## Sauce of Learning

*From Dr John Hunter*                    *20 October 1984*

Sir,

Am I alone among your readers in deploring the loss of that much loved and most piquant of French primers − the label on the HP sauce bottle?

If unfortunate circumstances decreed that there was nothing else to read at the breakfast table one could always turn to the HP sauce bottle for a little French revision. It will be sadly missed.

Yours faithfully,

J. H. HUNTER

*From Mr H. J. G. Richards*                    *25 October 1984*

Sir,

Dr John Hunter is not alone. There must be many who miss the opportunity to polish up their Franglais by constant study of the description of the virtues of HP sauce.

Perhaps it was omitted from the label after a prolonged but unsuccessful attempt to capture the French market for bottled sauces. This would not be surprising; HP sauce, like most others produced in this country, is admirably suited for Anglo-Saxon cooking, as it disguises rather than enhances the taste of our food.

It is said that a Frenchman, on recovering from his first application of the sauce, studied the bottle intently and opined that it could be more briefly and just as accurately labelled in his language as *une sauce incendiaire*.

Yours faithfully,

H. J. G. RICHARDS

*From Lieutenant-Commander J. H. McGivering, RNR (retd)*
25 October 1984

Sir,

*Pace* Dr John Hunter, give me the multi-lingual Angostura
label at any meal!

Your obedient servant,
J. H. McGivering

*From Mr John Lomas*                    27 October 1984

Sir,

Like Dr John Hunter I too regret the passing of the French
label on the HP Sauce bottle.

It used to contain the sentence '*elle est absolument pure*'
which I used in my French classes to teach my students that 'it'
in French was just as likely to be 'elle' as 'il'. They never forgot
it.

Yours faithfully,
JOHN LOMAS

*From Mr E. H. Moore*                    2 November 1984

Sir,

If HP Sauce is not already regarded universally as a national
institution, surely the fact that it merits discussion in the
correspondence columns of your famous newspaper finally
confers on it this status. Naturally I am delighted because my
grandfather was the founder of the company which invented it
and my father played a leading role in its introduction, which
transformed a fairly prosperous family vinegar brewery into a
company of national and international fame.

I am not sure which of the two dreamed up the brilliant idea
of a discourse in French on the label, but this was much
in character with the inspiration and imagination which
accompanied the rest of its launch — the name itself, Houses of
Parliament Sauce, shortened to HP (my grandfather's favourite
dictum was 'condense'); the fact that it was the first thick sauce
to be distributed nationally; and sales promotion by, among
other things, giving away free miniature bottles of sauce from
miniature carts drawn by miniature Shetland ponies or donkeys
which toured the streets of all the towns in the UK. The original
idea was to use zebras, but this proved impossible!

As possibly the last family contribution to the popularity
and prosperity of this national institution, may I be permitted
to join your other correspondents in deploring the present label
and suggesting that the present proprietors would do them-

selves a lot of good by reverting to the original label in its
entirety.

Yours faithfully,<br>E. H. Moore

*From Miss Phyllis Birt*       *5 November 1984*

Sir,

I, too, regret the passing of the French label on the HP sauce
bottle. What does this portend?

Already the officer and his Indian servant on the Camp coffee
bottle have become much smaller, and the last time I bought a
bottle of Dr Collis Browne's medicine the testimonials from
Whymper and the doctor struggling against cholera in India had
disappeared.

Will the lion disappear from the Tate and Lyle syrup tin?

Yours faithfully,<br>Phyllis Birt

*From Mr C. P. McFie*       *7 November 1984*

[Secretary, Tate & Lyle]

Sir,

Let me assure Miss Phyllis Birt that there is no item on the
board agenda to consider the removal of the lion on our syrup
tin.

Judges, ch XIV ('Out of the strong came forth sweetness') is
of greater antiquity and carries more authority than some of the
recent bottle coverings – designed, dare one suggest, to conceal
the contents!

Yours faithfully,<br>Colin McFie

*From Mr Adrian Room*       *8 November 1984*

Sir,

I was very interested to read the letter from Mr E. H. Moore
regarding the origin of the name of HP Sauce, since, when I was
researching this name for my book, *Dictionary of Trade Name
Origins* (Routledge, 1982), I was informed in a letter from the
Group Product Manager (Sauces) of Smedley-HP Foods Ltd
that, alas, there was no firm evidence that the initials did
actually stand originally for 'Houses of Parliament'.

Company records show that a Mr Sampson and a Mr Moore
(no doubt Mr E. H. Moore's grandfather, whom he mentions)
first started to make HP Sauce in Birmingham in the 1870s,
having purchased the name from a Mr Garton in Nottingham.

263

The latter was marketing the product then as 'Garton's "HP" Sauce', although there is nothing to indicate why he chose this particular name.

The name itself was first registered in the *Trade Marks Journal* of May 22, 1912, by 'Edwin Samson Moore, trading as The Midland Vinegar Company, The Trade Malt Vinegar Company, and as F. G. Garton & Co.' The company was then based at Aston Cross, near Birmingham, where it traded as 'vinegar brewer and sauce and pickle manufacturer'.

Yours faithfully,

ADRIAN ROOM

*From Dr John B. Poole*　　　　　　　　　　*10 November 1984*

Sir,

Miss Birt should not be too despondent. Proctor's Pinelyptus Pastilles are still being recommended by Mme Sarah Bernhardt, Miss Ellen Terry and Sir Henry Irving.

Yours faithfully,

J. B. POOLE

# British Justice in a Questionable Guise

*From Mr J. N. Archer*　　　　　　　　　　*17 December 1984*

Sir,

I have just spent 2½ days at Knightsbridge Court answering, at the age of 63, my first summons for jury service. This is described in the explanatory leaflet as one of the most responsible duties that the individual citizen can be called to undertake, but I have not been allowed to undertake it.

On two occasions when I was about to be sworn in the defence counsel challenged me and I was sent back for a further long stint in the waiting room before my services were finally dispensed with.

After my first challenge, I was advised not to wear a pin-stripe suit the next day. After my second challenge it was suggested that I should wear casual clothes next time, but I needed to return to my job in the City in the late afternoon and I had an evening engagement.

Nor did I see why I should match the open-neck shirts, pullovers and jeans of most of the other jurors in order to be allowed to exercise the fairness, honesty and impartiality that the explanatory leaflet says is required, and for which a long career in the Army, the Civil Service and now with an international organization in the City should qualify me.

It may be an important principle of British justice that individual jurors can be objected to without a reason being given, but when it is apparently based on appearances it seems absurd.

I am opposed to any form of discrimination in this country especially when, as on this occasion, I was discriminated against! However, I suppose I should be thankful not to have to sit in court, or more likely the jurors' waiting room, right up to the Christmas holiday.

Yours faithfully,
JOHN ARCHER


## Dressing Down

*From Sir Robin Hooper*                                      *27 December 1984*

Sir,
Though I still, from time to time, wear a pin-striped suit, advancing age exempts me from jury service, so I have no personal axe to grind. But Mr John Archer's account of his experiences leaves one fighting back an unworthy suspicion that defending counsel's objections to him had less to do with doubts whether their clients would get a fair trial than with possibly justified fears that they might.

Yours faithfully,
ROBIN HOOPER


## Tongue-Tripping

*From Mr Ned Sherrin*                                           *4 March 1985*

Sir,
The best genuine malapropisms regularly committed these days come from one of the most talented and beautiful actresses to appear with the National Theatre in recent years.

Authenticated instances include her comment on a best friend who, 'went to live in Israel and worked on a kebab'; her dismay at the treatment of, 'the ostriches'. 'What ostriches?' 'The ostriches in Iran'; her dislike of, 'ejaculated lorries'; her admiration for the actress 'Joan Playwright' and her work at the 'RAC' and, perhaps most surreally, her recovery from a back-flip when she arrived at an upright posture saying, 'I'm Tallulah Bunkbed! Whoops! Sorry, I mean Tallulah Handbag!'

While training for her career she sought advice on how to be a better actress. She was advised to read Stanislavsky. She asked how the name was spelt. 'S.T.A.N. . . .' She looked hurt. 'I know how to spell his first name,' she said.

Yours faithfully,

NED SHERRIN

## People and Places

*From Mr Pat Adams*                                    *18 January 1985*

Sir,

'What a wealth of fictional names lies there' — how right Miles Kington (January 11) is about our villages.

Not long ago, in the Lincolnshire Wolds, a friend saw a signpost which said: 'To Mavis Enderby & Old Bolingbroke'.

Someone had added ' — a son'.

Yours faithfully,

PAT ADAMS

*From Mr Tim Heald*                                    *21 January 1985*

Sir,

Apropos Miles Kington's piece some of us 'genre' writers have been raiding the atlas for years in search of names for our characters.

My first ever chief constable was called Sir Erris Beg after the well-known Irish hill and like other sleuths (Paris, Dover, Cork, Wexford) my running character is named after a town, Bognor Regis. I've now started naming characters after reviewers. Thus (to appear shortly) Lord Justice Berlins and Chief Inspector Lejeune (aka Lejeune of the Yard).

Come to think of it, Miles Kington is a perfectly plausible name for a craggy hamlet high on the moors above Vanbrugh's magnificent ducal mansion at Sheridan Morley.

Yours faithfully,

TIM HEALD

*From Mr J. C. Newbold*                                *22 January 1985*

Sir,

What a delightful 'Moreover'. Mr Kington has invented an amusing game for the family to play while motoring on holiday.

Had his eyes wandered north east across the map to Lincolnshire he would have found cream with which to top the fruit of his genius in the characters of Boothby Graffoe (The

Hon, of course), Brant Broughton (expatriate US Air Force officer), Carlton Scroop (historian, novelist and Mrs Thatcher's uncle), Ashby Puerorum (Fellow of Trinity), Cherry Willingham (a real pretty chick), and many others.

Yours, with the yellowest of bellies,

CLIFFORD NEWBOLD

*From Mr Adrian Room*          *25 January 1985*

Sir,

We must be grateful for Mr Clifford Newbold's letter introducing us to some splendid Lincolnshire worthies.

But he and family holidaymakers should not overlook Devon for some equally agreeable personages. There one can find Sydenham Damerel (retired Cockney coiffeur), Curry Mallet (ex-All India croquet champion), Mary Tavy and Peter Tavy (husband and wife children's writers), Bovey Tracey (rising 'gender bender' rock singer), and Broadwood Kelly (noted Irish pub pianist).

And I should not be at all surprised to come across Mr Newbold himself on some Midlands map one day!

Yours faithfully,

ADRIAN ROOM

*From Mr Alec Clifton-Taylor*          *26 January 1985*

Sir,

There is a signpost in Lincolnshire which reads New York 2, Boston 11.

Just nine miles between them!

Yours faithfully,

ALEC CLIFTON-TAYLOR

*From Mr D. J. Corney*          *29 January 1985*

Sir,

Between London and Colchester one may make the acquaintance of Sible Hedingham (her ladyship), Ivy Chimneys (her daily), Tolleshunt D'Arcy (her lover), Margaret Roding (her rival) and, of course, Black Notley (her downfall).

Yours sincerely,

D. J. CORNEY

*From Lady Tudor Evans*          *29 January 1985*

Sir,

Mr Adams may care to have the latest scandal from the Wolds. Our local gossip, commonly called Bag Enderby, alleges that Lord of the Manor, Sir Claxby Pluckacre, was the protector of Mavis Enderby long before Old Bolingbroke, in his dotage, publicly announced the notorious liaison.

The New Bolingbroke refuses to comment.

Yours etc,
SHEILAGH TUDOR EVANS

*From Dr John R. Bennett*                    *5 February 1985*

[who lives in Remenham House]

Sir,

Miles Kington's influence extends to the Far East. Last week a letter from South Korea addressed me as 'Professor Remenham House'. Had the University of Hull not already had one Professor House on its staff I would readily have adopted the distinguished-sounding appellation.

Yours faithfully,
JOHN R. BENNETT


# Pay for Directors

*From Mr R. G. Opie*                    *23 March 1985*

Sir,

It was naughty of you to publish on the same day (March 20) the details of both Mr Lawson's Budget and that of eight directors of ICI, in particular of that of its chairman. The chairman's pay, you report, has risen from £170,999 (accuracy is important in these matters), or £3,288.44 per week, to £5,524.25 per week, a mere 67.99 per cent extra.

Now, Sir, my admiration for Mr John Harvey-Jones is considerable but, unlike his pay, it has not increased by 67.99 per cent, at least not within one year. You quote him as saying: 'It is not for us to say if we are worth what we are paid. Uncle Tom Cobbleigh and all will do that, and rightly so.' Very well then.

His excuse for these rather handsome increases is 'the responsibilities that all ICI directors carry (and incidentally relish)'. But, Sir, if they *enjoy* their job, why pay them so much more for what they already do so happily? And have these 'relished' responsibilities become 67.99 per cent more onerous within one year?

What has increased is not their responsibilities but ICI's profits. And that upsurge in profits was not the result of 67.99 per cent extra or harder work, but of the fall in the sterling/dollar exchange rate. In other words, the ICI directors have simply grabbed what they could get, or what their cleverly written contracts specified.

A number of questions arise. Will the wages and salaries of all the ICI staff also rise by that amount this year? And why should Mr Harvey-Jones receive an extra 67.99 per cent for his (extra?) responsibilities when teachers are offered 4 per cent, i.e., a real salary cut, for theirs? And if the Chancellor's views on these things are valid, are not the directors of ICI in danger of 'pricing themselves out of a job'?

Yours faithfully,

R. G. OPIE

## The Cuckoo's Finest Hour

*From Professor J. K. Hyde*                    *28 March 1985*

[Department of History, University of Manchester.]

Sir,

Mrs Thatcher's reported remarks (March 25) to the Conservative Central Council in Newcastle marks a further stage in the insidious politicization of the institutions of this country. Not only is it suggested that dons are under some kind of obligation to instil supply-side ethics whether they believe in them or not, but it is also clearly stated that churchmen of the Established Church who criticize Government policies are cuckoos, that is, guilty of extreme ingratitude.

So, just as the view has recently been promoted that Civil Servants owe their ultimate loyalty to the Government of the day rather than to the Crown, the Prime Minister now implies that the bishops owe their office to herself and her ministers rather than to the Queen.

To suggest that the bishops do not enjoy the freedom of speech which is the birthright of everyone but should trim their words to the susceptibilities of a temporarily dominant faction within a particular party is to incite them to disloyalty to their consciences and to God. Can arrogance be carried any further?

Yours faithfully,

J. K. HYDE

*From the Reverend Arthur Moss*                    *28 March 1985*

Sir,

The report of the first cuckoo of spring is always eagerly anticipated but less experienced bird-watchers frequently get it

269

wrong, confusing the call of *Columba palumpus* for *Cuculus canorus*.

The good lady from Westminster, having heard several as widely apart as Canterbury, Liverpool and Durham, to mention but a few, as early in the year as February and March, might have had second thoughts and known that what she heard was the much rarer *Novum Testamentum*.

Yours faithfully,

ARTHUR MOSS

## Lieutenant-Colonel Alfred Daniel Wintle, MC

[to whom this book is not dedicated]

Our anti-hero must be 'Freddie' Wintle, lovingly remembered by R. V. Jones in *Most Secret War*, who, in 1940, was sent to the Tower for producing a pistol in the presence of the Director of Air Intelligence. The most serious charge at his Court Martial was that he had threatened to shoot the Air Commodore, along with himself, and had 'said words to the effect that certain of His Majesty's Ministers, all Officers of the Royal Air Force above the rank of Group Captain and most senior Army Officers ought to be shot.'

Wintle did not deny the charge as regards the Ministers but insisted it was a patriotic duty. So saying, he read out a list of the Ministers concerned; at No 7, Kingsley Wood (see page 123), the Prosecuting Advocate withdrew the charge. Asked if it had been his intention to intimidate the Director of Air Intelligence, Wintle replied, 'Intimidate the Air Commodore? Oh dear me, no! Why, I have worked with the Air Commodore for over a year, and I well know that he is the type of officer that if you rushed into his room and shouted at the top of your voice "The Air Ministry's on fire!" all he would do would be to take up his pen and write a minute to someone about it!' Shaw's General Burgoyne would doubtless have been convulsed by this discomfiture of the Prosecuting Advocate. After further hilarity, Wintle escaped with a severe reprimand.

His finest, non-military, hour came in 1958. Deciding that a solicitor had tricked one of his female relatives into making over some money, Wintle lured him to a secluded flat and there removed his trousers. The solicitor, clearly not an admirer of Whitehall farce, summoned Wintle for assault. The de-bagging of a solicitor being a more serious offence than the threatening of the Director of Air Intelligence with a pistol, Wintle was sentenced to six months imprisonment.

Emerging in need of a snifter, Wintle fought his case, unaided, against the solicitor to the House of Lords, where he won — not on a point of law but on one of fact. *The Times* hailed his triumph: 'Cavalry officer jumps last fence to win', while the junior barristers of Lincoln's Inn drank a toast to Wintle, congratulating him on his legal expertise.

A hero in peace as well as in war, Wintle was no delight to the Cuckoo. Indeed, with a race of Wintles, the Cuckoo would not be in business. The following letter did not appear in the correspondence columns of *The Times*, though it did make the diary on the occasion of Wintle's death in 1966, and also *The Times: Past Present Future* (to commemorate the 200th birthday) in 1985, some 39 years after being written.

*From Lt-Col A. D. Wintle*                    *6 February 1946*

[Written from the Cavalry Club]

To the Editor of *The Times*.

Sir,

I have just written you a long letter.

On reading it over, I have thrown it into the waste paper basket.

Hoping this will meet with your approval.

I am, Sir, Your obedient servant

A. D. WINTLE

# INDEX

## Letter-writers' names are in CAPITALS

273

274

George VI, King: coronation 105; death 151; in London during Blitz 152

Germany, Nazi: anti-Semitism 105–6, 119; attitude to foreign journalists 97, 105–6; attitude to foreign visitors 95–6; concentration camps 137; immunity of forests 123; propaganda 118–19, 124–5; Vervoerd, a student in 167

ghost writing 16

GIBB, FRANCES 208

GIBSON, MRS EVELYN 186

GIBSON, SIDNEY LANIER 122

Gladstone, W. E. 7, 109–10

GLOAG, JULIAN 214–15

Gloucestershire, illegal tobacco plantations in 127

GOBLE, MISS ELIZABETH 62–3

GODDARD, AIR-MARSHAL SIR VICTOR 64

GODDEN, MRS MARY 250

GODDING, MARK 202-3

GODFREY-FAUSSETT, T. P. 166

Goebbels, Dr Josef 105, 118–19

going a-maying 80

GOLDBERG, RABBI D. J. 199

GOLDBERG, RUBY D. 63–4

GOLDING, MISS RUTH 250

GOODCHILD, JOHN 16

GOODHART, ARTHUR M. 26

GOOLD-ADAMS, RICHARD 153–4

graffiti 223, 266

GRAHAM, REV. D. L. 205–6

GRAVES, ROBERT 65, 133–4

GREEN, STEPHEN 220

green, clothes-moths' preference for 6, 154

Greenwich meridian 211–14

GREGG, DAVID 219

GREGORY, PROFESSOR ROY 215

GRENFELL, REGINALD 103–4

GRIMWADE, CANON J. G. 221

grouse, red 59, 60, 62, 65, 66

GROVE, DR VICTOR 131

GROVES, DR N. D. 251

Grundy, Mrs 6, 78–9

GUBBINS, NATHANIEL 172–3

*Gulliver's Travels* 82

HAILSHAM, LORD 237

Hampton Court Palace 78–9

Hannibal 205–9

Hardwicke, Sir Cedric 71

Hardy, Thomas 55, 74

harmonious motorists 26

HARMSWORTH, ST JOHN 202

HARRIS, JOHN 116

HARRIS, WALTER B. 91

Hart, Basil Liddell 133, 216

hassock-stuffing, new use for 127

hats, English 95–7

Haviland, Julian 220

HAVINDEN, MISS E. 143

HAWKINS, (SIR) A. H. 31–2

HAWKINS, REV. D. F. C. 200

HAWORTH, J. 251

Hawthorne, Nathaniel 222

headlines 3–4

HEALD, TIM 266

Healey, Rt. Hon. Denis 202

Heath, Rt. Hon Edward 87, 189

Heathfield, Peter 242–3

heliotropism 256

HEMMING, H. R. 77

Henderson, Brig. Gen. David 129

HENDERSON, GERALD W. 60

HENSON, RT. REV. HERBERT HENSLEY 246–8

HERBERT (SIR) ALAN P. 5, 117–18, 148–9

Hero of Alexandria 135

HETHERINGTON, ERNEST C. 62

'Hickey, William' 12

HIGHLOCK, STEPHEN 183

high tea 93–4

HILL, RAGLAN 148

HINDE, THOMAS 207

Hitler, Adolf 33, 56, 76, 220

hockey 165–6

Hobhouse, Miss Emily 16

HOLMES, REV. CECIL 89–90

Holmes, Sherlock 96

HOME, LORD. *See* Dunglass, Lord

honorary degrees 6, 84–7, 148

HOOPER, SIR ROBIN 265

hooter neuroses 24

'HOPE, ANTHONY' 31–2

'hopefully' 195

horse: archers 133–4; life saving 144; conveyance by train 197; loin-cloth 76–7; racing 42–4, 110; riders 159

HORTON, ROBERT F. 20

hospital visiting 90

Hotson, Leslie 175

HOWELLS, CANON D. L. 257

HOWIESON, CAPT. S. A. J. 118

Hoyte, John 206, 208

HP sauce 261–4

Hull University 268

humanity 180

Hume, Cardinal Basil 220

HUME-ROTHERY, R. 178

humour, sense of 258–9

Oak-Apple Day 80
obstreperousness at ticket-barrier 19
Ockley 12
octogenarians 42, 99–101
odd-one-out problems 165–6
OGLE, R. J. 196–7
OLIVER, L. H. 64
OLIVIER, (SIR) LAURENCE
174–6; (mentioned) 148, 190
OLIVIER, SIR SYDNEY 47
Olympic Games 32, 256–7
Omdurman, Battle of 135
OMMANNEY, MRS J. 173
OPIE, R. G. 87, 268–9
ORDE, LADY EILEEN 110
Orwell, George 239
Oxford: armorial bearings 63; athletics
31–2; Dictionary 74; gas works
146–7; graduate's legacy 50–1;
honorary degrees 86–7, 148;
Marxist dons 86, 87; opera-going
don 162; Rhodes Scholars 33, 156;
rowing blue 55; towpath sign 249;
University MP 117–18, 148–9
oyster-shell diet for hens 82, 83

Paddington Station 177
PALMER, G. H. 117
PALMER, R. A. 158–9
PALMER, MRS STELLA 81
paper-eating at Eton and in Greece
111
PARKER, JOHN 156–7
parliamentary: bastardy 140; behaviour
161–2; linguistic usage 112,
195–6; pay 6, 27–8
PARMITER, GEOFFREY DE C.
185–6
participles, unattached 122
PARTRIDGE, CHARLES 157–8
PAULLEY, HAROLD 60
pay: directors' 268–9; dustmen's 184,
188; farm labourers' 23; miners'
228; MPs' 6, 26–8; Princess
Elizabeth's 27; RAF 108;
shepherds' 108; tax inspectors'
106
Peacehaven 212
pedestrianism, obsessive 202–3
peers' identity problem 164
'penny dreadfuls' 110
PERCIVAL, SIR IAN 86
PERCIVAL, RT. REV. JOHN 17
PERRY, ROGER 59
PERTWEE JOHN D. 194
'Philip' 114
PHILIPSON, A. G. 127
Picasso, Pablo 140–1

picketing 229–34, 248
pigeon's egg 8, 132
PIGGOTT, A. H. 212
pigs 119–20
pins, superfluity of 159–60
PINSON, E. R. 250
pipe-smoking 125–6
place-name(s): chosen by competition
212; personalising 266–7;
pronunciation 121
PLOWRIGHT, ROBERT O. 221
poets: Mrs M. W. Adams 151;
anonymous 54, 128, 158; Deor 69;
Masefield 145–6; Ogden Nash
12; Mark Twain 176; Theocritus
69; Virgil 111, 130; Sir William
Watson 55; P. & W. Whitehead
16
police: Canadian 52; Churchill's
defence of 28; commissioner 76;
in miners' strike 229–32, 248;
patience in Poplar 28; Tsarist 75;
'useless' in pocket-picking cases
77
poltergeist 47
Polybius 207, 208
polygamy 209, 215
polyglot labelling 262
polysyllabism 117–18
POOLE, DR JOHN B. 264
Poplar 28
'P.O. Prune' 117
postal service 173
POWELL, PREBENDARY J. H. 115
preacher in miniskirt 15
prebendaries 115
'presently' 196
PRIEST, DR PAMELA 13
PRIESTLAND, GERALD 251
principles, Victorian 164
prisoners of war 49–50
Proctor's Pinelyptus Pastilles 264
Promenade Concerts 189, 259
pronunciation: 'Adlai' 176; BBC 195;
'Dynasts' 74; 'isolate' 74;
'lamentable' 195; 'prebendary'
115; 'primarily' 195; stage 174–5;
telephonic 121–2
PRYOR, E. J. 63
pun, episcopal 203
*Punch* 110, 117–18
punctuation 199, 249–53
PURCELL, MRS C. P. 206

quadrangle-haunting thrush 19
quartermasters' terminology 216–19
QUICK, A. O. H. 238–9

279

280

281